Follow the
Blue Blazes

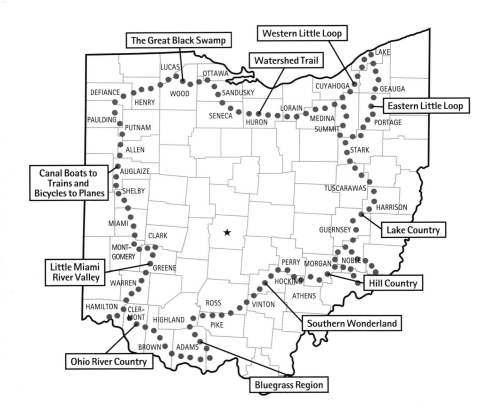

The Great Black Swamp

Western Little Loop

Watershed Trail

LAKE

LUCAS

OTTAWA

DEFIANCE

WOOD

SANDUSKY

CUYAHOGA

GEAUGA

HENRY

Eastern Little Loop

PAULDING

SENECA

LORAIN

PORTAGE

PUTNAM

HURON

MEDINA

SUMMIT

ALLEN

STARK

Canal Boats to Trains and Bicycles to Planes

AUGLAIZE

SHELBY

TUSCARAWAS

HARRISON

MIAMI

GUERNSEY

Lake Country

CLARK

MONT-GOMERY

Little Miami River Valley

GREENE

PERRY

MORGAN

NOBLE

WARREN

HOCKING

Hill Country

HAMILTON

CLER-MONT

ROSS

VINTON

ATHENS

HIGHLAND

PIKE

Southern Wonderland

Ohio River Country

BROWN

ADAMS

Bluegrass Region

Follow the Blue Blazes

A Guide to Hiking Ohio's Buckeye Trail

Second Edition

Connie Pond and
Robert J. Pond

Foreword by
Steven M. Newman

Ohio University Press
Athens

Ohio University Press, Athens, Ohio 45701
ohioswallow.com
© 2014 by Ohio University Press
All rights reserved

To obtain permission to quote, reprint, or otherwise reproduce
or distribute material from Ohio University Press publications,
please contact our rights and permissions department at
(740) 593-1154 or (740) 593-4536 (fax).

Printed in the United States of America
Ohio University Press books are printed on acid-free paper ⊗ ™

24 23 22 21 20 19 18 17 16 15 14   5 4 3 2 1

This guide is made possible, in part, by the generous support of the
Buckeye Trail Association.

Photographs not otherwise credited are by the author.

Library of Congress Cataloging-in-Publication Data

Pond, Connie.
    Follow the blue blazes : a guide to hiking Ohio's Buckeye Trail /
Connie Pond and Robert J. Pond ; foreword by Steven M. Newman. —
Second edition.
        pages cm
    Includes index.
    Revised edition of: Follow the blue blazes : a guide to hiking Ohio's
Buckeye trail / Robert J. Pond. 2003.
    ISBN 978-0-8214-2121-5 (paperback) — ISBN 978-0-8214-4504-4 (pdf)
    1. Hiking—Ohio—Buckeye Trail—Guidebooks. 2. Trails—Ohio—
Buckeye Trail—Guidebooks. 3. Buckeye Trail (Ohio)—Guidebooks.
I. Pond, Robert J. II. Title.
    GV199.42.O32B836 2014
    796.51'09771—dc23   2014029647

This guidebook is dedicated to present and past members of the Buckeye Trail Association's board of trustees, staff, team members, and trail crew and to hikers and maintainers of the Buckeye Trail.

Contents

Foreword to the Second Edition   xi

Preface to the Second Edition   xv

Acknowledgments   xvii

How to Use This Guide   xix

CHAPTER 1   HIKING THE BUCKEYE TRAIL   1

The Need to Hike   3

Planning Is Crucial   4

   Day Hiking Checklist   6

Safety and Comfort on the Trail   8

Bicycling and the Buckeye Trail   11

Trail Markings   12

The Buckeye Trail Association   13

Contacts   15

CHAPTER 2   SOUTHERN WONDERLAND   16

Overview   16

Featured Hike 1—Old Man's Cave to Cedar Falls   23

Featured Hike 2—Tar Hollow State Forest   30

Featured Hike 3—Scioto Trail State Park   35

Local Contacts   39

Waypoint ID's   39

CHAPTER 3   THE BLUEGRASS REGION   41

Overview   41

Featured Hike 1—Pike Lake State Park   47

Featured Hike 2—Fort Hill   51

Featured Hike 3—Davis Memorial State
   Nature Preserve   57

Local Contacts 63

Waypoint ID's 63

CHAPTER 4 OHIO RIVER COUNTRY 65

Overview 65

Featured Hike 1—Shawnee State Forest 73

Featured Hike 2—Ripley 77

Featured Hike 3—East Fork State Park 83

Local Contacts 87

Waypoint ID's 88

CHAPTER 5 THE LITTLE MIAMI RIVER VALLEY 89

Overview 89

Featured Hike 1—Eden Park 98

Featured Hike 2—Fort Ancient State Memorial 103

Featured Hike 3—Glen Helen and Clifton Gorge 109

Local Contacts 116

Waypoint ID's 116

CHAPTER 6 CANAL BOATS TO TRAINS AND
BICYCLES TO PLANES 118

Overview 118

Featured Hike 1—Eastwood MetroPark and
National Museum of the USAF 128

Featured Hike 2—Johnston Farm and Indian
Agency Historic Site and the Locks
at Lockington 132

Featured Hike 3—The Miami and Erie Canal
Towpath Trail, St. Marys 138

Local Contacts 143

Waypoint ID's 143

CHAPTER 7 THE GREAT BLACK SWAMP 145

Overview 145

Featured Hike 1—Fort Defiance and
Independence Dam State Park ... 153

Featured Hike 2—Oak Openings Metropark ... 158

Featured Hike 3—Providence Metropark
to Roche de Bout ... 161

Local Contacts ... 166

Waypoint ID's ... 166

CHAPTER 8   THE WATERSHED TRAIL ... 167

Overview ... 167

Featured Hike 1—Wolf Creek Park ... 177

Featured Hike 2—Findley State Park ... 180

Featured Hike 3—Hinckley Reservation ... 186

Local Contacts ... 190

Waypoint ID's ... 191

**CHAPTER 9   CONNECTICUT'S WESTERN RESERVE:
BIG LOOP TO LITTLE LOOP** ... 193

Overview ... 193

Featured Hike 1—Brecksville Reservation ... 204

Featured Hike 2—Canal Fulton ... 209

Featured Hike 3—Chapin Forest ... 212

Local Contacts ... 216

Waypoint ID's ... 216

**CHAPTER 10   THE UPPER CUYAHOGA RIVER:
EAST BRANCH OF THE LITTLE LOOP** ... 218

Overview ... 218

Featured Hike 1—Mentor Marsh ... 226

Featured Hike 2—Mogadore Reservoir ... 231

Featured Hike 3—Quail Hollow State Park ... 235

Local Contacts ... 239

Waypoint ID's ... 239

CHAPTER 11 LAKE COUNTRY   241

Overview   241

Featured Hike 1—Fort Laurens to Zoar Village   252

Featured Hike 2—Clendening Lake   256

Featured Hike 3—Salt Fork State Park   262

Local Contacts   266

Waypoint ID's   266

CHAPTER 12 HILL COUNTRY   268

Overview   268

Featured Hike 1—American Electric Power
ReCreation Land   276

Featured Hike 2—Scenic River Trail in
Wayne National Forest   281

Featured Hike 3—Burr Oak Backpack Hike   285

Local Contacts   295

Waypoint ID's   296

**CHAPTER 13 MAKING IT ALL POSSIBLE—
THE BLUE BLAZES, OF COURSE!**   298

The Pioneers   298

The Maintainers   302

Appendix 1: Bedrock Geologic Map of Ohio   308

Appendix 2: Physiographic Provinces Sections
of Ohio   309

Index   310

Foreword
to the Second Edition

Any seasoned hiker knows well that the Great Outdoors of today is a nearly endless trove of natural and man-made wonders—all waiting to tease and inspire the mind and soul of every explorer, from the novice and to the veteran. This is particularly true in the Buckeye State. Indeed, it is Ohio's abundance of wildlife, fauna, and history that helped sway me over thirty years ago to make my home here in the heart of the USA.

Rarely a day passes at my rural cottage overlooking the Ohio River that I am not entertained by the sight of wild animals or gladdened by the lush vistas. Why just this morning I watched a glossy brown-furred mink rubbing his neck and cheeks against the rough bark of a creekside maple. And nearly every evening some fourteen deer graze in a field just yards from our kitchen window. If I could have a quarter for every time my wife, Darci, and I have been delighted by the wild critters, or by another bit of historical gossip concerning this hill, and or by a postcardlike scene in the surrounding forest, I would be a wealthy man. As if it isn't enough that Daniel Boone and countless bison as big as trucks once trod through the gap in our hill and that on the ridgeline above the cottage there are Indian graves, I've even had locals swear that the legendary Indian slayer Simon Kenton was once tied to the gargantuan gnarly oak behind our home.

And yet, as fascinating as my own little slice of Ohio may be, I well know from doing many long and short hikes throughout Ohio that our spread along the Ohio River holds but a smidgen of all the natural and historical delights to be found in the state as a whole—especially if one is fortunate enough to explore along the path of what is known as the Buckeye Trail. Thus, I was thrilled to learn that longtime hiking enthusiasts Connie Pond and Robert J. Pond would be updating and making even more user friendly his first edition of *Follow the Blue Blazes,* which has become one of the most popular (and definitely the most comprehensive) Ohio hiking guidebooks.

Follow the Blue Blazes has been an invaluable source of information whenever Darci and I have laced up our boots and hit our favorite sections of the Buckeye Trail. Not only do the book's detailed directions and uncluttered maps keep me from becoming lost (and thus too worried or tired to

enjoy the setting), but Robert's simple and folksy bits of background information on the plants and animals of the area keep me excited at what I
am—and may yet be—seeing. This book is like having along your personal
guide—one who deeply loves Ohio and wants to share as much as possible
with you. One who truly is hoping you will have as much fun as he
is having.

A perfect example of what I'm talking about is the hike at Fort Hill
State Memorial. Darci and I have often hiked that ancient Indian gathering
area, located not far from our home, and before we had Follow the Blue
Blazes to guide and teach us, it was a hike past unusual man-made dirt
formations, stream-eroded cliffs, the occasional beaver, and many spectacular old trees and colorful wildflowers. But when we took along Robert
Pond's guidebook, it was if we were on a completely different hike. Suddenly, the flowers and the trees had names and a surprising history; the old
cabin in the forest opening had faces and a purpose; the fort was not a fort
at all and—better yet—became more mysterious than ever. The guidebook
added so much clarity. And that clarity brought with it a heightened appre-
ciation of just how much humans and nature have transformed Fort Hill
into the treasure it is. And it isn't just the wilderness that Pond brings to
life with such keen precision. Many of the book's Featured Hikes lead the
reader into delightful cultural centers of rural and urban Ohio.

My favorite example is the charming river village of Ripley. This is
where I pick up our mail and prescriptions and do our banking. I have
walked the streets of that history-rich settlement more times than I could
count, and I thought I knew its abolitionist history and landmarks as
thoroughly as anyone. Not so. *Follow the Blue Blazes* showed me that
somehow I had missed out on the basketlike coffin made of wooden slats
in the Ripley museum and that many of Ripley's residents had actually
returned escaped slaves to their owners for the bounty money.

As adept at philosophizing as at instructing, Robert Pond makes the
varied worlds and winding paths of each of the Buckeye Trail's sections so
much easier to appreciate and navigate. In following Robert Pond through
the pages of *Follow the Blue Blazes,* I find myself at turns in the company of
a sharp scout, a kindly neighbor, an inspirational teacher, and—if I may say
so—a kindred spirit to the likes of Thoreau and Robert Louis Stevenson.

The wealth of anecdotes and the concise, easy-to-follow format of
this book ensures that it will be a welcome addition to any hiker's knap-
sack. Robert Pond has long been experienced in the art of teaching, and it

shows in the disciplined and comfortable manner in which he guides us though each segment of the Buckeye Trail. Whereas other guides might prod us along for the sake of merely hiking, Robert Pond, the wise teacher, encourages us to pause, to gaze more closely, to think—even to be inspired. And that, dear friend, is exactly the sort of guide something as special and fascinating as the Buckeye Trail should have.

Steven M. Newman
Worldwalker Hill

Preface
to the Second Edition

Ohio's Buckeye Trail has changed greatly since *Follow the Blue Blazes* was published in 2003. Thanks to the efforts of the many volunteers who participated with the Buckeye Trail Crew in organized work parties, dozens of miles of new off-road trail has been established. The reader will have to participate in new trail building with hand tools in order to appreciate what 1 mile of newly benched trail involves (one estimate is up to 500 man-hours per mile of new off-road trail). The new Marietta "Little Loop" has been developed to showcase the Wayne National Forest—Marietta Unit, with its Archers Fork Trail and the Easternmost section of the Ohio River and has added 114 miles of on-road and off-road trail. Indeed, the association has changed as well, with new leadership determining the next evolution of this now over 1,400-mile trail around Ohio. The association now has a full-time executive director and an office in the small southeastern town of Shawnee. The 1888 Century Barn on Tappan Lake, near Deersville, has also been renovated for meetings and overnight gatherings of members and volunteer trail workers.

This second edition offers many enhancements, including photos and art in color, and GPS data to aid in navigating the trails used in the 33 Featured Hikes found in the book. The new Overview Maps beginning each chapter have been revised while also offering the reader more information on how to navigate to the chapter's interest points. The 33 hikes have all been walked once again and modified as needed.

The Featured Hikes in the book are for the most part in the same locations as in the original edition, but many are shorter. On many of the most popular hikes—for example, Old Man's Cave—you will find the trail well used to about 1 mile from the starting point. After a mile, there is dramatically less use. This led us to the conclusion that shorter hikes would be better. They are designed to accommodate the families who purchase *Follow the Blue Blazes* to introduce their children to the natural world of Ohio. Seniors, too, will find most of the hikes fairly easy, while younger, stronger, or more experienced hikers will find more challenging hikes such as those at Burr Oak and Clendening Lakes. Hopefully, the hiker will find either the longer or shorter hikes will take them to secret places where time stands still.

Hiking each of the 33 hikes seemed an insurmountable project until my wife Connie presented a plan for overnight visits to the various hike localities. The visits would be reminiscent of our nine-year adventure when we hiked the entire Buckeye Trail. Then, we would take two cars, park a car at each end of the day's hike and walk the miles in between. This time, we could take one car, do the short hike and visit favorite restaurants and overnight establishments. While completing our circuit hike, the number of miles we walked was often more important than what we saw. This time, the hike's vistas, natural wonders, and the historical significance of the area was more important.

Our lives have been enriched by our walks around the state. The periphery of the state includes miles of peaceful forest trails, canal towpaths, and the banks of picturesque rivers and streams. All of which are interspersed by quiet country roads connecting small Ohio towns and villages that you walk through, often meeting and talking with the residents. The people you meet along the way feel you are more approachable because you carry a day pack or, in our case, are accompanied by our canine friend, a boxer named Buckeye.

Even the busier urban areas like Cincinnati and Dayton the BT passes through are picturesque due to their parks and natural spaces as well as their museums and historical sites. Lovely Eden Park in Cincinnati is one terminus of the BT along the Ohio River, while the other terminus is the natural area at Mentor Headlands along the Lake Erie shoreline and its picturesque lighthouse.

Much of the periphery of the state the trail passes through is of historic, geologic, and ecological importance. It is around the edges of Ohio that European pioneers settled, resulting in epic battles against the Native Americans wanting to keep their beautiful lands. Yet it is also the less visited by most of the state's residents. Even more reason for you to get out and hike!

Connie and I hope you enjoy the descriptions in *Follow the Blue Blazes* and try some of the hiking experiences offered by the book. Let us know how you find the material in these pages. Contact us at buckeyetrail.org or, better yet, write a review on the Amazon website, on Facebook, or on any blog. All proceeds from book sales go to the Buckeye Trail Association.

Robert Pond

Acknowledgments

This second edition again acknowledges the efforts of all those who helped with the first edition and have made significant contributions to this edition.

Richard Lutz, GIS Coordinator for the BTA, taught us how to use the GPS and then translated that data into the maps for this book. We had a great time adding the "blue" (rivers and streams) to the maps. Thanks, Richard.

Darlene Karoly, Graphics Editor for the BTA, added her magic to page design and layout for both the first and second editions. All of us in the BTA sing her praises each time she joins our efforts.

Pictures for this book were a special effort because we wanted high-quality color photos and pictures from all along the trail. Who better to turn to than those who have recently walked the entire trail and have a knack for taking great photos: Andy "Captain Blue" Niekamp and Brent and Amy Anslinger. Many of the great photos were provided by organizations that are charged with guardianship of Ohio's beauty: Ohio History Connection, Five Rivers MetroParks, Miami and Erie Canal Corridor Association, Toledo Metroparks, Cleveland Metroparks, and Quail Hollow State Park.

In April 2014, the BTA did a campaign asking our membership to donate to help provide funding for this second edition. More than 60 members and friends will be receiving an autographed edition of the new book when it is released. Special thanks go to Marc Vincent as a Bronze Leaf contributor and Garry and Sidney Dill as Gold Leaf contributors.

How to Use This Guide

Chapter 1 introduces the Buckeye Trail (BT) and the Buckeye Trail Association (BTA). It helps you understand how to follow the blue blazes and use the detailed maps produced by the BTA. The chapter also explains the basics for safe and enjoyable hiking.

Each of chapters 2 through 12 begins with an Overview describing the path of the Buckeye Trail throughout that chapter. The chapters are arranged so that you will follow the BT clockwise around the state. You may read the overviews from each chapter serially in order to become familiar with the entire Buckeye Trail. For each chapter, a map of the trail traveled in that chapter supports the overview.

Three Featured Hikes are described in each of these chapters—a total of 33 hikes. The descriptions are designed to be read before, after, and during your hikes. Each Featured Hike is supported by a map. The characters on the maps are International Recreation Symbols. Each hike has been walked with a GPS, waypoints have been established, and specific coordinates are noted at the end of each hike. The GPS waypoints are in decimal degrees, and your GPS or phone should be set accordingly. Estimated hiking times assume a pace of about 1 mile per hour for off-road walking and 2 miles per hour on hard surfaces. Terrain, elevation changes, and the hiker's fitness level and experience affect hiking times.

In each of chapters 2 through 12, we present features of Ohio's geology (see also the appendix), tell how it has affected present flora and fauna, and point out specific animals and plants to look for in many of the Featured Hikes. Listed at the end of each chapter, find Local Contacts for more information about individual hikes or points of interest.

Although we have made this guide as accurate as possible, trail relocations do occur and trail conditions change. The best way to keep up with those changes is to become a member of the BTA. The *Trailblazer*, published quarterly, will keep you up to date on trail relocations as well as group hikes and opportunities to help maintain the trail. On the Web, visit www.buckeyetrail.org for timely trail alerts.

KEY TO MAPS

△	Camping	🚻	Park Office
🏛	Museum	🚻	Rest Rooms
🏠	Cabins	$	Fee
⚑	Point of Interest	🏞	Scenic View
🏪	General Store	⛺	Shelter
◉	Historic Site	🍴	Food
▭	Lodging	☎	Telephone
P	Parking	🗼	Viewing Tower
🏕	Picnic Area	🥛	Water
🏕	Picnic Shelter	•	Waypoints

T-129	Township Road	------ Buckeye Trail
C-5	County Road	—•—— Power Lines
P-2	Park Road	
22	US Route	▬▬▬▬ Featured Hikes
70	Interstate	----- Other Trails
41	State Route	—— Local Roads
🍁	Buckeye Trail	▬▬▬ State Routes
		—— Rivers
		▬▬▬ Lakes

Hiking the Buckeye Trail

To the roughly one thousand members of the Buckeye Trail Association (BTA), the title of this guidebook is familiar and even nostalgic. They already know of the joys and benefits of hiking the BT by following the familiar trail markers. Many nonmembers also enjoy the fruits of the BTA's efforts, some as they walk small portions of the trail near their homes, others by backpacking it end to end. All users find the generous efforts of BTA volunteers are free and open to all.

Follow the Blue Blazes is designed to get you outdoors to discover Ohio at a slower pace. The present Buckeye Trail (fig. 1.1), the longest loop

Figure 1.1 Buckeye Trail today

trail in the country and the only one to encircle the major portion of a state, traverses more than 40 of Ohio's 88 counties. (The section titles in figure 1.1 correspond to BT 50-mile section maps that may be ordered from the BTA.) In 1999 the BT was designated Ohio's Millennium Legacy Trail. (There is only one such designation per state.) The BT connects the four corners of the state, following old canal towpaths, abandoned railroad rights-of-way, rivers, lakeshores, and farmlands. It passes through the Wayne National Forest as well as many of the state's parks and nature preserves. It is considered a neighborhood trail, for wherever you live in Ohio the trail will be within a short drive. From central Ohio, you can reach a segment of the BT within 1 hour.

If really long hikes are your intention, the coast-to-coast American Discovery Trail (ADT; fig. 1.2) connects the BT to other great national trails. The 6,800-mile ADT links cities, wilderness areas, forests, and deserts across America. It begins at Cape Henlopen State Park, in Delaware, and ends at Point Reyes National Seashore, in California. From east to west the ADT first connects with the Appalachian Trail, then with the Continental Divide and Pacific Crest Trails, all running north to south. It uses the Buckeye Trail to traverse southern Ohio from West Virginia to Indiana. The American Hiking Society and *Backpacker* magazine began planning this first coast-to-coast hiking trail in 1989. (For the ADT's starting and ending points on the BT, see chaps. 5, 12.) Another long-distance trail that uses the Buckeye Trail is the North Country Trail (NCT), a 4,600-mile National Scenic Trail that crosses New York, Pennsylvania, Ohio, Michigan,

Figure 1.2 American Discovery Trail

Wisconsin, Minnesota, and North Dakota (see chaps. 7, 11). Both the ADT and the NCT are recognized as National Millennium Trails.

The blue blazes lead you to experience lovely landscapes, intriguing historical sites, quaint villages, and even major cities. If you travel, whether day-hiking or backpacking (fig. 1.3) the entire BT, the terrain will change from relatively flat and open land in the west to steep ridges or hills in the east. History will become more meaningful as you visit places of historic importance. The variety of plants and animals you see in Ohio may surprise you. Colorful villages abound along the trail. You will pass through wealthy neighborhoods as well as inner-city areas. Rich or poor, most of the people you meet will be eager to talk to the wayfarer. Most important, following the blue blazes will bring feelings of accomplishment and satisfaction.

THE NEED TO HIKE

What makes hiking such a pleasant pursuit? The activity seems too primitive for a world rich in material possessions: cars to transport us, television sets to amuse us, and computers bringing us into the realm of virtual reality. The answer is that, advanced as we are, our primitive roots are very much intact. These roots require nature's nurturing balm of sights, sounds, smells, and feelings. We must step away periodically from a technological and materialistic culture threatening to alienate us from our natural world.

Figure 1.3 Backpackers (Andrew Bashaw)

Some of society's greatest discoveries originated during a walk. Many breakthroughs came from the rhythm of walking, which frees the mind from intense concentration on a problem. A long walk can work just as well to solve your own problems or, at least, put them in proper perspective.

Research reports on the health benefits of walking are numerous. Sedentary adults who become walkers benefit by trimming waistlines, strengthening bones, improving heart health, and boosting aerobic fitness. Add to the list balance and physical coordination.

Many people eventually lose interest in more aggressive programs that require going to a gym or classes. Walkers find it easier to keep on walking. Research also credits walking with reducing stress, alleviating depression, and even improving mental prowess, all of which improve overall attitude.

Our children definitely need more quality time outdoors. They probably experience the outdoors less than you did as a child. Children who experience the great outdoors by camping and hiking, especially with their parents, will achieve more in school, grow up to be more confident and self-assured, become more flexible in their responses to life's problems, and be proud of and recognize their immense capabilities. Seeing and feeling nature firsthand is the best way for children to get to know their own natures, giving them a perspective that computer simulation software and virtual reality games can never impart.

Your catalyst for getting out periodically and hiking the Buckeye Trail could be a new dog that needs a walk. It could be a child or grandchild who needs to spend some quality time with you. Walking could also aid you in finding connections with a new or longtime partner in life, solving a perplexing problem, or rejuvenating a relationship with someone you already know. The list is endless. *Get out and hike!*

PLANNING IS CRUCIAL

No matter where in Ohio you live, it is only a short drive to some portion of the Buckeye Trail. (Central Ohioans are fortunate to be closest to all parts of the trail.) However, finding the trailhead on many township or county roads takes careful planning, especially for families that have always lived in the city. Be sure to check the weather forecast at the location for the hike. Weather can make roads to trailheads impassable and the trails themselves dangerous. If flood warnings are posted or severe weather is expected, do not attempt to hike.

Before driving to a hiking site, make sure you know the specific directions to the parking area. It is best to write them out. A map of the state, appropriate Ohio county maps, and especially the *Ohio Atlas and Gazetteer* can supplement your BT section maps. The *Gazetteer* (available in most grocery stores) and the official state map (available in many welcome centers at designated interstate rest areas) mark the Buckeye Trail. (For more on maps, see Contacts at the end of this chapter.)

Always travel with a companion and let a friend or family member know where you are planning to hike. Give them a copy of your map if possible. They can then direct emergency or safety personnel to the area should you not return. A cell phone can be useful on the hike, but don't count on reception in remote areas. Sometimes reception may be enhanced by walking up on a ridge from a valley or "holler."

Some hikers may wish to take two cars for long, linear hikes on the BT. (This is usually not necessary for the Featured Hikes in this guidebook.) With a car waiting at either end, the need to walk "out-and-back" is eliminated. The authors used the two-car method to hike the entire BT, one section map at a time. Hikers attempting to traverse a full section map may aim to complete a section of the Buckeye Trail (about 50 miles) in a few days of day hiking. You may even become motivated to walk around the state. A surprising number of people have hiked the entire BT. Many of these "circuit hikers" have accomplished their goal by day-hiking on weekends, a project that takes several years. Some circuit hikers have been in their 80s. (Figure 1.4 shows hikers preparing to walk a segment of trail.)

Another interesting way to hike the long stretches of the Buckeye Trail involves bicycling. Enterprising hikers will tote a bike along with them, secure the bike at a safe spot at the planned end of the hike, and drive back to the beginning of the hike. One hiker currently hiking the trail in this manner cautions others to consider the elevations of the hike. Do you want to walk downhill and bike up, or vice versa?

Proper preparation is crucial to a safe and successful hike. And planning a hike is often as much fun as the hike itself. Involve your children in the planning phase, as they will enjoy the process and learn valuable lessons from it. Notice how involved they become in helping you find the roads to the parking spot, and how proud they are when you arrive at that precise place on the map (though you might find that children have a limited sense of geography or have not learned the cardinal points of the compass.)

Make a checklist of necessary items and consult it before every hike. Each item should be checked off. Use the following list as a seed that may grow into your own personal list.

Figure 1.4 Circuit hikers (C. W. Spencer)

DAY HIKING CHECKLIST

EMERGENCY PHONE NUMBERS Contact information for family or friends can be listed here. For individual hikes, see the contact information on applicable BTA maps and the Local Contacts section at the end of each chapter.

DAY PACK

CELL PHONE FOR TIME AND EMERGENCIES

FIRST-AID SUPPLIES May include moleskin, bandages, scissors, tweezers and matches for removing ticks, lip balm, sunscreen, soap or wet wipes for poison ivy. Anyone allergic to insect stings should carry a bee sting kit to help prevent anaphylactic shock.

INSECT REPELLENT

HAT

FLASHLIGHT AND BATTERIES

RAIN GEAR Ponchos are best, but other recreational rainwear will work on cleared trails without briars.

EXTRA SOCKS On some trails you may get wet fording a stream. You may wish to cover your feet with plastic bags secured with rubber bands (trash bag waders).

HIKING SHOES Before long hikes, break in new shoes.

NOTEBOOK WITH PEN Reference books on birds, animal tracks, flowers, trees, and so on are also useful.

WATCH Can dispense with this if a cell phone is carried!

GROUND CLOTH

WALLET For cash as well as ID.

COMPASS

WATER BOTTLES Always carry plenty of water. Safe drinking water is often not available on the BT.

MAPS Carry BTA maps for the section(s) you plan to walk. See Contacts, at the end of this chapter. The Buckeye Trail Association offers maps for short hikes in the series Hiker on the Go. They are available for Chapters 2, 5, 8, 9, and 12.

HIKING POLES Very useful, especially while hiking rough terrain. It is surprising how efficiently a set of two poles can aid in balance, coordination, and improving the ability to cover miles.

GAS FOR CAR Always fill up before venturing into remote areas.

FOOD Carry supplies adequate for hikes longer than anticipated. And an afternoon lunch on a ground cloth or log can be very enjoyable as well as restful after a couple of hours on the trail.

CAMERA

SUNGLASSES

CAR KEYS Check that your keys are with you before locking the car and leaving it. Have a hiking partner carry an extra set of keys.

TRASH BAGS Large kitchen trash bags make good waders for fording creeks.

A more appropriate checklist for backpacking can be found by checking out the Burr Oak Backpack Hike in chapter 12.

SAFETY AND COMFORT ON THE TRAIL

Danger may be encountered in any activity, and walking outdoors is no exception. Experienced hikers know how to anticipate, avoid, and deal with these dangers. For instance, to avoid reckless drivers, they will not walk on the berm of the road if there is good footing in the drainage area. If they must walk the berm, they walk on the left side of the road, facing oncoming traffic, and stay alert. They can thus spot a speeding car early and avoid it. (Most roads on the BT have little or no traffic and offer great hiking experiences.)

Experienced hikers will patiently wait out a thunderstorm in a local barn (with permission, if possible) or other shelter. If in woodlands, they will avoid taller trees. A jacket or poncho or even a small umbrella carried in a day pack can help prevent hypothermia.

A compass and map prevent experienced hikers from becoming lost, even in a clear-cut area. If they are unsure of getting through safely, they remain calm and simply retrace their steps to blazed trail and a safe return to the parking area. If you become lost and unable to find any blazes from the way you came, don't panic. Take the following immediate actions:

- Take a break to recall where you know you have been and to relax so you may hear cars on a nearby road or boats on a lake.
- Walk carefully; if you do not have a compass, determine a straight path by keeping landmarks in a straight line fore and aft.
- Use the sun or patterns of stars as a continuous reference.
- Walk downhill—it will lead you to a stream and eventually to civilization.

Always use a compass when hiking off-road, constantly checking the maps to be sure of your location. A Global Positioning System (GPS), found on many smart phones, is an excellent aid to navigation. The GPS uses information beamed from satellites to fix a position on earth. Marking your position as you hike allows the GPS to keep track of, and point out, a safe return to your car or any other previously marked point.

Experienced hikers are aware of the various hunting seasons and avoid hiking in wildlife areas during such times. Hiking during deer season in Ohio should definitely be avoided. Wear brightly colored clothing whenever hiking through potential hunting areas.

Ticks are small arachnids that attach themselves to people in order to suck their blood. In warm weather you must constantly check for ticks, as they can carry diseases such as Lyme disease, which can seriously damage your health or even result in death. White-tailed deer, making a comeback in Ohio, act as host for the species of tick that can be infectious. Ticks should be carefully removed as soon as detected, so as not to leave any part of them embedded. Carry tweezers on hikes and heat the tips with a match to get ticks out of your skin cleanly. Other precautions: wear light-colored clothes and tuck pant legs inside boots, use DEET insect repellent or organic substitutes, stay in the center of the trail, and avoid brushy areas.

If you see a snake it will most likely be nonvenomous (fig. 1.5), although southern Ohio woodlands have both copperheads and rattlesnakes, which are of course venomous. In the unlikely event you are bitten by what you believe is a venomous snake, never cut into or wash the wound. Pressure bandaging until you can reach a medical facility is recommended. Experienced hikers will testify that they seldom see snakes on the Buckeye Trail. This is because snakes avoid large animals—like humans—whenever possible, and their natural camouflage prevents them from being discovered. Always remember that most snakes in Ohio are nonvenomous, are highly beneficial, and do not pose a threat to your safety. Experienced hikers seldom kill any animals, even poisonous snakes.

Figure 1.5 Garter snakes (Brent & Amy Anslinger)

Coyotes are spreading into Ohio, even in urban and suburban areas. If you spot wild or feral dogs or coyotes, avoid them and notify authorities as soon as possible. Most dogs will not attack and can be kept away, or prevented from following on a road, by throwing a handful of roadside gravel at their feet. Mace or the less-toxic pepper spray may offer protection from attacks by vicious dogs. Carrying firearms for protection is never recommended.

Bears in Ohio? There were at least 65 black bears sighted in Ohio in 2012, and their numbers are increasing, according to the Division of Wildlife. Most sightings near the Buckeye Trail have been in southeastern Ohio. In 1999 a black bear was spotted east of Athens, gorging itself on the 17-year cicadas that emerged that spring over much of Ohio. Bears eat mainly insects and grubs. They normally avoid people. If you spot one, simply back off and do not try to take photographs. Report the sighting to the Ohio Department of Natural Resources as soon as possible. And remember, always being quiet and considerate of the wildlife around you, large or small, is in your own best interest.

Poison ivy is so abundant in Ohio that it should be the state plant. If you come in contact with this three-leafed plant, wash the exposed area as soon as possible. Wet wipes made especially for ivy can be carried in your day pack and used immediately after exposure.

Foot problems can occur; this is especially true for older hikers. Walkers of all ages should wear quality shoes that fit well and offer firm support. Soft shoes, like sneakers, will not offer adequate support for the ankles. Decent hiking shoes or boots are strongly recommended. To prevent blisters, keep feet as dry as possible and wear good socks. In warm weather take your shoes off during breaks to allow feet to cool. Apply moleskin if blisters or hot spots develop.

When you hike on the trail remember that only you can assume the risk for accidents or illness. Stay on the trail as much as possible—this not only protects you but spares the delicate environment as well. Obey the regulations of nature preserves. For instance, pets are most likely not allowed. Always obey posted signs, leave gates as you find them, and carry out litter. Be careful with fire and smoking. A good summary of courtesy on the trail is the oft-cited phrase "Take only pictures and leave only footprints."

Lunch on the trail can be a truly enjoyable experience. Carry a ground cloth to sit or lie on. To prevent dehydration, always carry and drink plenty of water, even when hiking on cold winter days, when you may not be thirsty. You will be surprised how good it tastes after a couple of miles of hiking.

The BT follows several miles of bike paths, especially those that follow the Little Miami River, the Mad River in the Dayton area, and the miles of canal towpaths on the east and west sides of the state. The rules for these paths can usually be found on signage along the paths. One rule for all is to stay to the left of the path to allow bicyclists to pass (sometimes without warning).

No matter where you are along the BT, relax and enjoy the adventure of walking. Ask yourself why you are hiking—to enjoy nature and a relaxing adventure, or to race against time. Hurrying or trying to complete a trail in record time is a good way to get in trouble or lost. Remember, stay alert and keep those blue blazes in sight.

BICYCLING AND THE BUCKEYE TRAIL

Many parts of the Buckeye Trail offer great bicycling, especially in northern Ohio. Bicycling (fig. 1.6) offers many of the health advantages and pleasures of walking. The Ohio River Trail Council's Bicycle and Trail Advisory Committee supports the increased use of bicycles in the state. Most of the roads that make up the Buckeye Trail are not for bicycles alone; automobiles and motorcycles use them as well. Be alert at all times.

Figure 1.6 Biker on trail (Barb Compton)

For off-road bicycle enthusiasts there are "single-track" trails for mountain biking, many of them on or near the Buckeye Trail. The Ohio Division of Natural Resources (ODNR) and the Ohio Department of Transportation (ODOT) both offer information regarding these trails. The International Mountain Bike Association (IMBA), Ohio Horseman's Council, and the BTA host the Ohio Trails Partnership (OTP), in which bikers, horseback riders, and hikers join together to build and maintain trails. See the section "The Buckeye Trail Association" for more on the joys of trail building.

TRAIL MARKINGS

The blue blazes are the 2x6-inch vertical blazes used to mark the Buckeye Trail. The standardized paint used is known as Sweeping Blue, and the blazes are painted on trees, utility poles, and specially designed Carsonite signs (fiberglass-reinforced composite markers). Turn blazes, indicating a turn in the trail, utilize two blazes with the upper blaze offset in the direction the trail turns (fig. 1.7). For example, if you arrive at an intersection of two roads and see a double blaze on a telephone pole with the upper blaze offset to the right, you will need to turn right. After turning, you should soon see a single blaze that will let you know you are still following the BT.

Using blue for the BT's blazes came from the founding members of the BTA back in the late 1950s. Many of them, like "Grandma" Gatewood (see chap. 13), followed blue-blazed alternate or side-trails of the mighty Appalachian Trail. This fact makes the blue blazes decidedly appropriate today, for the North Country and American Discovery Trails now link the Buckeye Trail with the Appalachian Trail. These national trail systems will be featured in later chapters.

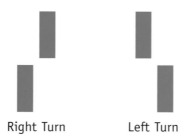

Right Turn   Left Turn

Figure 1.7 Double blazes announce turns

THE BUCKEYE TRAIL ASSOCIATION

If you wish to hike the Buckeye Trail, you should definitely consider becoming a member of the BTA. Membership is very affordable and supports the efforts of the association, as well as keeping you up to date on trail happenings around the state through the BTA's quarterly newsletter, the *Trailblazer*.

At the BTA's annual spring meeting, known as the TrailFest (fig. 1.8), you can join other hikers on scheduled hikes and learn how you may contribute as a volunteer to this dynamic organization. You may even wish to take part in building and maintaining the longest loop trail in the United States by becoming a maintenance volunteer and adopting a section of the trail or joining the trail maintenance crews that travel to work sites for a weekend. You will enjoy camping, work with experienced maintainers from all over the state, and learn quality trail building.

Membership in the BTA also means discounts on maps, a must when hiking the Buckeye Trail. Maps of each section of trail (45 to 60 miles) are currently available for members or nonmembers. All BTA maps, produced by all-volunteer mapmakers, will easily fit into your pocket, include high-quality detail, and are waterproof as well. Visit buckeyetrail.org to order section maps.

The cover of each of the BT's section maps shows the title of the map section and a map of Ohio with the location of the section circled. Section maps are often named after small, off-the-beaten-path towns, many of which you may not be familiar with. For example, the New Straitsville section map (fig. 1.9) is named for the town in the Hill Country (chap. 12)

BuckeyeTrailFest.org

Figure 1.8 Logo for TrailFest

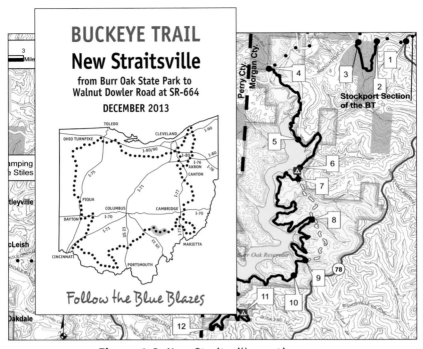

Figure 1.9 New Straitsville section map

that is home to the Moonshine Festival. (See the Overview in that chapter.) The part of the map shown in figure 1.9 covers Points 1 through 11. Each map includes a legend that shows the abbreviations used in the trail log. In addition, in both maps and text, township roads are prefixed with a T-, county roads with a C-, forest roads with an F-. For example, at Point 1, a county road (C-58, Pleasant Valley Road) intersects with SR 78. In the maps the number of a state route appears inside a white circle (in text the abbreviation SR is used: SR 55). The number of a U.S. highway appears on maps inside a white shield (in text: U.S. 250).

A new series of maps called Hiker on the Go (fig. 1.10) has recently been developed by the Buckeye Trail Association. To date there are five short hikes in this book that are supported by Hiker on the Go maps. These maps offer very detailed descriptions of each short hike and interesting facts to tease your curiosity. And, best of all, they can be downloaded onto smart phones and carried with you on the hike. As you prepare for a hike, look for the notation that a Hiker on the Go map is available.

Supporting the maps is information on the BTA website at www .buckeyetrail.org. Trail Alerts found there describe trail conditions of

Figure 1.10 Hiker on the Go map

immediate concern and deviations from current maps, such as a recent trail rerouting, a bridge damaged by flooding, or a lack of blazes in a particular section. The website is continually updated, and hikers of the BT are encouraged to submit items. If there are any significant changes to the short hikes described in this book, they will be noted on Trail Alerts.

Ohio offers an exceptional hiking experience, including a wide variety of plant and animal life. Recent comebacks of animals like beaver, wild turkey, pileated woodpecker, white-tailed deer, and wood duck are largely due to the reestablishment of forests over the last half-century. The great Ohio outdoors is our best-kept secret and the Buckeye Trail—seen from a car, by bicycle, or on foot—is a convenient avenue to exploring it. Don't wait to take that trip to a faraway place. Like Thoreau, who found a whole new world in his backyard, visit the back roads and neglected sites of Ohio, stopping to pet a cow's nose poked through a fence, or enjoy the wildflowers in one of Ohio's beautiful state parks or forests.

CONTACTS

- American Discovery Trail. www.discoverytrail.org.
- Buckeye Trail Association. www.buckeyetrail.org.
- National Park Service. www.nps.gov.
- North Country Trail Association. www.northcountrytrail.org.
- Ohio Atlas and Gazetteer available in most bookstores.
- Ohio Department of Natural Resources. http://ohiodnr.gov/; ODNR Division of Wildlife, http://wildlife.ohiodnr.gov/.
- Ohio History Connection. www.ohiohistory.org.
- Ohio State Parks. http://parks.ohiodnr.gov/.

Southern Wonderland

BTA SECTION MAPS Old Man's Cave, Scioto Trail.

COUNTIES TRAVERSED Hocking, Vinton, Ross, Pike.

DISTANCE COVERED 107 miles.

The Hocking Hills Regional Welcome Center, distinguished by a rustic waterwheel, offers a great beginning point to learn about the Hocking Hills. You will find the Welcome Center (Point 2) by turning south on SR 664 from U.S. 33.

OVERVIEW

Southern Wonderland is the term many use to describe the beauty of the Hocking Hills area. Eroded sandstone walls rise as natural cathedrals from gorge bottoms. The cavelike conditions support unique plant communities that thrive in the gorges' cooler summer temperatures while offering moderate shelter in winter. The human population of this wooded countryside is sparse except on summer weekends, when tourists descend on the area. Plenty of bed-and-breakfasts, campgrounds, stores, and recreational areas exist for those visiting the gorges, the most famous of which is Old Man's Cave.

The oceans of the Paleozoic Era (300 to 500 million years ago) created all of Ohio's bedrock, which extends miles below the earth's surface. Layers of this sedimentary rock are composed of sand as well as the plant and animal life existing at the time. (See appendix 1 for a chart of Ohio's bedrock.) The land described in this chapter was formed during the Mississippian Period (325 to 360 million years ago), when sandstone and shale were formed from the breaking up of the rocks (igneous and other) that made up the earth's original crust. These equatorial seas (Ohio was near the equator) also formed limestone from organic material like coral. Since the glaciers from the north never quite reached this area (see appendix 2), the landscape was shaped by erosion, from wind and mostly from water.

Hocking County is named for the Hocking River, which flows through it. The BT crosses the river at the quaint village of Enterprise, which lies just northwest of Logan. The Hocking River was an early highway used by Native Americans (Delaware, Shawnee, and Wyandot) to get to the Ohio River from central Ohio. The historic Belpré Trail ran east to west through this area connecting Shawnee villages on the Scioto River near Chillicothe to the Ohio River near Belpre and, farther east, to other villages in West Virginia.

The river's drainage basin was used to construct the Hocking Canal, which joined the Ohio and Erie Canal at Carroll. From there it passed through Lancaster and Logan, with a southern terminus in Athens. Early development in the area was attributed to canal transportation. The canal prism (bed profile) and one restored lock are visible along U.S. 33 north of Nelsonville.

Soon after crossing the Hocking River, the blue blazes cross U.S. 33, which follows the Hocking River's drainage basin north to Lancaster and south to Athens and the impressive campus of Ohio University, the oldest university in the Northwest Territories.

The BT crosses the north end of Lake Logan on a levee (Point 1). Lake Logan State Park offers a campground and other facilities. The lake, one of the best fishing lakes in Ohio, supports some infrequently observed birds such as ospreys and great egrets. Bald eagles have also been spotted here. On the west side of the levee is the beginning of the Bill Miller Trail (chap. 13).

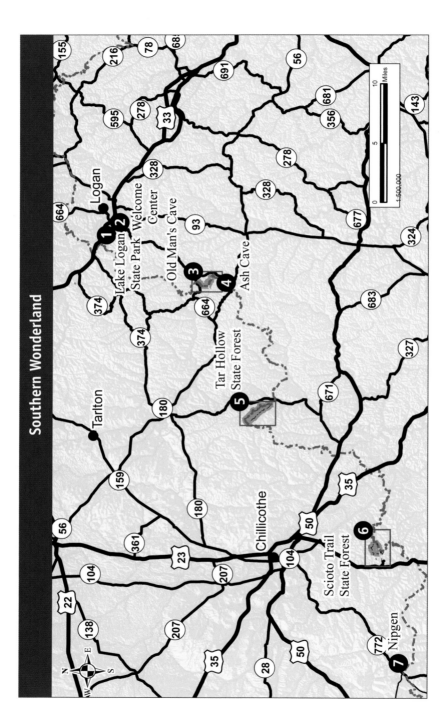

Hocking Hills Welcome Center (Point 2) is located on SR 664 near Lake Logan. A tourist's visit to the area should begin here.

From the Bill Miller Trail the BT is blazed on picturesque county and township roads on its way to the Old Man's Cave rappelling area. Two nature preserves, Scheick Hollow and Saltpetre Cave State Nature Preserves on Big Pine Road, require permits from the Ohio Department of Natural Resources. American Indians and early pioneers used saltpeter to make gunpowder and cure meat.

Six separate areas make up Hocking Hills State Forest, and the first Featured Hike will visit two of them, Old Man's Cave (Point 3) and Cedar Falls. The BT continues southwest at Cedar Falls to pass through Ash Cave (fig. 2.1; Point 4), the last of the three connected areas in Hocking Hills State Park. Ash Cave got its name from the large mounds of ashes found by early settlers. It is certain that Native American families visited this gorge in earlier times. The cave is the largest rock shelter in Ohio, as

Figure 2.1 Ash Cave (Andrew Bashaw)

well as showcasing a 90-foot waterfall. It is said that certain places in the recess echo like a whispering gallery. The quarter-mile trail to Ash Cave from the parking lot is wheelchair accessible. After leaving Ash Cave the BT continues southwest on SR 56.

Traveling west on the BT brings you to Tar Hollow State Forest, at the border of Vinton and Ross Counties (Point 5). This secluded area is the location of our second Featured Hike. A 22-mile network of hiking trails winds through the forest, while 17 miles of paved roads offer scenic drives through the hills and "hollers." As the Buckeye Trail leads you through the hills of southern Ohio, treasures are often given up (fig. 2.2).

Historic Chillicothe, the county seat of Ross County, is west of the Buckeye Trail as it turns south from Tar Hollow. The mighty Scioto River, which in the Wyandot tongue means Deer River, flows through the city to eventually connect with the Ohio River. Always subject to flooding, the Scioto was the site of the Great Flood of 1913 and another devastating flood as recently as 1959. Compared to the Hocking River that the BT crossed earlier, the Scioto River was the American Indians' superhighway.

The ancestors of the Eastern Woodland Indians were most likely the Hopewell and other prehistoric mound builders, who built many mounds in the Scioto valley. The Hopewell Culture National Historic Park in

Figure 2.2 Derelict cabin (Jeff Yoest)

Chillicothe offers evidence, at its five sites, that a long, straight road connected this area to the Hopewell Earthworks (4-square-mile complex) in Newark, Ohio. If this is true, the roadway would have been built more than a century before the Anasazi or Maya built their networks of similarly long, straight roads. Most impressive, the Hopewell built theirs across woodlands and not across desert and plains.

Driving north from Chillicothe on U.S. 23 you pass Mount Logan off to the east. This high hill inspired the Great Seal of Ohio (fig. 2.3). Great Seal State Park is at the southern edge of the glaciated part of Ohio. To the north and west are gentle slopes and rich farmland. To the south and east rise the unglaciated land with steep slopes and poor soils, like those in Tar Hollow. The BT continues south from Tar Hollow in the unglaciated land to cross the fertile Scioto River valley. After climbing a very steep hill from the Scioto River valley, the blue blazes enter Scioto Trail State Forest from the east (Point 6), the location of this chapter's third and last Featured Hike.

After visiting Scioto Trail, you can see a part of Zane's Trace on the BT at the village of Nipgen on SR 772 as it runs south out of Chillicothe. Also known as the Wheeling Road, Zane's Trace ran between Wheeling, Virginia (now West Virginia), and Maysville (then called Limestone), Kentucky. Planned and built by Colonel Ebenezer Zane in the late 1790s,

Figure 2.3 Hills of Chillicothe (Andy "Captain Blue" Niekamp)

it became the earliest frontier road of such length in Ohio (fig. 2.4). At first the road was merely a narrow path through the forest, with stumps protruding from the roadbed. Instead of bridges, ferries were used to cross the rivers. Crude as it was, Zane's Trace offered a much-needed path to many on the frontier. The BT will be near this pioneer road as it travels south and west to the Ohio River.

Before the invention of the steamboat, Ohio pioneers used Zane's Trace for commerce and travel between the east and the south. Boatmen, returning upriver after taking their wares to New Orleans on rafts, also used the road much as they used the Natchez Trace, in the South.

The community store in Nipgen (Point 7) is worth a visit. From Nipgen, the BT goes into Pike Lake State Forest. The journey on the Buckeye Trail, for this chapter, ends at Pike Lake State Park. This hidden gem will begin our next chapter. To find and follow the Buckeye Trail around the state consult the Overviews in chapters 2 through 12. Also, you should plan to hike one or more of the Featured Hikes found below to learn more about the BT in the Southern Wonderland.

Figure 2.4 Diagram of Zane's Trace

FEATURED HIKE 1
OLD MAN'S CAVE TO CEDAR FALLS

DISTANCE A loop of slightly over 5 miles.

TIME At least 3.5 hours (includes time to enjoy the natural world encountered along the way).

DIFFICULTY Moderately easy. Although there is an elevation change of over 200 feet from the bottom of Cedar Falls to the Visitor Center, most of the climb takes place on the wooden staircase at Cedar Falls. Families with young children regularly make this trip.

There is a Hiker on the Go map for this section of the Buckeye Trail.

Park in the large parking lot at Old Man's Cave, just off State Route 664. Stop first at the Visitor Center (WP 1), just south of the parking lot. The building houses a great collection of art and artifacts describing the biological and human drama of the caves. Among the treasures is the story of Richard Rowe, the Old Man of Old Man's Cave. Born in 1774 in Tennessee, he moved with his family to the Ohio Valley in 1796. Rowe became familiar with the new land by hunting and trapping and wandered into the Hocking region by way of Salt Creek and Queer Creek. He lived alone in what is now known as Old Man's Cave. You will find the cave and see the ledge he was buried under on this Featured Hike.

Take the paved walkway leading northeast from the Visitor Center to the upper falls. The gorge is to the right. Do not venture near the edge, and keep reminding yourself and others that the edges are not marked and it would be easy to fall as much as 75 feet, resulting in death or serious injury. You should always stay on the trail when hiking in a state park, a practice that protects not only you, but the delicate environment as well.

A monument to Grandma Gatewood stands above the Upper Falls (fig. 2.5). The Gorge Trail between this point and Ash Cave, several miles south, is dedicated to this founding member of the Buckeye Trail Association. The Gatewood story is found in chapter 13. The blue blazes lead you to the steps descending into the gorge.

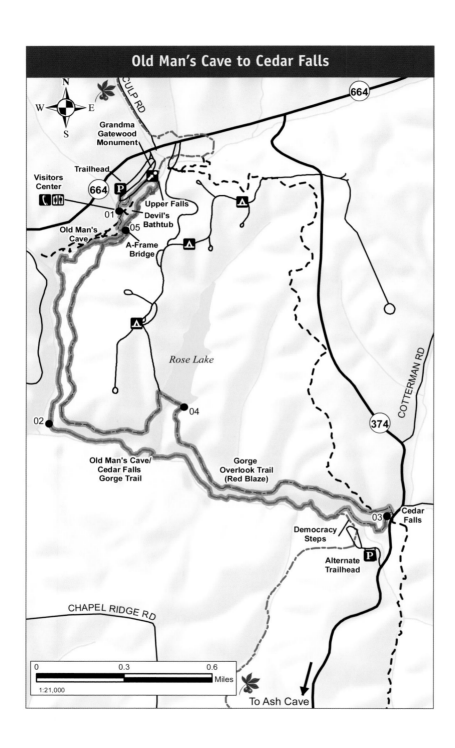

Old Man's Cave to Cedar Falls

N W E S

CULP RD

664

Grandma Gatewood Monument

Trailhead

Visitors Center

664 P

Upper Falls

01 Devil's Bathtub

05

Old Man's Cave

A-Frame Bridge

Rose Lake

04

02

Old Man's Cave/ Cedar Falls Gorge Trail

Gorge Overlook Trail (Red Blaze)

COTTERMAN RD

374

03 Cedar Falls

Democracy Steps

P

Alternate Trailhead

CHAPEL RIDGE RD

0   0.3   0.6
                              Miles
1:21,000

To Ash Cave

Figure 2.5 Grandma Gatewood Memorial Hiking Trail

From the bottom, look up over the Upper Falls (fig. 2.6). Imagine how the sandstone, formed eons ago from the sands of an ancient sea, would have been hundreds of feet higher. Glaciers, stopping 6 miles north of this area, dumped meltwater that removed much of the sandstone and carved many of the gorges. Old Man's Creek is continuing the erosion process, and you will follow it through the gorge. From the Upper to the Lower Falls is blackhand sandstone, which resists erosion in its upper and lower layers. Erosion of the softer center sections formed the dramatic rock shelter caves.

Over time, the sand from the ancient sea became cemented into the many horizontal layers in the sides of the gorge (see appendix 1, Mississippian Period). The slanted cross-bedding lines are evidence of an ancient sandbar shaped by changing ocean currents. The honeycomb patterns on the rock's surface were caused by water percolating through from above. Iron ore within the sandstone causes the red hues. The layering of the sandstone in the large slabs that have fallen from the sides of the gorge was horizontal, before the slabs fell.

At the Upper Falls the vegetation is often nonexistent, due to people climbing and playing on the sides of the gorge. Still, you may see *Sullivantia*

Figure 2.6 Upper Falls (Andy "Captain Blue" Niekamp)

(Sullivant's coolwort), a very rare wildflower with white flowers that people travel from afar to see. This is an example of the ancient and rare plants that can be found in this sheltered climate.

Shortly after leaving the Upper Falls, heading south into the gorge, you will see the pothole known as the Devil's Bathtub (fig. 2.7). Local legend has it that the pool's bottom is in Hades. Water levels may change rapidly in the gorge. When the water level is up, the swirling waters create a deafening sound in the basin. In 1998 the water level, due to heavy rains, would have been well over your head here. The 1998 floodwaters wiped out or weakened bridges that had survived since the 1930s. Further along, try to find the whale in the wall, a huge protrusion in the rock cliff face on the left (east) side of the gorge.

You will next pass under an A-frame bridge (WP 3) that crosses the gorge high above your head. You will walk across this bridge later, at the end of the hike, on the Gorge Overlook Trail.

Soon you will come to Old Man's Cave, off to the right (west side) of the gorge, and shortly after that the trail passes through a tunnel. A bridge and another tunnel allow access to the cave. The large overhang to this rock shelter cave was created by running water gouging out the soft center

Figure 2.7 Devil's Bathtub (Andy "Captain Blue" Niekamp)

of the sandstone cliffs. This is the cave where Richard Rowe lived and died. In the winter of 1857 a friend sent to check on him discovered his body: at the age of 83 Rowe had apparently shot himself accidentally while using the butt of his gun to break the ice in the creek. While here, look for an interpretive sign about a rock formation shaped like the head of a sphinx that has become the logo for the state park.

The 40-foot drop of the Lower Falls marks the end of the Old Man's Cave area. Steps here lead up the west side of the gorge to an overlook on the Old Man's Cave Trail. But our hike continues in the gorge by following the blue-blazed BT and the Old Man's Cave/Cedar Falls Gorge Trail. After 1.5 miles into the hike, the park has provided benches for a peaceful sit-down (WP 2).

In the warmer months, take time to notice the life in the clear, cold stream. Look for water striders and minnows like the blacknose dace or the creek chub. Look hard and you might find a rare minnow, the mottled sculpin, walking on ventral fins across gravel bottoms. Even some small fish, such as bluegill, might be seen.

All through the gorge area you will see giant eastern hemlocks. The larger trees have to be very old, over 300 years, for they receive little in nutrients from the sandstone floor they are rooted in, and growth is slow. A cross-section of an oak in the Visitor Center shows a tree's amazing life span. The hemlocks are being threatened today by the hemlock wooly adelgid. This invasive insect has the potential to drastically change the gorge environment. Other trees to look for are sweet (or black) birch, tulip, and sourwood (sorrel-tree). In midsummer, when other trees have already lost their flowers, the sourwood will bloom with a multitude of white blossoms reminiscent of lily of the valley.

Sometimes a giant tree will fall in the gorge because of its weak anchorage on sandstone. When a large tree falls, the environment is dramatically altered. Sunshine penetrates areas that had been shaded, allowing wildflowers and new saplings to spring forth. Birds and other animals will move into the newly created niche. The broken trees become dens or food sources for raccoons and pileated woodpeckers. Wildflowers in the gorge include partridgeberry (red berries in July) and white baneberry (berries July–September). The baneberry's highly poisonous white berries with black dots give the plant another common name: doll's eyes. You might even be lucky enough to see the rare pink lady's slipper, an orchid that blooms in May or June.

Cedar Falls makes a great lunch stop on this Featured Hike (fig. 2.8). The name was given to this area by early pioneers who mistook the hemlocks for cedars. Before you get to Cedar Falls, you will notice the Democracy Steps, off to the right (south) side of the gorge and leading up to the parking area. The blue blazes go up these steps. According to a Hocking Hills visitor's guide, these steps were specially designed by artist Akio Hizume to be "mathematically and physically attuned to the human gait." Restroom facilities can be found in the parking area at the top.

Near the falls (WP 3), find a set of wooden steps that take you to the Gorge Overlook Trail (not to the Cedar Falls parking lot). At the top of the steps, follow the clearly defined path to the suspension bridge crossing to the Gorge Overlook Trail. Keep the red blazes (indicating a park trail, not the BT) in sight as you follow this trail. This trail is most beautiful in the winter, when it is frosted with snow and ice and the gorge can be seen more easily. Always stay on the trail and never get close to the rim of the gorge.

The pine plantation to your right was planted in the 1950s. Each year that a pine tree lives, it produces a new ring of branches. By counting the number of whorls of limbs on a tree its age can be confirmed. Soon, the woods open to reveal the dam at Rose Lake (WP 4). This is a favorite spot

Figure 2.8 Cedar Falls (Brent and Amy Anslinger)

for anglers fishing for bass and rainbow trout. Take a hard left (south) after passing over the dam; do not follow the service road up the hill to the campground (which permits group camping).

During the summer in the gorge you may hear the clear, ethereal notes of the hermit thrush. You may also spot this migrant, slightly larger than a sparrow, on the red-blazed park trail. Look for the gray-brown bird's rust-colored tail.

The A-frame bridge (WP 5) spanning the gorge near the end of this Featured Hike is the one you walked beneath earlier in the hike. It will return you to the Visitor Center.

FEATURED HIKE 2
TAR HOLLOW STATE FOREST

DISTANCE 6 to 7 miles.

TIME At least 4 hours.

DIFFICULTY Difficult. This is one of the most strenuous hikes in this book. The elevation change is almost 300 feet from the creek along Clark Hollow Road to the fire tower on South Ridge Road. A compass and the map provided here are indispensable in following the correct trail among others in the forest. Parents of small children should plan a modified hike. Plastic bags with drawstrings can be used to cover the feet while fording one or two creeks.

Tar Hollow is a little over 10 miles east of Chillicothe on SR 327, the highway to the park and forest. At Londonderry, U.S. 50 intersects SR 327 from the south. From the north take SR 56 from Circleville to SR 180 and head south to Adelphi and SR 327.

Enter the park through the main entrance, on Tar Hollow Road (F-10). The large sign for the state park is found at the junction of SR 327 and F-10. Follow Tar Hollow Road to the Park Office to get a recent brochure and other information. Other features on Tar Hollow Road include a general store and nature center, camping and horseman areas, and Pine Lake. Mountain bikers will enjoy the 3.5-mile loop trail along the lakeshore as well as other trails in the park.

Continue on serpentine F-10 until it Ts into South Ridge Road (F-3). Follow this road left (south) to the fire tower parking lot and picnic area with toilets. The total distance to the fire tower from SR 327 is 5 miles. There is also a backpacker's campground here. In winter, when the forest roads are icy and snow covered, hikes may begin at the trailhead just north of the former forest headquarters on Clark Hollow Road, or F-2. This trailhead (between WP 4 and WP 5) is identified later in the hike.

If you are ambitious enough to climb the Brush Ridge fire tower (fig. 2.9), you will see that the ridge tops approach the same elevation. This feature is characteristic of the unglaciated region of Ohio. First, meltwater from nearby glaciers and later the streams flowing in the defined hollows carved out the ridges over centuries. Before the 1930s the land was too poor to produce good crops. Moonshiners supplemented their low income, but revenuers could make life difficult for them. Because of

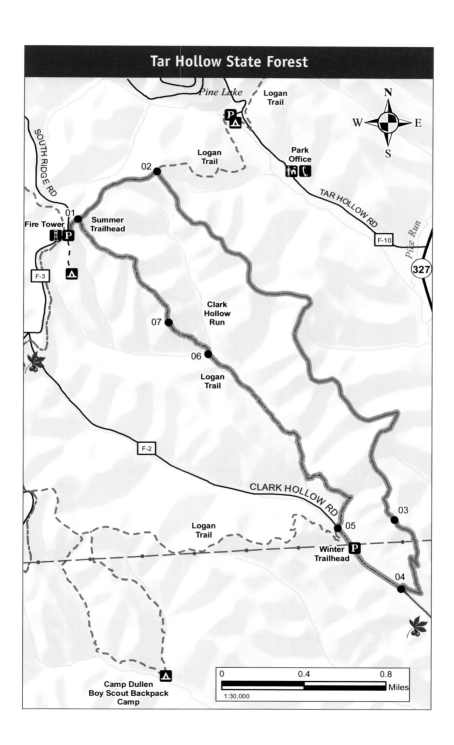

Tar Hollow State Forest

Pine Lake

Logan Trail

Logan Trail

Park Office

SOUTH RIDGE RD

TAR HOLLOW RD

F-10

Pine Run

327

02

01

Fire Tower

Summer Trailhead

F-3

Clark Hollow Run

07

06

Logan Trail

F-2

CLARK HOLLOW RD

05

03

Logan Trail

Winter Trailhead

04

Camp Dullen Boy Scout Backpack Camp

N
W   E
S

| 0 | 0.4 | 0.8 |
Miles
1:30,000

Figure 2.9 Fire tower (Richard Lutz)

the settlers' poverty, the government bought the land that presently makes up the forest, paying the settlers enough to move on. But much of the forest you see here did not exist in the 1930s. Forests today cover more than 30 percent of Ohio's land, compared to only 12 percent at the turn of the century.

Tar Hollow is so named because of the native pitch pine growing on its poor, hilly soils. The tree's heartwood and its many knots yield pine tar, which was once used for such varied applications as horse liniments and wagon wheel lubricants. Look for a grove of pitch pines at the fire tower as well as others scattered throughout the hills and hollows on your hike. It is distinguished from other pines in the same area by its 3-to-5-inch, stiff needles in bundles of 3 (white pine, bundles of 5; red pine, bundles of 2).

The shy timber rattlesnake is an endangered species living in these hills, but it is unlikely that you will see one. These reptiles, although poisonous, are usually not aggressive. If you do see one, leave it alone and report the sighting to a park ranger. Other wildlife in the area includes a large number of wild turkey and deer, as well as the less frequent bear or bobcat. Several varieties of lizards and salamanders can be seen in the summer. In the early spring enjoy the redbud trees and a variety of wild-flowers. The Mushroom Festival in the spring brings many people to Tar Hollow to enjoy hunting for the delicious morel mushroom.

Begin the hike at the northeast corner of the fire tower (WP 1). The Carsonite sign here shows that you will be traversing the BT, the ADT, and the North Country Trail (for descriptions of the NCT and ADT, see chaps. 1 and 11). You will see *both blue and red blazes* on the trees. Both the BT (blue blazes) and the north loop of the Logan Trail (red blazes) parallel South Ridge Road for a while before turning more to the east.

The wildflowers will be quite different here, on a north-facing slope, than on south-facing slopes you will hike later. In about 10 minutes you will encounter a side trail, identified as Brush Ridge Trail, leading to a picnic area at Pine Lake. In about 20 minutes, there is a clearly marked junction (WP 2), with the red blazes of the Logan Trail going straight ahead (northeast) and the blue blazes heading south.

A Carsonite sign with the familiar blue blaze reinforces the direction of the BT and of our hike. This nicely benched (flat) trail built on a steep hillside is a credit to the maintenance volunteers of the BTA. Orient your-self also to the ravine on your left and notice the young beeches along the way. (Old beeches are a sign of a mature wood, but, as noted previously, this area had been farmed until the 1930s.) Also look for signs of a pile-ated woodpecker's work—large rectangular holes in the trees, with wood chips at the base of the trunk.

About 40 minutes into the hike you will ascend to a high point on the ridge where you can look north to view a river of pines in the ravine below. Twenty minutes later the BT broadens as it joins an old logging road, then narrows once again as it leaves the shared trail. This is why it is important to follow the blazes rather than clearly defined paths that can mislead you. (For a description of turn blazes, see chap. 1.) Continuing higher on the ridge you might begin to hear traffic on SR 327. The BT begins to turn more to the southwest, but the trail is still on the north side of the ridge. You should soon be able to see houses along the highway. The 300-foot plateau offers excellent views from which early settlers may have spotted the "revenooers." In a few minutes you will begin descending and may notice a line of larger trees along the ridge that could be an old fence line.

After about 2 hours of hiking you will cross a gravel road (WP 3). Go left and reenter woods to your right. You will see a memorial post dedi-cated to a scout who succumbed to heat exhaustion when working on the nearby Logan Trail (fig. 2.10). Next you will enter a clear-cut area under power lines. There is a good view of the trailhead along the power lines' path and adjacent to the road. This trailhead, mentioned at the beginning of the hike, may be used for a winter parking area when the forest roads are snow covered.

From here, as you descend the steeper slopes, switchbacks will ease your passage. Some rocks here are composed of an interesting quartz-sandstone conglomerate. At the bottom of the ridge you will see forestry buildings on the road below, across from Clark Hollow Run. Cross the stream (WP 4) and follow Clark Hollow Road to the north. About 200 yards after passing a parking area under the power lines you will encounter the Logan Trail, marked in red (WP 5). This trail is a section of the South Loop of the Logan Trail. Follow the red blazes to the right (east), heading back to the fire tower.

As you follow the red blazes into the lowland, you might get lucky and jump a grouse or two in this area, for a grouse management area in the

Figure 2.10 Memorial to Scout (Andy "Captain Blue" Niekamp)

forest's northwest corner has increased their numbers. The red-blazed trail is named for Chief Logan, an early American Indian leader famous for a speech in which he stated reluctantly that he had to make war on the "long-knives" because they were murdering his people. The site of his speech was the Logan Elm, now a state memorial, which stood until 1964 in the Pickaway Plains, a little south of Circleville. Boy Scouts have maintained the Logan Trail in Tar Hollow for many years. As with the blue blazes of the BT, if you do not see any red blazes while on this trail, be sure you have not lost the trail.

Moving generally northeast at first, begin climbing a ridge above the stream. After walking on the ridge for a short time, descend again to the stream and a wide logging road heading north. The BT used this route at one time before it was moved to the higher ridge to the east.

About half an hour from the beginning of the Logan Trail, you will cross the confluence of two streams (WP 6), near the intersection of the Hocking, Vinton, and Ross county lines. After the fording, using plastic bags if necessary, you begin a steep climb. Be careful, for part of this trail is rocky, with a difficult grade. Both red pine and pitch pine grow along the trail. In a little more than an hour after beginning the Logan Trail, you will arrive at the top of the ridge (WP 7), where the trail turns westerly. A feathery-barked grove of sweet (or black) birch will be found along the trail here. The walk on top of the ridge is easier and soon you may spot the angular fire tower through the treetops. After crossing a gully you will soon reach the fire tower, where this Featured Hike ends.

FEATURED HIKE 3
SCIOTO TRAIL STATE PARK

DISTANCE 2.75 miles.

TIME At least 1.5 hours for the hike from Caldwell Lake, up to the ridge, and then down to the environs around Stewart Lake.

DIFFICULTY Difficult. The elevation change is 300 feet from the Caldwell Lake parking area to the highest points on the hike. One or two stream fordings.

Take U.S. 23 south from Chillicothe to get to Scioto Trail State Park and Forest. The entrance is on the left (east) side of the highway. Enter the park on SR 372, which is also Forest Road 1 (F-1) and Stoney Creek Road.

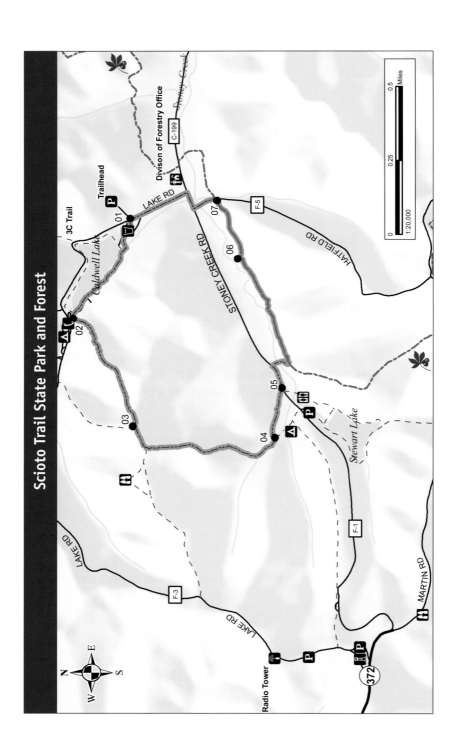

Before beginning the hike you may wish to visit the scenic overlook on Martin Road (F-4), the first right turn after entering the park and near the old fire tower. From this vantage point you will see the transition boundary between Mississippian and Devonian bedrock (see appendix 1). To the north, along SR 23, is the southernmost penetration of glaciers in this area (see the glacial boundary, in appendix 2). As you look south the bedrock hills become more prominent. Characteristically, the blue blazes stay to the south of the glacial boundary, leading into the higher ridges.

Such historic figures as Tecumseh and Daniel Boone once traveled the historic Scioto Trail, which followed the Scioto River flowing east of Scioto Trail State Park and Forest. At least three Shawnee villages were located along the Scioto River in the Chillicothe area during the 1700s, and the forest served as part of the hunting grounds for the Shawnee.

Return to Stoney Creek Road and bear right (northeast). Note the Buckeye Trail sign just beyond Stewart Lake. This trail accesses the blue blazes as they pass to the east of Stewart Lake. At the forestry buildings at Lake Road (F-3), turn left (north) to visit the Park Office and obtain further information on the park and forest. There is parking in the area near the maintenance buildings and office. There is also ample parking across the road and a picnic area with restroom facilities.

Begin your hike by climbing the stairs from a parking area (WP 1) to the top of the dam. Follow a trail around to the left or west side of Caldwell Lake to the camp store. On the east side of the store see a trail (WP 2) going up the ridge that gives the distances to the fire tower (2.25 miles) and Stewart Lake (1.75 miles). (Stewart Lake will be our destination.)

The trail climbs steeply southwest above Caldwell Lake. This is a well-defined trail with no blazes. In about 15 minutes the trail will bear right (west). The top of the ridge rises to the left and a ravine drops off to the right as you walk a fairly flat portion of the trail. The trail turns back to the southwest and becomes steeper as it leads to the top of a very narrow ridge. A large variety of birds may be seen here. Good views of the other ridges to the northwest and southwest reveal they are all at the same elevation as the ridge you stand on. Just as at Tar Hollow, the ridge tops are at the altitude of the original unglaciated plateau and the ravines have been formed over centuries by erosion.

In another 15 minutes, after reaching the top of the ridge (WP 3), you will see a trail diverging to the right, back to the campground. Go straight ahead to the Fire Tower and Stewart Lake Trails. In a few minutes, as they diverge, good signs here show clearly that the Stewart Lake Trail turns left (south). Follow the trail to Stewart Lake. Soon the trail will come to a hiker's overlook with a view across a ravine that drops off quickly. After the overlook the trail also drops rather steeply. At the bottom of the ravine is a small stream to cross that could be a ford in wet weather. Here the trail flattens out along the watershed and turns from south to east as it nears Stoney Creek Road. At WP 4 the trail turns left and crosses a wooden bridge, bringing you to a utility building and Stoney Creek Road (Park Road 1).

Cross the road (WP 5) and head left (east). At the end of the picnic area you will come upon a brown sign saying Buckeye Trail. Enter the woods at this sign and cross Stoney Creek. The path is unmarked but well defined. In about 30 feet, you will come upon the blue blazes of the Buckeye Trail (fig. 2.11). Follow the blue blazes to the left (east), across a small gulley on a footpath. After this turn, there is another quick turn left. Follow the blue blazes.

If conditions make fording Stoney Creek unfeasible, return to the road and walk east. Shortly you will encounter a multipurpose trail leading into the woods. This trail does not join the BT immediately but turns

Figure 2.11 Scioto Trail (Andy "Captain Blue" Niekamp)

left (northeast) along the creek, passing through a peaceful white pine forest. These trees have needles in bundles of five. By counting the whorls of limbs you can estimate that this pine planting occurred about 50 years ago (much later than the forest lands developed in the 1930s). The entire area was used for target practice during World War I.

If you took the trail using the bridge, it will be blazed in white and merge with the blue blazes at WP 6. After WP 6, follow blue and white blazes to Hatfield Road (F-5) (WP 7). Turn left and walk the road to Stoney Creek Road, turn right and return to your car.

After your hike and as you leave the parking lot on Lake Road, you might wish to turn left and drive Stoney Creek Road east instead of west to explore Three Locks Road (C-205), which follows the Scioto River. The road is so named because the Erie Canal followed the Scioto and there are remains of locks and other canal infrastructure along this road. The BT exits the Scioto Trail area to the north and eventually crosses Three Locks Road at the bridge over the Scioto River, where a ditch reveals the remains of the Ohio and Erie Canal, opened in 1832.

LOCAL CONTACTS

- Adena Mansion and Gardens. www.adenamansion.com.
- Great Seal State Park. www.parks.ohiodnr.gov/greatseal.
- Hiker on the Go map for Old Man's Cave. www.buckeyetrail.org.
- Hocking Hills State Park. http://parks.ohiodnr.gov/hockinghills.
- Hopewell Culture National Historical Park. www.nps.gov/hocu/index.htm.
- Ohio Department of Natural Resources. www.ohiodnr.gov.
- Ross County Historical Society. www.rosscountyhistorical.org.
- Scioto Trail State Park and Forest. http://parks.ohiodnr.gov/sciototrail.
- Tar Hollow State Park. http://parks.ohiodnr.gov/tarhollow.
- Tecumseh! Outdoor Drama. Summers, Monday through Saturday. North of Chillicothe. www.tecumsehdrama.com

WAYPOINT ID'S

WAYPOINT ID	DESCRIPTION	LATITUDE	LONGITUDE
	OLD MAN'S CAVE		
1	Visitor Center	39.43467400	−82.54143500
2	Bench	39.42368900	−82.54590000

WAYPOINT ID	DESCRIPTION	LATITUDE	LONGITUDE
3	Wooden steps at Cedar Falls	39.41902500	−82.52432300
4	Rose Lake dam	39.42454700	−82.53727600
5	A-frame bridge	39.43367200	−82.54103400
	TAR HOLLOW		
1	Fire tower	39.37635200	−82.76173600
2	Jct BT and Logan	39.37993000	−82.75456400
3	Gravel road	39.35446500	−82.73273800
4	Stream	39.34970700	−82.73199000
5	Jct BT and Logan	39.35267300	−82.73625900
6	Confluence two streams	39.36645900	−82.74978600
7	Top of the ridge	39.36876800	−82.75343900
	SCIOTO TRAIL		
1	Parking at dam	39.22718300	−82.94864100
2	Trail at camp store	39.22985600	−82.95500400
3	Top of ridge	39.22700000	−82.96178100
4	Trail turn	39.22030700	−82.96245900
5	Road crossing	39.21999300	−82.95932100
6	Jct White Trail and BT	39.22210300	−82.95117300
7	Hatfield Road	39.22309400	−82.94748100

The Bluegrass Region

BTA SECTION MAP Sinking Spring.

COUNTIES TRAVERSED Pike, Highland, Adams.

DISTANCE COVERED 53 miles.

OVERVIEW

Whether you take U.S. 50 or SR 32 into the Bluegrass Region, the drive itself will be a treat. SR 32, known also as the Appalachian Highway, is magnificent in spring, when the eastern redbud and the white flowers of the dogwood are in bloom. Driving west on SR 32, notice how cedars suddenly appear just to the east of Peebles. The presence of the eastern red cedar (actually a juniper) indicates your arrival on limestone-based,

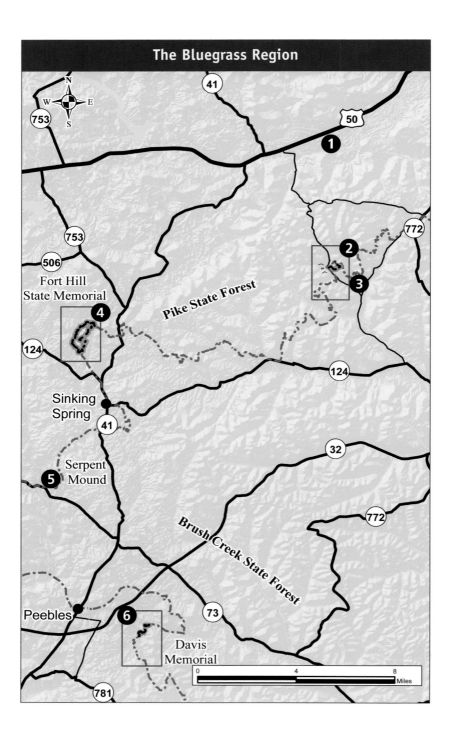

The Bluegrass Region

alkaline (sweet) soils created during the Silurian Period (see appendix 1). The other Ohio soils are more acidic and not as friendly to the red cedars.

If you are coming to this area from Chillicothe on U.S. 50, visit Seip Mound (Point 1 on the Overview Map). The second-largest Hopewell mound, Seip Mound is an Ohio History Connection site with an interpretive kiosk. Artifacts found in the mound indicate how extensive the Hopewell trading routes must have been. There were pearls from the Gulf Coast, copper and silver from Lake Superior, mica from the Appalachian Mountains, and silver from Canada. Several skulls found in the mound were adorned with copper noses.

We begin this chapter's Featured Hikes in Pike County at Pike Lake State Park (Point 2 on Overview Map). The county's land west of the Scioto River was part of the Virginia Military District, exclusively settled by Virginia's veterans of the Revolutionary War. The pioneers of this region came after 1795, when the Treaty of Greenville was signed and the Shawnee had to relinquish their homelands.

Pike County is also where the last reported passenger pigeon was found in the wild (1900); these birds once darkened the skies with their enormous numbers. The last one in captivity, Martha, died in 1914 at the Cincinnati Zoo. This marked the first known extinction by humans of a native American animal.

Near Pike Lake State Park is the Eager Inn (Point 3, fig. 3.1) at the intersection of Morgans Fork Road and Pike Lake Road. The historic inn

Figure 3.1 Eager Inn

was used by a contingent of Morgan's Raiders as the Rebs traveled—without permission, of course—through Ohio during the Civil War. The group was later captured in eastern Ohio (chap. 11). A sign in front of the building indicates that you are on the old Zane's Trace. On the back of the building are the date 1797 and the name Eageren. Mr. Eageren built the inn here, known as the Eager Inn, when Ebenezer Zane oversaw the building of his road. Inns were established about every 8 miles along this important pioneer road.

By the second Featured Hike along the BT you will discover a little piece of Kentucky at Fort Hill (Point 4, fig. 3.2). In geological terms this small triangular area is known as the Bluegrass Region, noted for its limestone and dolomite bedrock. Appendix 2 shows Ohio's landform regions, both unglaciated and glaciated. Known as a physiographic map, it shows the landscape and terrain of the land caused by erosion and/or glaciations that occurred in more recent times than the millions of years taken for the formation of the bedrock. This type of glaciated and unglaciated landform caused erosion that often resulted in flat hills as well as more striking features such as sinkholes, created when water dissolves limestone, forming subterranean holes.

Karst is the name given by the geologists to this landform and, like landslides or coastal erosion, it is a geological hazard. (Another significant karst region is discussed in chap. 8.) The area around Peebles is a part of

Figure 3.2 Fort Hill (Darryl Smith)

Figure 3.3 Serpent Mound (Courtesy of Ohio History Connection)

the 2 percent of Ohio that has this landform. A cave 2,323 feet long near Peebles, which only a few professional spelunkers visit, is noteworthy for its length and for having an entrance that has never been modified by humans. The underground shaft is also the home of a blind beetle found nowhere else in the world.

Sinking Spring, just south of Fort Hill and north of Peebles and at the intersection of SR 41 and SR 124, has in its park the only octagonal schoolhouse in Ohio. South of the village you will enter Adams County, the third-oldest county in Ohio.

Further south on SR 41 is the intersection of SR 73. Taking this road west will lead you to the enigmatic Serpent Mound, an earthwork in the shape of a reptile that seems to be intent upon engulfing an egg (Point 5; also see fig. 3.3). Over a quarter mile long, it is the largest known effigy mound in the U.S. and perhaps the world. This curious work sits above the surrounding landscape on the uplift of a 10-mile-wide (6 km) bowl in the earth formed by a prehistoric meteorite.

Researchers are still attempting to determine who built the effigy and why. Adena, Hopewell, and Fort Ancient Indians lived near the site from 800 b.c. to after a.d. 1000, and Serpent Mound is believed to have been constructed around a.d. 1000. As with all prehistoric knowledge, there are differing views as to who constructed the effigy. As for why, worship of serpents and other animals by both "primitive" and present-day peoples is well known, and prehistoric peoples built serpent effigies in at least four other states in the U.S. The famous stone effigy of Loch Nell (not to be confused with the more famous Loch Ness monster) in Scotland is of prehistoric origin.

Peebles is the site of one of the largest events ever to take place in Adams County, the fifth annual World's Plowing Match and Conservation Exposition, in 1957, in which competitors from 14 nations participated, attracting some 250,000 people. The BT leads east from Peebles on Portsmouth Road (C-198), where it crosses SR 32. The Plum Run Quarry is located there. Further east the blue blazes lead to Pine Gap Road (C-25), where a limestone-dolomite conveyor crosses overhead, carrying the rocks 3 miles to the processing plant where they are crushed and screened. Ohio ranks fourth in the nation in limestone production, producing 12 percent of total U.S. output. Most of the limestone and dolomite from this area is used for building (concrete) and road construction.

Just past the conveyor, the Buckeye Trail goes cross-country to Beaver Pond Road. This land, part of 7,000 acres, is owned by General Electric, which tests jet engine thrusts of up to 150,000 lbs. at a facility here. At predetermined times, the jet engines will roar to life. This is another anomaly with Adams County, a test operation that produces horrendous noise and at the same time protects thousands of acres as a wildlife preserve. The facility's weapons ban creates a wildlife refuge where biologists have found an outstanding number of plants and animals. Over 100 species of birds listed as rare or endangered have been identified on the property.

We end the chapter at Davis Memorial State Nature Preserve (fig. 3.4), our third Featured Hike (Point 6). This hike is a fitting finale when discussing a portion of trail that is renowned for its collision of geology and biology. Davis Memorial offers an up-close look at dolomite formations, earth faults, and the flora resulting from the chemical makeup of dolomite—calcium magnesium carbonate.

Figure 3.4 Davis Memorial boardwalk (Andy "Captain Blue" Niekamp)

FEATURED HIKE 1
PIKE LAKE STATE PARK

DISTANCE 1.2 miles.

TIME 1–2 hours.

DIFFICULTY Moderately difficult. There is a 400-foot climb to the top of the ridge, but the trail is well benched (trail builders carve out of the slope a flat surface to walk on).

Pike Lake State Park is one of Ohio's hidden gems. This hard-to-find area doesn't attract as many visitors as other parks, offering the hiker a more restful visit.

Park at the dam and visit the Park Office, on Pike Lake Road (T-348), for information about the park, forest, and surrounding area. There is a general store near the dam.

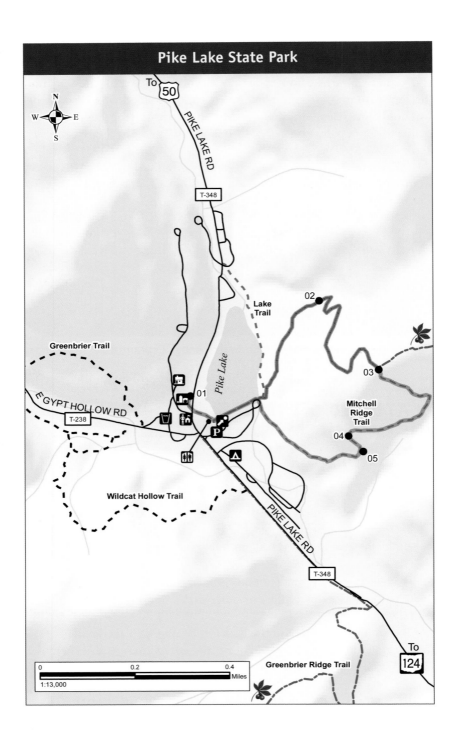

This hike is on the 1.2-mile Mitchell Ridge Trail. The Buckeye Trail follows the Mitchell Ridge Trail to the top of the ridge. Walk to the dam at the south of the lake (WP 1, fig. 3.5). As you begin to cross the dam, find the lonely tombstone of an unknown Union soldier who died of his wounds before reaching home (fig. 3.6). After crossing the dam, where the dam and the woods meet, follow the Buckeye Trail (blue blazes) and the accompanying ridge trail (red blazes) to the left (north). The hike parallels the lake, so you have views of the water while walking through mature woods. At the north end of the lake the trail turns more uphill alongside a stream.

At WP 2, a bridle trail will merge with the BT and Mitchell Ridge Trail. You will now be following red, white, and blue blazes. Notice that the trail is much wider now that it has joined the bridle trail. The trail will be quite muddy during wet weather because of the horse traffic. While on this hike, it is critical that you do not get distracted by intersecting trails.

Figure 3.5 Pike Lake (Andy "Captain Blue" Niekamp)

Figure 3.6 Grave of Unknown Soldier

If you encounter horses, avoid reaching out to them or startling them in any way. Step off the path and let them pass.

The Mitchell Ridge Trail climbs steeply to the south once again and then levels out near the top. After about one-half hour of climbing, the bridle and BT trails lead off to the left from the Mitchell Ridge Trail to continue east to Scioto Trail State Park (chap. 2) (WP 3). At this point follow only the red blazes, which continue south. The trail is now narrow but clearly marked. The descent will be a bit rugged as it descends through stream beds. In May and June, the woodland flowers, such as cohosh, are abundant. Black cohosh is used as a tonic and can even be found in herbal stores.

Further down the hill you will encounter a white-blazed bridle trail (WP 4). Follow the red and white blazes to the left. In this area watch for American chestnut sprouts among fallen trees. At WP 5, the Mitchell trail goes to the right. One consistent focus throughout this hike is the red blazes. Always stay with the red. Finish the hike by crossing the dam, or follow the lilac-blazed Lake Trail for a shoreline walk around the east side of the lake and then follow the road south back to your car.

FEATURED HIKE 2
FORT HILL

DISTANCE 4 miles.

TIME Allow at least 3 hours to appreciate the natural world revealed along the trails.

DIFFICULTY Difficult. Approximate elevation change is more than 500 feet and there are precipitous climbs and descents.

Fort Hill State Memorial is off SR 41, which connects U.S. 50 and SR 32. These two highways cut across southern Ohio from east to west. The sign directing you down Fort Hill Road will be found south of Cynthiana and 4 to 5 miles north of Sinking Spring.

The Arc of Appalachia Preserve System maintains this park, which has been designated a National Natural Landmark by the National Park Service. A Natural Landmark is created by geological time or possesses rare plant life. You will find both attributes here, as well as the earthworks of earlier humans—the Hopewell mound builders. Before your hike, visit the museum to acquaint yourself with the features you will see. There is no charge. The museum is open from May to October, noon to 5 p.m. on Saturdays and Sundays. Check the website.

Four out of five of Ohio's land-forming regions conjoin here. To the east, the hills of the unglaciated Allegheny Plateau are pronounced (see appendix 2). Immediately to the northeast is the glaciated Allegheny Plateau, formed by massive ice sheets that flattened hills and changed the course of rivers. To the west is the Till Plain, an area rich in glacial material (till), deposited by retreating glaciers. To the south is the unglaciated Bluegrass Region. The dolomite bedrock here creates a karst landscape, with the natural bridges and arches you will see on this hike.

Because of the differing types of bedrock in these geological regions, an amazing 675 different plant species live here. The area hosts rarities not found in popular wildflower books, such as Walter's violet, Canby's mountain-lover, and American columbo. The wildflower American columbo takes up to 25 years to mature, produces a 4-foot flower stalk, and then dies. Identify this plant by its large leaves arranged in basal whorls up to 2.5 feet across. Hiking in the spring is best for viewing some of the rarer plants, as well as enjoying more common wildflowers such as Canada violet, with its thin heart-shaped leaves; wild geranium, sporting rose-lavender flowers; and the ubiquitous showy trillium.

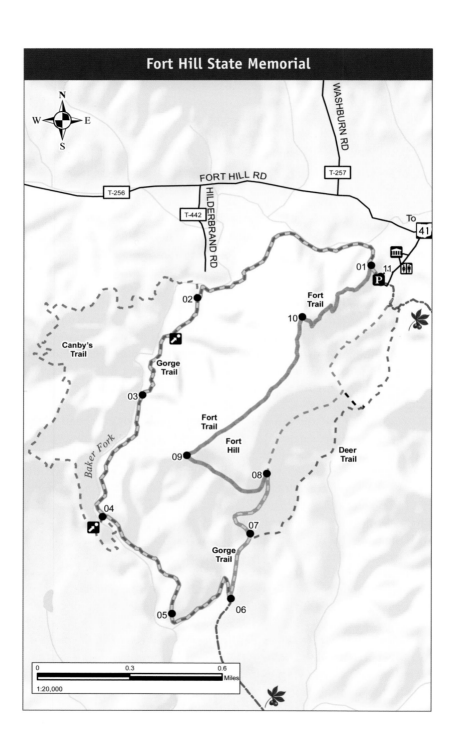

Fort Hill State Memorial

Perhaps plant diversity and the striking landforms at this magical place attracted the earlier inhabitants who left their mark on this land. You will see on this hike the ceremonial mound of the Hopewell Indians—previously thought to be a fort. The ceremonial mounds of Newark in Licking County were probably created about the same time—about 2,000 years ago—and the two villages may have traded. Artifacts of Vanport flint mined in Licking County have been found in this area. This flint—used to make spear points at first and arrowheads later—was probably traded by the Hopewell culture and has been found as far south as the Gulf of Mexico.

Although no cultural artifacts have been found in the earthworks at the top of the hill, there was a ceremonial lodge in the valley to the south, and in that area were found the implements and ornaments characteristic of the Hopewell. One such discovery was an item made of obsidian, which had been fractured, making it possible to date the piece by a process known as hydration dating. Astonishingly, the piece, fractured in a.d. 306, was traced to an ancient mine, the Obsidian Cliff, in Yellowstone National Park.

Begin the hike at the kiosk (fig. 3.7) near the picnic shelter where four trails intersect: the Gorge Trail, the Buckeye Trail, the Fort Trail, and Deer Trail (WP 1). The trailhead is on the southeast corner of the parking lot.

Figure 3.7 Fort Hill kiosk

For most of the hike, you will be following the Gorge Trail (yellow discs) and Buckeye Trail (blue blazes). The Fort Trail to the top of the fort is a very strenuous 500-foot climb. We will use the Fort Trail as we descend from the top of the fort. As you begin the hike, you will see Baker Fork, on your right. It will be a constant companion for more than half the hike. Please stay on the trail to protect the environment as well as yourself. The park manager has had to rescue several visitors annually who fell on the rough terrain off the main trail.

The riverine sycamores in the area are distinctive for their bone-white limbs. These large trees are often hollow and provided shelter for early settlers. The comparatively old trees are actually second growth, because of two early sawmills that operated here. Tannin to make ink and preserve leather was produced from the many chestnuts, which no longer survive here, and the chestnut oaks, which still thrive.

As you move deeper into the cool gorge you will begin to see some of the many ferns—more than 30 species—that abound along the sides of the rock formations. Among the ancient plants that thrive in the cool, damp gorge are the Christmas fern and the walking fern, as well as the liverworts and mosses. Coal was formed from abundant plants like these.

Wild ginger, identified by its small brownish flower in the crotch between stalks, grows here. American Indians reportedly used it to flavor their hominy grits. After climbing for a while you will come to a fairly steep downhill section with exposed roots on the trail surface, which makes it treacherous. At the bottom of the hill watch for a sharp left turn. After beginning another climb, look for the delicate walking fern, with its long tendrils, on exposed dolomite rock surfaces.

At WP 2 Canby's Trail goes off to the right. Go left with blue and yellow blazing to visit a historic cabin. This reconstructed dwelling was the home of a freed slave, Jesse H. Burdette, who built it near this location shortly after the Civil War. Around this area you will see evidence of past human activity. Look for day lilies and a row of black locust trees that were originally planted to be used for fence posts.

White snakeroot is also found here and throughout the park. This plant with fuzzy white flowers was responsible for milk sickness. Pioneers found that if cows ate snakeroot as they grazed woodland areas, their milk would turn poisonous. Abraham Lincoln's mother is said to have died from snakeroot-tainted milk.

Early explorers and surveyors used the presence of spicebush—a small aromatic shrub of the laurel family that also grows in this area—to identify the rich deep soil that would grow good crops. One of these early surveyors was George Washington, who wrote about the search for this harbinger of fruitful labors.

Follow an 80-year-old township road south from the cabin. Ruffed grouse love the red seeds of the partridgeberry, found in this area. Interestingly, only two species of partridgeberry exist—one in the U.S. and the other in Japan. Further uphill the soil becomes more acidic due to the shale bedrock formations. Look for the big leaves (12 in.) of the pawpaw as you occasionally drop back down to the stream.

After a mile on the Gorge trail, you may see rock bridges and arches in and over the stream (natural bridges—arches with water underneath; natural arches—no water underneath). This will be a good test of observational talents, for these natural wonders are not easily seen from the trail. Witch hazel grows on the moist slopes around some of these formations. The leaves turn bright yellow in fall, and spidery, fragrant yellow flowers appear early in the spring.

At a large overhanging rock overlooking the broadening stream, Baker Fork, the trail turns a little to the left. Watch for a side trail to an overlook where you might be able to see Walter's violet blooming in April and May. Deer prefer to not graze near cliffs, which probably has saved this rare plant as well as the Canadian yew, also found here. Before the last glacier, Baker Fork flowed northward to join Paint Creek. The glacier blocked the stream in the valley north of the park, known as the beech flats. Imagine a chunk of ice hundreds of feet high that, when melted, created a lake. The lake then overflowed, cut the gorge here, and turned the stream south toward Serpent Mound.

Take the 44 wooden steps down to the wooden bridge (WP 3). Look over the vertical flower garden on the rock face to your left. *Sullivantia,* with its scalloped leaves, is present (third hike in this chapter). Sullivantia is very rare, but found in Adams county on the dolomite outcroppings. Clear signs of beaver activity appear further down the stream. Bordering the wet and slippery trail is touch-me-not, or jewelweed. Their seedpods explode when touched—try it. In the summer the spicebush swallowtail butterfly— the larvae feed on the spicebush—might be seen pollinating the plant.

At WP 4 the Canby Trail intersects with the Gorge and Buckeye Trails. Look across the stream to see one of the larger natural bridges, Keyhole Bridge especially beautiful in winter. Ignore any blazing near the river and ascend the hill following the Gorge Trail. On the way up you will encounter the shale bedrock again. The soil is more acidic here, so it supports different plants. Look for black huckleberry, often called whortleberry. In the summer and early fall this shrub will produce blue-black berries with tiny, gritty seeds. Here also are the massive chestnut oaks, their bark dark brown to black, which like the shale footing. The Ohio black shale is so called because it appears black when wet. At WP 5, there is another set of steps (fig. 3.8). Go left at the bottom of the steps and continue to follow the blue and yellow blazes. At WP 6, the blue blazes head south out of the park. There is a sign pointing in the direction of the Buckeye Trail to a circle mound that may be visited.

To get the top of the fort make a sharp left going north and continue following the Gorge Trail. At WP 7, the Deer Trail intersects. If you take the Deer Trail, it will lead to the parking lot, but you will miss the top of the fort. By staying on the Gorge Trail, you are beginning the serious ascent to the top.

Continue following the Gorge Trail uphill. At WP 8, take the Fort Trail (green discs) to the left (west). The shale gives way to sandstone here. The walls of the earthworks were built by digging from the inside. Note the resultant borrow pit facing inward rather than outward, as a defensive moat might—one piece of evidence that you are viewing a ceremonial mound and not a fort. There are also 33 openings in the walls. What was their purpose? Some experts speculate that they could have been used to

Figure 3.8 Fort Hill steps

monitor the phases of the moon or other astrological signs, possibly for agricultural purposes. No artifacts have been found here, but the valley to the south has more earthworks. Excavations there have uncovered pottery fragments, spear points, and flint knives that have been associated with the Hopewell culture. The postholes of a rectangular structure similar to the longhouses of the Shawnee and other woodland Indians are also found here.

At WP 9 the Fort Trail goes straight uphill for 50 feet. A hard ascent, but the views from the top are worth the effort. Continue walking to the north end of the fort and then begin the descent (WP 10). The parking lot is to the north, one-third of a mile. A walking stick would be a useful tool as you make your way down. After your descent, you will come upon an intersection of four trails. Make a sharp right on the blue to take a short walk to the parking lot. Once, in October, swarming ladybugs, the state insect, accosted me in the parking lot.

As you leave Fort Hill State Memorial, watch for evidence that this region conjoins four out of five of Ohio's physiographic regions (appendix 2). If you take SR 41 to the north, think of the huge sheet of ice that once carved this beautiful valley known as the beech flats. Also notice the difference between the glaciated and unglaciated plateau to the east. If driving to the south note the striking hills bordering the Allegheny Escarpment to the east, while along the roadway stand the characteristic red cedar thriving in the dolomite bedrock soils of the Bluegrass Region.

FEATURED HIKE 3
DAVIS MEMORIAL STATE NATURE PRESERVE

DISTANCE 2 miles out and back.

TIME 1 hour.

DIFFICULTY Easy.

Just east of the intersection of SR 41 and SR 32, go south on Steam Furnace Road. Make an immediate left onto Davis Memorial Road. Davis Memorial Road becomes a gravel road before it turns into a narrow paved road and reaches the parking area at Davis Memorial. Davis Memorial property was donated to the Ohio Historial Society (now Ohio History Connection) in 1961 by Davon Stone, Inc., and was dedicated as a State Nature Preserve in 1993.

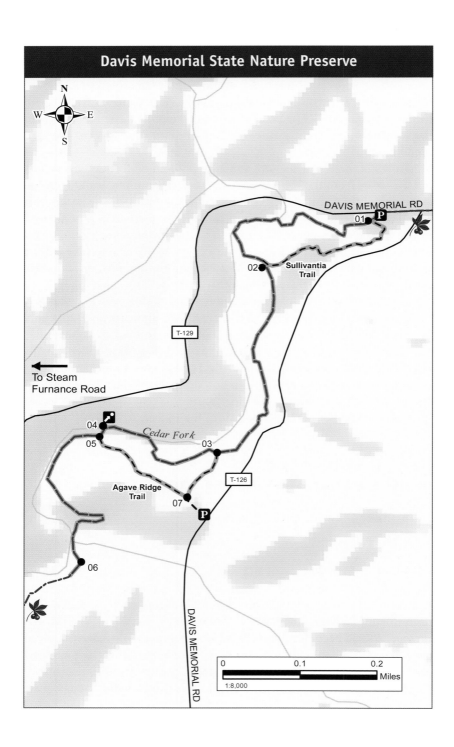

Davis Memorial State Nature Preserve

N
W ⊕ E
S

DAVIS MEMORIAL RD

01 **P**

02 **Sullivantia Trail**

T-129

To Steam Furnance Road

04

05 *Cedar Fork*

03

Agave Ridge Trail

07 **P**

T-126

06

DAVIS MEMORIAL RD

0   0.1   0.2
                                  Miles
1:8,000

Begin the hike at the kiosk and follow the blue blazes down a narrow wooded trail to Cedar Fork Creek. There you will encounter a boardwalk with dolomite rocks on one side and the peaceful waters of Cedar Fork Creek on the other. Dolomite is magnesium-rich bedrock. Adams County is one of the few places in Ohio where dolomite is exposed. Here in Davis, you will find two types of dolomite: Peebles and Greenfield. Greenfield dolomite is layered above Peebles dolomite. As they are exposed, the Peebles weathers in graceful curves. The Greenfield has a blocky appearance.

As you walk the boardwalk (fig. 3.4), you will be passing Peebles dolomite. Above the exposed rock, you will see red and white cedars. The white cedar, not commonly found in Ohio, migrated to the state during the glacial period. It continues to thrive in cool moist areas such as this. The white cedar has smooth flat needles that distinguish it from the prickly needles of the red. White cedar is also called arbor vitae, tree of life, because of its long life span. It is reported that French explorer Jacques Cartier used a concoction of arbor vitae to treat his men who were suffering from scurvy, a disease caused by a lack of ascorbic acid in the diet.

Red cedar occurs in virtually every county and grows in slightly alkaline soil. It is commonly used for fence posts and cedar lumber. The distinctive odor of red cedar is used in chests and closets to repel moths. Red cedar is a juniper, not a true cedar. Here in the relatively shallow soils of Davis Memorial, red cedar grows very slowly and trees of only 8 inches in diameter may be 100 years old. The soils at the top of the ridge were depleted further by local farming practices 100 years ago.

Along the face of the dolomite, you will see *Sullivantia* (fig. 3.9), which, like the white cedar, is a remnant of the glacial period. This small flat plant hugs the sides of the rock faces and is found in cool moist environments. It has a fluffy white bloom in early June. *Sullivantia* is named for William Starling Sullivant, who discovered it on rocky cliffs above Paint Creek in Highland County. William was schooled as a businessman, but his hobby of botany made him renowned. Sullivant's father, Lucas, was the founder of Franklinton, which is now a part of Columbus, Ohio.

As you climb away from the creek, the vegetation changes to those plants that exist in a more acid soil. Just a few yards apart, the soil pH can be much more acidic or alkaline. For example, the top of the ridge is capped by Ohio black shale, which is very strongly acidic, whereas nearer the creek the dolomite bedrock, alkaline in nature, controls the pH of the soil. There are interpretive signs along the hike that alert you to types of vegetation that will be seen. Look for the rare Walter's violet, which grows

Figure 3.9 *Sullivantia*

in just a few scattered locations in the region. At WP 2 the Sullivantia Trail and Buckeye Trail intersect. Bear right and follow the blue blazes.

On the ridge, maple, oak, hickory, and Virginia pine cover the hillside, and wildflowers such as purple coneflower (*Echinacea*) and tall larkspur grow along the trail. Look also for the dwarf iris. From September through December, the hardy stiff gentian (or five-flowered gentian) brings color to the woodland with its upright pale blue flowers.

WP 3 is the intersection of the Agave Ridge and Buckeye Trails. Bear to the right and stay with the blue blazes. There is an interpretive sign at WP 4 that tells the tale of the fault (fig. 3.10), or crack in the bedrock, found here and directs you to look behind the sign to the fault line that may be visible in Cedar Fork. You may notice a slight riffle below the water at this point that would indicate a rise in the level of the bedrock. This fault is 6 miles long and is visible here on the surface. Also notice the dolomite on the opposite bank. A chunk of Peebles dolomite to the left of the fault line and a chunk of Greenfield dolomite to the right are sharing the same strata. This abnormal stratification is evidence of an upheaval.

After walking away from the fault line, find the second intersection of the Agave Ridge and Buckeye Trails (WP 5). Bear right and stay with the blue blazes. The Buckeye Trail will continue another half mile, until it

Figure 3.10 Davis Memorial fault
(Courtesy of Ohio History Connection)

exits Davis Memorial. If you continue on the Buckeye Trail, you will climb a set of steps (WP 6) that leads up to a cedar glade forest. You will pass above an intermittent waterfall and pass by a sinkhole. Stop at the sinkhole and listen for the sound as water droplets fall into a hidden pool. Whether you are ending your hike or are going to continue on the BT for a while, when you return to the first intersection of the Agave and the Buckeye Trails, take the Agave Ridge Trail and follow it for another woodland experience.

While on the Agave Ridge Trail you will encounter a trail going off to the right (WP 7); bear left and stay on Agave Ridge Loop. Do not take the trail to the right, which leads to another parking lot on the southern leg of Davis Memorial Road. As you walk Agave Ridge, notice alongside the path the plant with needles covering its stem and branches. This is ground pine, named because of its evergreen quality. Actually, it is a club moss whose origins can be traced back 3 million years. The moss is endangered because of its slow growth rate and uncontrolled commercial use. The plant has been used as Christmas decorations, and the flammable spores were used by early photographers as flash powder. You will not see the club moss anywhere on this section of the BT except on the Agave Ridge Trail.

When you reach WP 3, go to your right with the Buckeye Trail's blue blazes (fig. 3.11). At WP 2, make a right on the Sullivantia Trail and head back to the car. The Sullivantia Trail leads through an area that was farmed 100 years ago. The farming depleted the soils and as the farms were deserted, the sun loving Virginia pine took over. Now, the Virginia pines are dying and the hardwoods are making a comeback (succession). As you near the parking lot, you will come upon a copse of river cane, the only bamboo native to the eastern U.S. You can reach out and touch it. It is also called canebrake bamboo, and before European settlement it covered thousands of acres of bottomland in Ohio and Maryland. It reaches a height of 15 to 20 feet.

Figure 3.11 Trail in Davis Memorial

Cane, the hard stems of this and other plants, was an extremely important resource for local Indians. They used the plant to make everything from houses and weapons to jewelry and medicines. Eastern Woodland tribes were known to have used the bamboo for flutes. As you pass the bamboo, you reach the parking lot and the end of the hike.

LOCAL CONTACTS

- Davis Memorial State Nature Preserve. www.ohiohistory.org; http://naturepreserves.ohiodnr.gov/davismemorial.
- Fort Hill. www.arcofappalachia.org.
- House of Phacops. Good information on the area's geology and fossils. E-mail: www.rockshop@cinci.rr.com.
- Pike Lake State Park. http://parks.ohiodnr.gov/pikelake.
- Serpent Mound. www.arcofappalachia.org.

WAYPOINT ID'S

WAYPOINT ID	DESCRIPTION	LATITUDE	LONGITUDE
	PIKE LAKE		
1	Parking lot	39.15970042	−83.22150721
2	Jct of horse trail, white blazes	39.16242345	−83.21640875
3	Jct Mitchell Ridge Trail and BT	39.16057306	−83.21411203
4	Bridle trail intersects	39.15847155	−83.21528155
5	Mitchell Trail goes to the right	39.15797660	−83.21469641
	FORT HILL		
1	Jct Fort, Gorge, and BT	39.12237455	−83.39761368
2	Jct Gorge, Deer, and BT	39.12066246	−83.40809751
3	Wooden steps	39.11583784	−83.41133670
4	Jct of BT and Canby	39.10992281	−83.41365606
5	Wooden steps	39.10524085	−83.40938682
6	Jct of BT and Gorge	39.10601065	−83.40583515
7	Jct of Gorge and Deer	39.10918420	−83.40471860
8	Jct of Fort and Gorge	39.11209540	−83.40376851
9	Fort Trail up hill	39.11293586	−83.40860982

WAYPOINT ID	DESCRIPTION	LATITUDE	LONGITUDE
10	Scenic view	39.11978739	−83.40173808
11	Kiosk	39.12182663	−83.39703575
DAVIS MEMORIAL			
1	Jct BT and Sullivantia Trail	38.93999079	−83.35366040
2	Jct Sullivantia Trail and BT	38.93904732	−83.35620196
3	Jct of Agave Ridge and BT	38.93550136	−83.35720310
4	Fault line	38.93591275	−83.35999394
5	Jct Agave and Buckeye Trail	38.93326800	−83.36047715
6	Waterfall and a sinkhole	38.93570236	−83.36006787
7	Agave Ridge Loop	38.93453971	−83.35794155

Ohio River Country

BTA SECTION MAPS **SHAWNEE,** West Union, Williamsburg.

COUNTIES TRAVERSED Adams, Brown, Clermont.

DISTANCE COVERED 161 miles.

OVERVIEW

Adams and Brown Counties were the first settled but are among the slowest to grow economically of Ohio's counties. These southern counties are undiscovered jewels, combining early Ohio history with the pristine beauty of the Ohio River lands. The sparse human population allows the visitor a relaxing sojourn in this southern borderland.

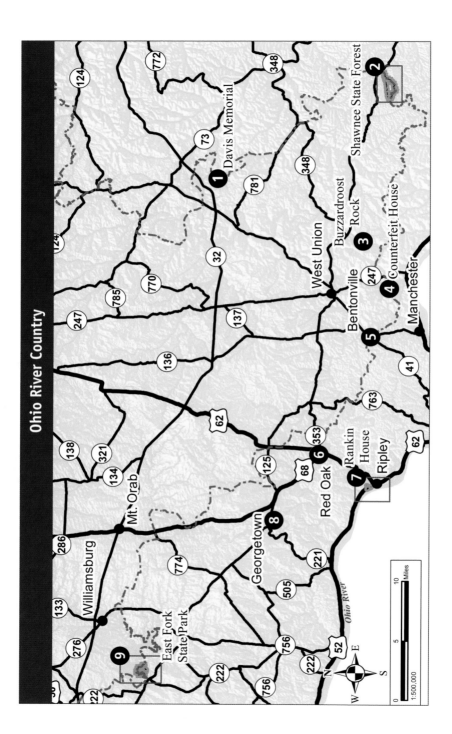

Ohio River Country

While traveling through Adams County from east to west it is useful to understand the changing geological conditions. The eastern edge of Adams County is part of the unglaciated Allegheny Plateau, displaying the picturesque "Little Smokies" terrain at Shawnee State Forest (Featured Hike 1).

As the Buckeye Trail continues west from Point 2, the landscape changes. Just west of Shawnee State Park, there will be a dramatic change from the edge of the Allegheny Plateau (the Allegheny Escarpment) to the Bluegrass Region (see appendix 2), which parallels the banks of Ohio Brush Creek (fig. 4.1). Fossil finds have proven that the great bison, or American buffalo, 7 feet high at the shoulders, once roamed here. The plain has the underlying limestone and shale that leads to the karst formations mentioned in the last chapter. Sinkholes can quickly appear and steep slopes may rapidly erode, which limits agriculture in this region.

Buzzardroost Rock (Point 3) is part of a preserve known as the Edge of Appalachia. Well-known botanist E. Lucy Braun first noticed the biodiversity of the area. The rocky slopes of the Allegheny Escarpment, interspersed with an extension of the great tallgrass prairies of the West,

Figure 4.1 Ohio Brush Creek (Andy "Captain Blue" Niekamp)

harbor many rare and endangered plants and animals. Buzzardroost Rock
has been named a National Natural Landmark because of the promontory
prairie at the top. This rare plant community once was common on the
hillsides of Adams County before farming stripped the poor soils of the
native plants. Please stick to the path in the Edge of Appalachia Preserve
to avoid harming this area. The other two main areas of the preserve are
Lynx Prairie and the Wilderness. Spring comes early to this entire southern Ohio area. The wildflowers found here—columbine, violet, trillium—
are some of the earliest to bloom in the state.

While in the Edge of Appalachia, the Buckeye Trail offers a walking or
driving tour beginning on SR 247. Drive north on SR 247—from U.S. 52—
for about 2 miles until you encounter the blue blazes at Gift Ridge Road
(C-2; Point 4). The first house on the right on C-2 is the privately owned
Counterfeit House (fig. 4.2). Built in 1840, the house was used for counterfeiting 50-cent pieces and 500-dollar bills. According to the BT's West
Union section map, the house was designed with "special door locks which
only could be opened by the 'right' people, slots in the tops of interior doors
to conceal coins, and a secret room—now the kitchen—with an entrance
only through trapdoors where the counterfeiting work took place. There
were seven chimneys, five of which were dummies but could give off smoke,
used as spy openings to check on visitors. The small gable window was used
to signal riverboats with a special light when a fresh batch of counterfeit
money was ready to sell." The house is falling into sad disrepair.

Figure 4.2 Counterfeit House (Brent and Amy Anslinger)

Continue following the blue blazes on Gift Ridge Road to Bat Roost Road, T-466. Follow this road southwest and you will soon arrive just northeast of the river city of Manchester, where you can see islands in the river. Only two islands of the original three now exist since dams have increased the river's depth. Many aspiring settlers met an untimely end here at the hands of the Shawnee, who could easily ambush them from the trees on the islands. The Indians were simply fighting for their right to the land north of the Ohio River, a land promised them by the Treaty of Fort Stanwix. This treaty was negotiated in 1768, before the American Revolution, and was not recognized by the citizens of a new country desiring the rich Ohio lands. In spite of Indian harassment in the three-islands area, Manchester became the first white settlement in Adams County, as well as the last stockaded village to be built in Ohio. The islands in the Ohio River, presently administered by the U.S. Fish and Wildlife Service, are open daily to visitors from sunrise to sunset.

Some rivers have bluffs on both sides, making them rather inaccessible. The Ohio River is a pleasant exception, for U.S. 52 is built on top of the rich bottomland along its low banks. There is even a vineyard, with its associated winery and restaurant, west of Manchester. As you drive along U.S. 52 you will understand why the French traders called the Ohio "la Belle Rivière."

Ohio's namesake is a mighty but relatively new river. According to Denison University geology professor William Tight, it came into being a mere 6,500 years ago. By studying river drainage patterns he concluded that glaciers blocked the ancient Teays River, which originally flowed north and west across Ohio. The trapped frozen water melted into a huge lake in eastern Ohio called Lake Tight. The lake, seven-tenths the size of Lake Erie, found an outlet and drained into what is now the Ohio River and its tributaries.

The Ohio's watershed covers 14 states, which makes it central to American history. The ancient ones or the mound builders must have navigated it as they traded with other tribes. Their probable descendants, the Shawnee, lived on its tributaries. The White Man used it to open the West. Bridges did not span it until after the Civil War, so escaping slaves found it a formidable barrier.

Returning to the blue blazes, in Bentonville the BT crosses SR 41 (Point 5), which roughly follows the former Zane's Trace (see chap. 2). Twenty-five yards south of the blue blazes, along the highway, stands an unusual monument commemorating the Bentonville Anti–Horse Thief Society, founded in 1853 (fig. 4.3). John Switzer, columnist for the

Figure 4.3 Bentonville Anti–Horse
Thief Society monument

Columbus Dispatch, reports that he "has never had a horse stolen since joining that organization." If you are interested in preventing equine theft, check out the Anti–Horse Thief Banquet, held each April.

As we continue further west from the Edge of Appalachia, to Brown and Clermont Counties, the Bluegrass Region gives way to the till plain (see appendix 2) created by the Illinoian glacier over 13,000 years ago. The glacier, as it melted over hundreds of years, deposited huge piles of rock and other debris. Some of these moraines are miles wide and hundreds of feet high. Cutting through some of the land are wide valleys created by glacial outwash that filled the land underneath the streams with tons of sand and gravel. This most southern portion of the till plain is used primarily for tobacco farming. While in the area you might see trucks hauling this valuable product to Ripley, the only surviving tobacco market in Ohio.

The blue blazes turn north from the river near the small village of Red Oak (Point 6). The Reverend James Gilliland came to Red Oak from South Carolina in 1805, having been dismissed because of his antislavery beliefs. He was instrumental in establishing a key station in the Underground Railroad (UGRR). Runaways who made it across the Ohio River to Ripley were often transported as quickly as possible to Gilliland's Red Oak chapel, to avoid capture by slave hunters. Reverend Gilliland is buried in the Red Oak cemetery. Local historians tell the story of Rosa Washington Riles, whose visage we recognize from the box of Aunt Jemima pancake mix. Rosa is buried in the Red Oak Presbyterian Church (1817) cemetery which is found 5 miles north of Ripley on the east side of U.S. 62 and 68, just before the two highways split. Her tombstone carries the logo from the Aunt Jemima pancake box.

We leave the blue blazes to return to the Ohio River in Ripley (fig. 4.4) (Point 7), one of our oldest river towns. Its 55-acre historic district offers the walker a glimpse of the architecture and history of the 1800s. During the steamboat era Ripley was almost as well known as Cincinnati. At least 13 steamboats were built in its boatyards, one of which was at the mouth of Red Oak Creek. Ripley was also important to the UGRR and the anti-slavery movement (see Featured Hike 2).

While visiting the Ripley area, drive east of town to Aberdeen, which marks the end of Ohio's first major roadway, Zane's Trace. The striking cable-stayed bridge found here is made of steel, which is cheaper than concrete to construct and easier to maintain.

Figure 4.4 Ohio River from Rankin House
(Andy "Captain Blue" Niekamp)

Near Red Oak, the Buckeye Trail turns north to pass by historic Georgetown (Point 8), boyhood home of Civil War general and U.S. president Ulysses S. Grant. Walking-tour maps are available at the Brown County Chamber of Commerce, and tours of the Grant homestead can be easily arranged.

The BT continues on through Williamsburg to East Fork State Park (Point 9), site of our last Featured Hike. This park, one of the largest in Ohio, is only 25 miles from Cincinnati. The Illinoian glacier formed this land. It occurred much earlier than the Wisconsinan glacier, which covered most of Ohio excluding this area. The terrain has thus had longer to erode into well-defined gorges, prairie habitats, marshy grasslands, and swamp forests. The hills around William H. Harsha Lake offer rewarding vistas. The park is also home to Old Bethel Church (1867), on the site of a log church built about 1807 by the Reverend John Collins.

The BT in this chapter ends in Milford near the bridge crossing the Little Miami River on U.S. 50. At the Little Miami Scenic Trail the blue blazes divide. The BT to the left (southwest) is a trail spur ending at Eden Park, overlooking the Ohio River, in the Queen City. The trail to the right (north) is a continuation of the Big Loop, returning us eventually to our starting point in chapter 2. The triple blaze in Milford is shown in figure 4.5.

Figure 4.5 Triple blaze (Andy "Captain Blue" Niekamp)

FEATURED HIKE 1
SHAWNEE STATE FOREST

DISTANCE Buckeye Trail, 4 miles; return by Lampblack Road, 2.5 miles. To visit Backpack Camp 7, add 2.2 miles for round trip from Lampblack Road.

TIME 6 hours will allow you to stop and enjoy the views.

DIFFICULTY Difficult on BT; moderately easy on Lampblack Road.

Shawnee State Forest is the largest of Ohio's 21 state forests. Its 63,000 acres were the hunting grounds of the Shawnee. In the 1600s a large Shawnee village was located in Portsmouth where the Scioto River out of Columbus joins the Ohio. The Scioto was the Shawnee's highway into the Ohio Country.

This hike follows a portion of the 42-mile Backpack Trail in the forest. Many other trails here offer great day-hiking adventures. The two lakes (Roosevelt and Turkey Creek) in the park offer boating (electric motors only), fishing, and swimming (fig. 4.6).

Figure 4.6 Roosevelt Lake in Shawnee State Forest (Andrew Bashaw)

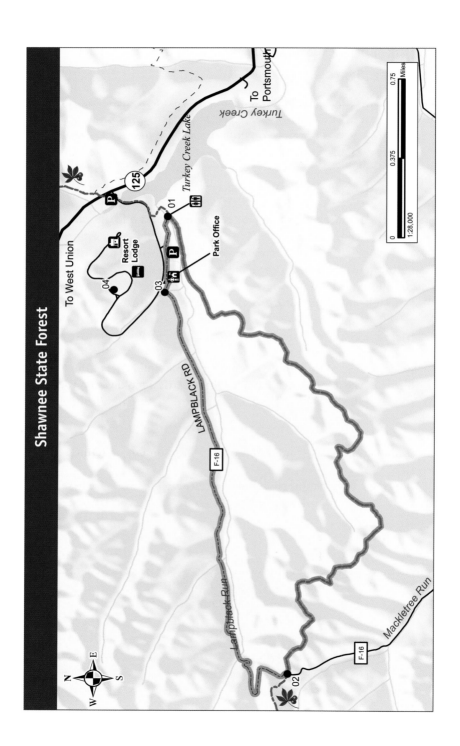

Shawnee State Forest

Park facilities also include a 50-room lodge with two swimming pools, a restaurant, a Class-A campground with flush toilets and laundry facilities, and 25 family cabins. The views from the lodge make it a must stop for visitors. Pets are allowed on the trails and in the Class-A campground. Pets are not allowed in the backpacking campgrounds.

Take U.S. 52 west out of Portsmouth, or drive to West Union to find SR 125. Find the trailhead for this hike by taking SR 125 to the main park road, west of Turkey Creek Lake. Lighted parking and overnight stays are available with backpacker registration. Registration forms and trail maps are at the Park Office near the parking lot. If you are day-hiking, you might wish to park in the beach parking lot, on the left, just east of the Park Office.

In Shawnee State Forest the BT is not marked by the traditional blue blazes. On this hike we will follow the main Backpack Trail, marked by orange blazes. Find the trailhead for the Backpack Trail (WP 1) just southwest of the toilets in the beach area. The trailhead is on a service road that goes south from the parking lot. There are trail markers identifying it as the BT as well as the North Country Trail (NCT; see chap. 11) and the American Discovery Trail (ADT; see chap. 1). You are on the correct orange-blazed trail if it rises steeply at first. In fact, when I hiked it with a backpack, it seemed that it rose steeply for a long time! Part of the Allegheny Plateau, the area is nicknamed Ohio's Little Smokies, for the hazy bluish views of the ridges. The haze is caused by the multitude of trees pumping moisture into the air. The Shawnee State Forest is in Ohio's southernmost climate zone, and some of the same trees, like tulip trees and white oaks, are also found in the Smoky Mountains of Tennessee and North Carolina.

The reward for all this climbing is a trail along the ridges, where beautiful views await. Try to identify the different plant life at different elevations. Spring wildflowers are abundant, including large-flowered, or giant, trillium with its three-petaled white flower that ages to pink. Even though you are hiking through second-growth forest, the presence of this trillium proves that it is old. I was most impressed with the relatively abundant dwarf iris that blooms in April. This striking flower, inspiring the fleur-de-lis of French royalty, is endangered and its range in Ohio is limited to southern Ohio. According to the state park brochure, you can also find several rare orchids: The small-whorled pogonia remains dormant underground for 10 to 20 years before reappearing and may be identified by five or six leaves beneath the greenish-yellow flower. The showy orchid has two wide basal leaves underneath its purple-and-white flower. Both orchids may be found from late April through June. These orchids, as well as the lady's slipper (both showy and pink), will not survive transplanting, so follow the admonition to take only pictures.

Wildlife is abundant here and many forest inhabitants are best viewed during early morning or late evening. In the spring and fall, migrating birds that winter in Central and South America—or neotropical species— pass through. The largest population of timber rattlesnakes in the state lives here, as well as copperheads, which prompted the following warning in a Shawnee Backpack Trail brochure: "Beware of poisonous snakes. Both rattlesnakes (endangered) and copperheads inhabit the forest. High leather boots or heavy leggings afford good protection. Watch where you sit and place your hands, especially in rocky areas. If bitten, seek medical aid immediately." The forest also supports large predators, such as coyote, bobcat, and an occasional black bear.

Later along the BT you will see evidence of a forest fire that occurred in 1981. To the left, the vista across a large valley is awesome. As with all the views from the top of the ridge, the spring, winter, and fall are peak times to visit, when the leaves are not present. You arrive at Lampblack Road (F-16) (WP 2), now closed to traffic, about half an hour from this point.

Here is where you may choose to visit, or stay overnight, at Backpack Camp 7. The camp is 1.1 miles south on the BT from Lampblack Road. The side trail to Backpack Camp 7 is marked by white blazes. Water is available here and a pit toilet has been built. Fires are allowed in the circles provided. Rocky Fork Road (C-96) provides access to this area.

If you are day-hiking you can retrace your steps along the BT or turn right (northeast) along Lampblack Road to complete the loop back to the parking lots at Shawnee State Park. The road follows lovely Lampblack Run, which widens as you travel east. There is one picnic table along the road. The culverts along this old road were constructed without cement by the Civilian Conservation Corps in the 1930s. This section of the hike is not as arduous as that along the Buckeye Trail. Near the end of Lampblack Road (WP 3) you will pass a service building and shortly intersect with the park road you came in on. Take a right and make your way back to the parking area east of the Park Office.

To make the hike a bit easier, consider walking Lampblack Road first and going east on the Backpack and Buckeye Trails, back to the parking area. Lampblack Road gently ascends the 400-foot ridge, whereas the Backpack Trail takes you up in a hurry. Lampblack Road is shown on the state park map as Lampblack Bridle Trail and as Forest Road 16. It is not open for vehicle traffic.

FEATURED HIKE 2
RIPLEY

DISTANCE 4 miles at most.

TIME Plan for a leisurely visit of half a day or more, including the museums along the way.

DIFFICULTY Easy, except for the climb of 100 steps to the top of Freedom Hill.

Find Ripley on scenic U.S. 52 where it intersects with U.S. 62 and 68. The Buckeye Trail is north of Ripley and crosses SR 353 just east of the village of Red Oak, which served as an important station on the Underground Railroad (UGRR).

From U.S. 52 in Ripley, turn west on Main Street, which terminates at the Ohio River. Turn right and park on the riverfront along Front Street. Enjoy the sights and sounds of the river as you begin the hike at the foot of Main Street by viewing the Liberty Monument. The monument was dedicated on Ripley's centennial, in 1902, and commemorates the Reverend John Rankin and others important to the antislavery movement in Ripley.

From the monument, walk northwest on Front Street along the river and watch for the following:

- 114 Front St. (WP 1). This Greek Revival home was built in 1815 by Dr. Alexander Campbell, Ripley's first abolitionist. The bronze plaque here tells more of his story. When the Ohio River flooded in 1937 the water reached the upper story. (David Gray, the current owner, played Doc Turner in the movie Coal Miner's Daughter.)
- 124–130 Front St. (WP 2). The row houses were built by Ripley's founder, Col. James Poage. The colonel lived in the house at 124 Front and his sons in the next two.
- 136 Front St. The house with the grand stone wall was once owned by Dr. Alfred Beasley, whose name also appears on the Liberty Monument. This house was elevated in 1913 to a level above the flood of that year, but it did not escape damage from the 1937 flood.
- 200 Front St. (WP 3). This is the house of Thomas Collins, a cabinet-maker who also made coffins. John Parker, a black freeman who lived further down the street, told the following story: "After the Fugitive Slave Law was passed, slave owners from the South were allowed to search Northern houses to retrieve escaped slaves. During such a search, I and

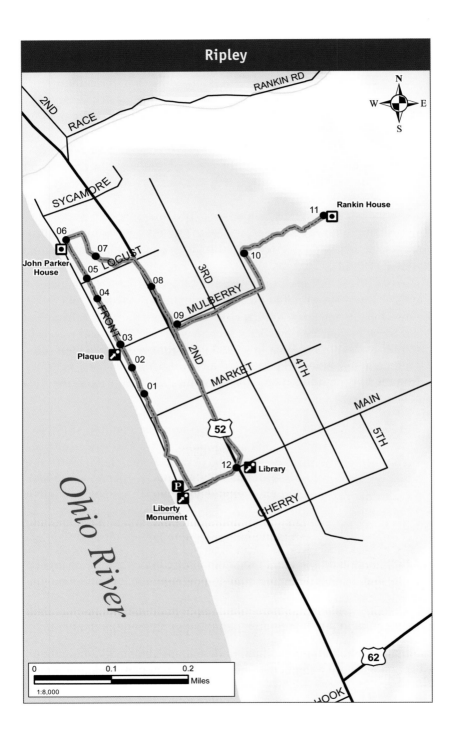

Ripley

RANKIN RD

2ND

RACE

N

W — E

S

SYCAMORE

Rankin House

11

06

07

LOCUST

10

John Parker
House

05

3RD

08

MULBERRY

04

09

FRONT

03

2ND

Plaque

02

MARKET

4TH

01

MAIN

52

5TH

12

Library

P

CHERRY

Liberty
Monument

Ohio River

62

HOOK

0   0.1   0.2

Miles

1:8,000

two escaped slaves hid in coffins at the Collins house. Either because of their own superstitions or their belief that slaves would be too afraid to hide in coffins, Southern sympathizers failed to look in the coffins."

Across Front Street, on the river's edge, is a plaque dedicated to the story of a fugitive slave, Eliza, who crossed the river on ice floes to escape capture.

- 220–224 Front St. The brick Federalist row house was John Rankin's first home. Known in his time as the father of abolitionism, Reverend Rankin lived in one unit and rented the rest of this complex out to businesses. He later moved to the "house on the hill," which will be visited later.
- 234 Front St. (WP 4). Signal House, now a bed-and-breakfast, was used by the owner to signal to Rev. Rankin that the waterfront was safe to transport slaves to freedom. A lantern was hung from a skylight as the signal.
- John Parker Memorial Park (WP 5). This park tells the story of Parker's habit of walking in the middle of the street to avoid ambush by thugs who would wish him ill. Note the footprints formed in the middle of the sidewalks in the park.
- 330 Front St. (WP 6). The brick home of John P. Parker (fig. 4.7) is central to the story of the UGRR and has been restored by Ohio History Connection and designated a National Historic Landmark. Iron implements and kettles from his foundry, located two doors north, are settled in the side yard.

Figure 4.7 Parker House

It is believed that John Parker was born in Virginia, in 1827, to a black woman and a white aristocrat. Nevertheless, his father treated him like a slave. When he was only eight years old he was chained to other slaves and forced to walk to Mobile, Alabama. John Parker managed to buy his freedom in the South and headed north to establish himself, eventually, as the owner of a foundry in Ripley. (The iron steps leading to the front door of the home were made in his foundry, Ripley Foundry and Machine Company.) He became quite successful as a businessman and inventor but never forgot his obligations to those yet to escape slavery. John Parker's adventures are described in the autobiography *His Promised Land*, available at the museums and historical sites in Ripley.

From Parker's house, turn west to look at the river. In antebellum days it was shallower than it is now; the locks built since have made the river more navigable. But even before the locks, the wide river basin, with its treacherous currents, represented a formidable barrier to a good swimmer. Runaway slaves had to cross the Ohio for even a chance at freedom. Fearing capture and punishment and usually not knowing how to swim, they often depended on abolitionists like Parker to connect with them, row a boat to the Kentucky shore, and then carry them to the Ohio side. Even then, safety was questionable, for most of Ripley's citizens were sympathetic to the institution of slavery. When they received news of runaways headed for the North, they would watch to intercept them and claim a likely reward for their return. Parker was a true American hero who faced imprisonment or death for his unselfish deeds before the Civil War.

Among the many exciting revelations in his autobiography, Parker describes his version of the dramatic escape of Eliza, the heroine of *Uncle Tom's Cabin*, written by Harriet Beecher Stowe. Stowe's book, which historians believe stirred up the feelings that led to the Civil War, was based on historical evidence that a black woman crossed the Ohio River on "rotten ice" with her baby. According to Parker, she fell through the ice twice, and had to fling the baby from her both times in order to hold on to the fence post she carried to help her up after falling. On reaching the shore, she was immediately discovered by what Parker describes as "one of the Ohio patrol." Rather than turning her in, the man said, "Any woman who crossed that river carrying her baby has won her freedom."

A play based on *Uncle Tom's Cabin* was extremely popular well into the 1900s. Theatergoers in those days attended the play year after year, mainly to see the ending, which depicted the heartrending sight of the white Little Eva, loved by the black Uncle Tom, rising up to heaven. (Of course, she was really raised into the rafters by a rope.) *Uncle Tom's Cabin* should be read by all who wish to learn from "a woman of the times" the attitudes of abolitionists and slave catchers and the social conflicts that were part and parcel of that historic era.

From the rear of Parker's house, in winter, you can look up to see the Rankin House (fig. 4.8), sitting prominently on Liberty Hill. A remnant of the old Parker foundry is still standing among the factory buildings to the north of Parker's house. Behind Parker's house, walk through the park to the east. At WP 7, look to your left at a large three-story building. This is a former piano factory that now serves as Ripley's antique mall, the Olde Piano Factory. Two examples of pianos made in Ripley are showcased here. Next, turn left onto Locust, then right onto Second Street (U.S. 52), which parallels Front.

The well-organized Ripley Museum at 219 Second St. (WP 8) is housed in an 1850 Federalist home. Here you will find a concise history of each of Brown County's towns. You will also learn what it meant to "go to hell in a handbasket": the horse-drawn hearse found in the museum holds a coffin made not of wooden panels but of strips of wood woven like a basket. This basket was used to carry bodies from homes to the funeral parlors. You must visit the 10 rooms of the Ripley Museum to fully appreciate the unselfish contribution by the citizens of Ripley and Brown Counties.

Figure 4.8 Rankin House (Courtesy of Ohio History Connection)

From the museum, go to Mulberry Street (WP 9) and turn left, up the hill. At Third and Mulberry you will find a large sycamore that was planted in 1816, when construction was begun on the First Presbyterian Church, the home church of abolitionist John Rankin. Final renovations were completed in 1867 on this Gothic and Romanesque Revival building. A monument to Reverend Rankin is near the church entrance. Continue up the hill on Mulberry to Fourth Street.

Turn left on Fourth and walk approximately 100 yards to a path on the right-hand side that is found before reaching a stone wall. From the road you will see the 100 steps (WP 10) leading up Freedom Hill to the Rankin House (WP 11, fig. 4.8). The house and grounds had major renovations in 2013 and can be reached by car using a driveway that winds up the hill from Second Street north of town.

Many frightened people once climbed this hill to the safety provided by John, his wife, and their 13 children. A Freedom Light on the hill served as a polestar to slaves on the Kentucky shore who were seeking the path to freedom. After they crossed the river and climbed the steep hill, the fugitives rested and were fed. "Conductors" on the UGRR would then escort them to freedom further north. While a guest at the Rankin home, young Harriet Beecher first heard the story of the brave mother pursued by dogs and slave catchers across the weak ice of the Ohio River.

When you come back down the hill, follow Fourth south and Mulberry west to Second Street. Follow Second Street south to the corner of Second and Main, where the Ripley Library (WP 12) is located. In 1914 the Ripley Progress Club received $10,000 from the Carnegie Foundation for the structure. Notice the many steps leading up to the front doors, built in the hope that the library would be high enough to escape flood damage. Nevertheless, the 1937 flood reached this level. There is a marker on the stairway to indicate the height of the 1937 flood. The exterior of the building is decorated with tiles made by Rookwood Pottery in Cincinnati.

There is a plaque on the cannon outside that tells the story of the squirrel hunters who wreaked havoc on the Rebel soldiers during the Civil War. Because of the abolitionist bent of the community of Ripley preceding the Civil War, the South already held grudges against Ripley. The Squirrel Hunter brigade and its sharp-eyed marksmen added insult to injury. It was said of the squirrel hunters that they never had to shoot at the same squirrel twice.

A visit to Ripley will provide a chance to experience one of the great river towns of southern Ohio. It will also offer a learning experience that cannot be duplicated in the classroom.

FEATURED HIKE 3
EAST FORK STATE PARK

DISTANCE 5 miles on the Buckeye and Steve Newman World Walker Perimeter Trails in East Fork State Park.

TIME At least 3 hours for a leisurely walk while enjoying the flora and fauna.

DIFFICULTY Moderately difficult. Even though the elevation change is less than 100 feet, you will cross several eroded tributaries of the East Fork of the Little Miami River that now lead into the lake. This means several ups and downs.

East Fork State Park is accessed from SR 125, which we have followed through much of the Ohio River Country. At the intersection of SR 222 and SR 125, turn north onto Bantam Road (C-112). You will soon see the East Fork State Park entrance on your left (Park Road 1). Turn left and note the Park Office on your right, just after Williamsburg-Bantam Road. You may wish to stop for current trail information.

Just north beyond the new Park Office, turn left onto an access road to the south parking lot. Follow the entrance to the south parking lot back between two ponds. Here at a large kiosk are descriptions of the trailhead for the Steve Newman Worldwalker Perimeter Trail (fig. 4.9) and other park trails. There are restroom facilities at this parking area.

Figure 4.9 Newman Trail sign (Brent and Amy Anslinger)

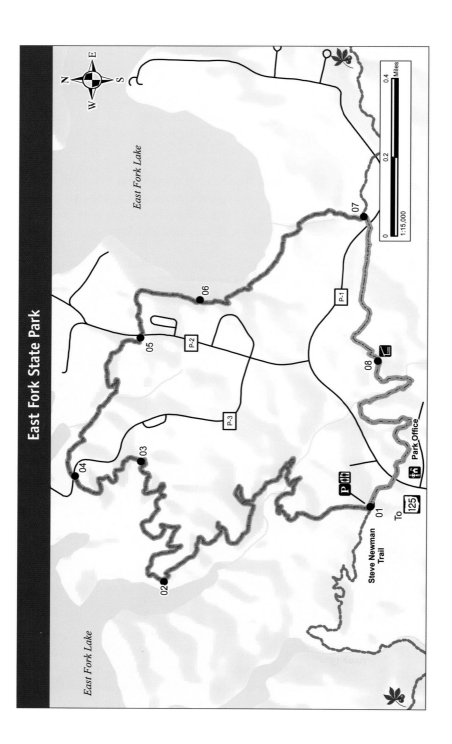

While the Buckeye Trail is in East Fork State Park, it follows the Steve Newman Perimeter Trail, the Backpack Trail, and at times the Mountain Bike Trail. A map of the trails is available in the park gift shop. The BT was rerouted in 1999 from the north side of East Fork Lake to the less horse-traveled, picturesque south side. The BT's present route comes in from the east, from Williamsburg. There is a ford across the East Fork of the Little Miami River. The trail then wends its way along the lakeshore until it arrives at your present location. From the south parking lot it continues west to a lovely saddle dam over the East Fork. The emergency spillway is popular for hunting fossils. Here are the U.S. Army Corps of Engineers visitor center, an overlook, and the Deer Ridge Trail.

To begin this hike, follow the blue blazes out of the parking area and to the right of the kiosk (WP 1). The post at this trailhead shows that you are walking the North Country Trail, the ADT, and the park's backpack mountain bike trails, as well as the BT. You will be following red/orange, yellow, and blue blazing. The serpentine trail moves generally north from here through a former field in late succession. This is a good example of plant succession, or encroachment, after a farm field has been vacated. Initially only a few plants from surrounding habitats can move in. Later, these so-called pioneer plants modify the habitat enough to allow other species known as intermediates in. Finally, the climax species take over. Ecologists can tell, by the types of plant and animal species living there, how long succession has been taking place. Note the small trees, known as pole trees, moving into the area. The scattered cedars are characteristic of both the till plains and the limestone bedrock exposed by the Illinoian glacier. Remember to always stay with the blue blazes. A few side trails are misleading. As always, if you lose the blazes for some time, retrace your footsteps to the last blaze seen. The trail is relatively flat and then descends into the first of several eroded gorges with small streams. Found in the streams are the characteristic well-worn fossiliferous rocks, limestone of the Ordovician Period (see appendix 1).

After walking for about 45 minutes and crossing some of the small tributaries in more mature woodland, you will view one of the bays of the lake as the trail turns more easterly (WP 2). There are so many switchbacks on this section of the hike, you may see yourself coming and going. Do not be tempted by some of the biker's shortcuts. Stay with the blue blazing.

During much of the year this is a birdwatcher's paradise and you will probably hear or see a variety of feathered residents. You may see a Cooper's hawk silently glide through the trees or rufous-sided towhees scuffing around in the brush. The red-shouldered hawk, once quite common in Ohio but rarely seen now, can be found in the area. Perhaps this bird will make a comeback, as has the bald eagle, which has also been sighted near the lakeshore. Ever present is the melodious wood thrush.

At WP 3, you will be on a stretch of trail that says NO BIKES, and will be crossing a bridge over a creek. Just after this bridge and a turn to the left, the yellow blazing (bike trail) goes off to the right and the blue and orange blazes go to the left. Do not be alarmed if a bike still comes up behind you because they are permitted to use this small section of the backpack trail to reach the Lake Tail just ahead. After the Lake Trail takes off, stay to your right and follow the orange and blue. Because of the hunting restrictions on this trail, you will often see the white-tailed deer.

Reptiles that may be spotted in the area include the ring-necked snake and the eastern plains garter snake. Numerous eastern box turtles can be seen in July. In July and August, in open areas near the roads or parking areas, you can find bushy clusters of wild bergamot. The leaves of this mint can be used for tea. Its lavender flowers attract hummingbird moths, which feed by day, and bumblebees. Raspberries and blackberries, in season, readily offer their sweet rewards.

After crossing a paved park road, Park Road 3 (WP 4), watch for a blue blaze on one of the posts along the road. You will now turn more to the east. Notice that without the bike traffic the path is much narrower. A field in early succession, with cedars, is to the right after the trail comes down from the elevated roadway. The trail turns right, crossing a bridge at a large tributary. At WP 5 you will cross Park Road 2. Soon you will be passing a camping area—bear left. At WP 6 you will make a sharp turn to the left and an immediate turn to the right (thus making an S). Note that a blue blaze on the top of a double blaze points in the direction of the trail.

At WP 7 you will see signs to Camp Area 2 and Camp Area 1. Turn right and head toward Camp Area 1. At this point, the blue blazes are leaving to the left. Immediately you will cross Park Road 1 and continue on an unblazed but widely mowed and easily followed trail. The backpack campground (WP 8) has two shelters and two his-and-hers pit toilets. Drinking water is not available here. At the far end of the campground are posts for hanging packs and gear. Here is an access trail to the Steve Newman Worldwalker Perimeter Trail. Turn right on the access trail and go west for about 200 yards to a wide creek that in wet times could be a challenging crossing and plastic bags would be useful. The green-blazed perimeter trail is just up the grade on the opposite side. Be sure to turn right (north) on the perimeter trail to pass through pole woods and then a field in early succession until you see the road. Cross the road (Park Road 1) to the access road to the south parking area and your car.

The 32-mile, green-blazed Steve Newman Worldwalker Perimeter trail, part of which you just traveled over, circles the lake and offers four primitive campsites like the one you visited earlier. In his book *WorldWalk*, Steven Newman describes his 20,000-mile trip—mostly walking—that began in April 1983. Near the end of his journey he camped in East Fork State Park. On the following day, April 1, 1987, he walked the final 5 miles of his around-the-world journey with about 300 people to his mother's home in Bethel (fig. 4.10).

LOCAL CONTACTS

- East Fork State Park. http://parks.ohiodnr.gov/eastfork.
- Edge of Appalachia Preserve System. www.cincymuseum.org.

Figure 4.10 Hero's homecoming
(Rocky Boots)

- John P. Parker Museum and Historical Society. www.johnparkerhouse .org.
- Rankin House. www.ohiohistory.org.
- Ripley Museum. www.ripleyohio.net.
- Shawnee State Park. http://parks.ohiodnr.gov/shawnee.
- Ulysses S. Grant. www.usgrantboyhoodhome.org.

WAYPOINT ID'S

WAYPOINT ID	DESCRIPTION	LATITUDE	LONGITUDE
SHAWNEE			
1	Trailhead	38.73767800	−83.19914000
2	Lampblack Rd & BT	38.72940200	−83.23894400
3	Forest Rd 16	38.73720500	−83.20645100
RIPLEY			
1	114 Front St	38.74693600	−83.84762600
2	Row houses	38.74744400	−83.84793400
3	Collins House	38.74789900	−83.84822000
4	Signal House	38.74879600	−83.84878700
5	John Parker Park	38.74920300	−83.84904200
6	John Parker Museum	38.74995300	−83.84955500
7	Rear Piano factory	38.74963500	−83.84883500
8	Ripley Museum	38.74905100	−83.84749000
9	Jct Mulberry and 4th	38.74831300	−83.84685900
10	Steps off 4th	38.74972000	−83.84527200
11	Rankin House	38.75048200	−83.84336600
12	Library	38.74528200	−83.84593500
EAST FORK			
1	Kiosk at parking lot	39.00671300	−84.14192800
2	View of East Fork Lake	39.01392700	−84.14565300
3	Bridge over creek bed	39.01484600	−84.14008300
4	Park Rd 3	39.01715800	−84.14082300
5	Park Rd 2	39.01496700	−84.13424500
6	"S" turn in trail	39.01290400	−84.13240000
7	Jct of trail to Camp Area 1	39.00718300	−84.12830100
8	Camp Area 1	39.00656800	−84.13510500

The Little Miami River Valley

BTA SECTION MAPS Loveland, Caesar Creek.

COUNTIES TRAVERSED Hamilton, Clermont, Warren.

DISTANCE COVERED 119 miles.

OVERVIEW

This chapter begins at an unforgettable overlook on the Ohio River that serves as the southern terminus of the Buckeye Trail (fig. 5.1) in lovely Eden Park, Cincinnati, Ohio. The first Featured Hike (Point 1) takes place here.

You may better experience this lovely city by following the American Discovery Trail (ADT; see chap. 1, fig. 1.2) from the southern terminus of the BT in Eden Park into Covington, Kentucky. The ADT's route from

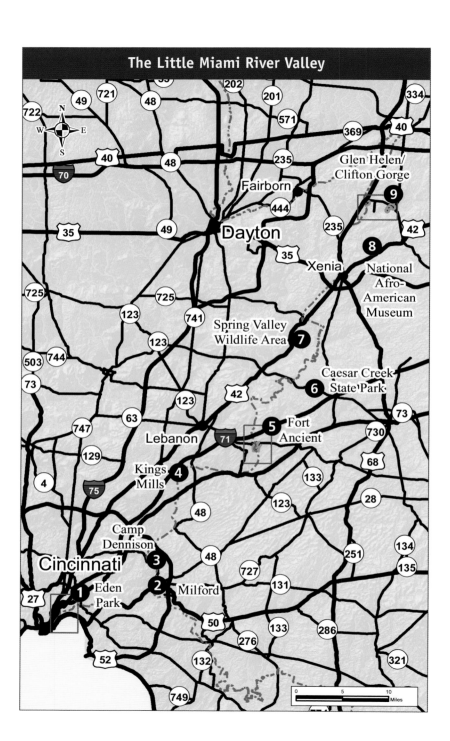

The Little Miami River Valley

Figure 5.1 Southern Terminus

Cincinnati to Covington (fig. 5.2) takes you by the stadiums at the riverfront and across the John A. Roebling Suspension Bridge. The trail ends at Devou Park, offering one of the best views of the Cincinnati skyline. Like the BT, the ADT has been designed to include metropolitan areas. This makes the trails more accessible, but, more important, the walk is a great way to experience these cities.

The Central Riverfront is situated between the Ohio River and Third Street. Bordered by Eggleston Avenue and Central Parkway, the area offers many other attractions for the walker, including

- a trip down Eggleston Avenue that covers the prism of the Miami-Erie Canal, where the final stage of six locks was located
- a sculpture garden employing symbols to describe Cincinnati's dynamic history
- a large-scale model of the Ohio River that will enable you to visualize the 28 locks and dams with their elevations
- a cross-section of the Miami and Erie Canal system
- a geologic timeline where every few steps take you through eons of earth's history
- a scaled version of a canal lock

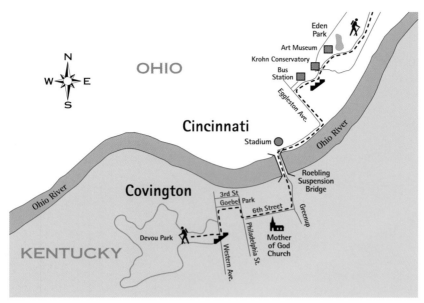

Figure 5.2 Map of ADT (Jonathan White)

You will even see the (in)famous Flying Pig sculptures. They commemorate a time when the Queen City was also known as Porkopolis for its many large porcine slaughterhouses.

Upon returning to the Buckeye Trail at Eden Park, look westward to take a last look at the mighty Ohio (fig. 5.3). The blue blazes now head northeast from the BT's southern terminus in Eden Park to rejoin the large loop continuing north to Toledo. The Harriet Beecher Stowe House and State Memorial are located just west of the blue blazes as they turn east on Madison Avenue. (For more on Stowe, see chap. 4, Featured Hike 2.)

The BT then passes northeast through the suburban village of Terrace Park and continues on to Milford, where it joins the main loop around the state (Point 2). Here is the juncture of the Williamsburg section, where three blue blazes arranged as a Y indicate that the BT heads in three directions (see fig. 4.5).

The blue blazes continue north in the Loveland section on the 70-mile Little Miami Scenic Trail (LMST), a rail-trail that follows the Little Miami River. This pristine waterway has been designated a federal and state scenic river. The North Country Trail (NCT; see chap. 11) also uses the LMST. Little Miami State Park maintains a portion of the LMST

Figure 5.3 Ohio River

that is really a trail corridor, or greenway. Hikers, bikers, inline skaters, horse riders, and skiers use the paved trail, and canoers access the Little Miami River from the parkway.

Between Milford and our next Featured Hike, at Fort Ancient, are three historic sites near the BT and the Little Miami Scenic Trail. The first is a small park that marks the location of Camp Dennison (Point 3), just south of SR 126 on Cunningham Road. This was a training center for soldiers who fought in the Civil War. Christian Waldschmidt House, at the camp, contains a Civil War museum. The BT passes the second site, the Butterworth House, an Underground Railroad site just north of Loveland (Point 4; also see chap. 4 for more information on the UGRR). Henry and Nancy Butterworth were members of the Society of Friends, commonly called Quakers, and their great-granddaughter still lives at Butterworth Farms, located near here. The third historic site, in the town of Kings Mills, is the now mainly abandoned building of the Peter's Cartridge Company, which made gunpowder during the Spanish-American War.

The BT continues north on the LMST to a connector trail that leads to Fort Ancient, Ohio's first state park, established in 1891 (Point 5). Today it is a state memorial owned and operated by the Ohio History Connection, which protects ancient Hopewell earthworks. Our second Featured Hike takes place in this area.

As we enter the Buckeye Trail map's Caesar Creek section, the blue blazes separate from the LMST and the NCT to head east to Caesar Creek State Park (Point 6). Caesar Creek was named for a black slave adopted by the Shawnee after his master was killed on the Ohio River. Caesar lived in the Shawnee village of Old Chillicothe, on the site of present-day Old Town, just north of Xenia on SR 68. There were at least five Indian villages in Ohio named Chillicothe, which means "principal town" in Shawnee.

According to its brochure, Caesar Creek State Park "sits astride the crest of the Cincinnati Arch, a convex tilting of bedrock layers caused by an ancient upheaval. Younger rocks lie both east and west of this crest, where some of the oldest rocks in Ohio are exposed." The sedimentary limestones and shales tell of a sea hundreds of millions of years in our past that once covered the state, as attested by the park's excellent fossil finds.

Along the Cincinnati Arch, at the nearby town of Lytle, drilling begun in 1987 produced one of the deepest cores east of the Mississippi. The plan was to drill through all the sedimentary rock—limestone and shale—to find the crystalline basement, composed of earth's original igneous and metamorphic rocks (like granite). The hole reached more than a mile before work was halted. The sediment deposited over the eons was so thick that the drilling never did reach the crystalline basement.

The oldest rocks in this area date from the Ordovician Period, up to 500 million years ago (appendix 1). Ohio was then near the equator, and the tropical sea that covered it, similar to the modern Caribbean, teemed with life such as ancient corals, snails, giant squids, and brachiopods (nearly extinct marine animals with a bivalve shell). The luckiest fossil hunters here have found large parts of a trilobite, which resembles the wood louse (sow bug) and is an ancestor to present-day insects, spiders, and lobsters. Trilobites were living 450 million years ago (more than 6 million human life spans). The cross-section of Ohio at the bottom of appendix 1 reveals that continuously younger rock formations occur as you travel east from the arch.

While visiting here, stop by the U.S. Army Corps of Engineers visitor center, just off Clarksville Road, on the north side of the dam. Here you can obtain a collecting permit. The fossil collection area at the spillway, which they will direct you to, is a favorite spot for local schools to bring children during the autumn and spring. I visited there in the spring while several busloads of children were collecting. The children's excitement over their discoveries helped me fondly recall my first fossil find and an emerging awareness of the earth's enigmatic and dynamic past.

The BT rejoins the LMST and the NCT north of Caesar Creek Lake, at the village of Spring Valley. The Spring Valley Wildlife Area (Point 7), just south of the village, has a trail called the Massasauga Trail. The name comes from Ohio's smallest rattlesnake (around 2 feet long). This endangered, venomous reptile enjoys such tasty items as meadow voles or mice and lives in crayfish burrows. Birding along the boardwalk is some of the state's best. (A white-blazed side trail of the BT also leads from the north end of Caesar Creek Lake to return to the LMST and NCT before they pass by the wildlife area.)

The city of Xenia is further north on the Buckeye Trail and the LMST, and here the trail's caretaker changes from the Ohio Department of Natural Resources to the Greene County Park District. The countywide system of trails is known as Greene County Greene Ways.

Xenia was devastated in 1974 by one of the largest tornadoes ever recorded in Ohio. Two hundred fifty people lost their lives and a large part of the city resembled European cities bombed during World War II. Today, the city has been rebuilt and is nicknamed Trail Town, USA, by the American Hiking Society. The old train depot is a hub for three trails—the LMST, which you have already been introduced to; the Creekside Trail, which heads east toward Dayton; and the Ohio to Erie Trail, which when completed will run from Cleveland to Cincinnati.

Wilberforce University, the nation's first university to be owned, operated, and supported by African Americans, was established in 1856 (Point 8). Central State University, which graduates about half the black teachers in Ohio, is just across SR 42. On its campus is the National Afro-American Museum and Cultural Center. A thought-provoking exhibit, From Victory to Freedom: Afro-American Life in the Fifties, shows how it was to live as a black person just before the civil rights struggle in America. Both universities are less than 3 miles from the BT at Xenia.

Further north on the LMST is Old Town. The Shawnee lived here in a town known as Chillicothe, thought to be the birthplace of the great war chief Tecumseh. (There is evidence that Tecumseh was born 12 miles north of here, at present-day George Rogers Clark Park.) In 1778, Simon Kenton ran one of three gauntlets here, any one of which would have killed a lesser man. Each time he was forced to run between a long line of Shawnee who tried to club him as he passed. When he miraculously survived, he was to be burned at the stake, but his friend Simon Girty saved him. Col. Daniel Boone was also a prisoner in Old Chillicothe.

The LMST and the BT next pass Glen Helen Nature Preserve, at Yellow Springs (Point 9), Featured Hike 3. The preserve is an important part of Antioch College (fig. 5.4), founded in 1850. The college's first president, Horace Mann, was a social and educational pioneer. His parting words to graduates still inspire current Antioch grads: "Be ashamed to die until you have won some victory for humanity." In 1920, Antioch president Arthur Morgan introduced one of the first co-op, or work-study, programs to provide real-life experiences in conjunction with formal education.

Glen Helen is adjacent to John Bryan State Park and Clifton Gorge (fig. 5.5), the location of the second phase of our third and final Featured Hike in this chapter. At the southern end of Glen Helen there are hiking trails into John Bryan State Park. It is one of Ohio's oldest state parks and offers one of only three public rappelling areas visited by the blue blazes.

Figure 5.4 Antioch College (Jennifer Koester)

Figure 5.5 Clifton Gorge (Marissa Fretz)

The trails along the Little Miami River at John Bryan are linked to the more striking gorge trails at Clifton Gorge, Ohio's most frequently visited nature preserve. Clifton Mill, on the east side of the gorge, was built in 1869 and is one of the largest water-powered gristmills still in existence. Tours there show how grain is turned into flour. The Millrace Restaurant serves breakfast and lunch and is popular with hikers in the area.

The chapter ends in Fairborn and the adjacent Wright-Patterson Air Force Base. This busy airfield, near where aviation was born, explains why you hear a lot of aircraft in the skies overhead. In the next chapter we will explore some of the places the Wright brothers frequented in the Dayton area.

FEATURED HIKE 1
EDEN PARK

DISTANCE Less than 3 miles.

TIME Allow at least 2 hours to enjoy the sights, sounds, and scenery along the paths in this wooded parkland positioned high above the Ohio River.

DIFFICULTY Easy. The elevation change is less than 100 feet, but you will go up and down a couple of times. The hike is made easier by conveniently placed concrete steps along the way.

Park at the Twin Lakes Overlook along Lake Drive. The directions to Eden Park were given at the beginning of the chapter. This overlook (WP 1) offers a magnificent view of the sharp curve of the Ohio River, 200 feet below (fig. 5.6). Dayton, Kentucky, sprawls along the south bank. The sternwheeler on the Kentucky side is one of many tour boats in this area

Figure 5.6 Ohio River

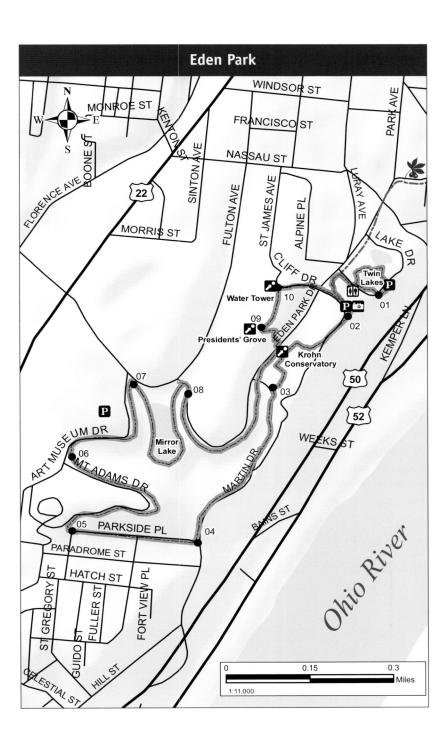

Eden Park

that may be rented. The floodwall there was built in 1937, after the Ohio rose to 80 feet and flooded much of the Kentucky communities Dayton, Newport, and Covington. Also, look for the prominent church with a burnished copper steeple just west of Dayton, in neighboring Bellevue, Kentucky. It appears as if it has twin spires, but one spire is on an adjacent building. This is the Sacred Heart Church, built in 1892, Bellevue's first house of worship.

You might spot a towboat pushing tons of coal in a train of barges to one of the many power plants located on the river. The large crane on the Ohio side is used to load bulky products that are efficiently transported around the world. Soon after the invention of the steamboat—and because of its location on the river—the Queen City became the fifth-richest city in the U.S.

West of the overlook is the Daniel Carter Beard Bridge, which carries traffic between the Ohio and Kentucky banks via I-471. Dan Beard was the founder of the Sons of Daniel Boone, one of the organizations that later became the Boy Scouts of America. Because of the golden arches on the bridge it is known locally as the Big Mac.

As you turn from the overlook and walk through the park, cross the concrete footbridge connecting the Twin Lakes. The lakes were formed from the mining of limestone for building materials. There are two statues on the other side; the first is of a cormorant fisherman. Note the ring fastened around the bird's neck to prevent its swallowing the catch. Near the bridge look for four large buckeyes, the state tree of Ohio. Walk to your right to the other statue, a bronze replica of Lupa Capitolina (fig. 5.7), the wolf that, according to mythology, nursed the twin builders of Rome, Romulus and Remus. At Lake Road, there are restroom facilities. Cross over Lake Road and walk toward Eden Park Road and find the blue blazes going to the left.

See the Melan arch bridge just ahead, with its powerful eagles carved from granite. The bridge crosses Eden Park Drive to the left (west) of Lake Drive. Built in 1894, this was the first concrete arch bridge in Ohio. Follow the blue blazes to the left of the bridge and climb 51 stone steps that will take you to the Upper Overlook and the sign announcing, "Buckeye Trail Southern Terminus. Follow the Blue Blaze" (fig. 5.1).

Beyond this sign is the Navigation Monument (WP 2), a 30-foot granite obelisk near the midpoint of the 980 miles of the Ohio River. The river originates at the confluence of the Allegheny and Monongahela Rivers, which surround Pittsburgh's Three Rivers Stadium, and ends at Cairo, Illinois, where it joins the Mississippi. The obelisk celebrates the completed

Figure 5.7 Lupa Capitolina

canalization of the Ohio, in 1929. Along the entire river 49 dams were built to make it deep enough for shipping.

Turn from the monument and look north across the Melan arch bridge to view the red-brick water tower. You will visit it up close on your return from the hike.

Turn southwest and follow the ADT for about 100 feet. You will find the steps down to Cliff Drive and the rear of Krohn Conservatory. There, in the harsher days of winter, the tropical rainforest and hot, dry desert environments are luxuriously comfortable to visit. The Art Deco greenhouse contains 5,000 of the world's most exotic plants, includes a 20-foot waterfall, and offers relaxation in a Japanese teahouse. Walk around the conservatory to the front to enjoy the gardens. Now follow the sidewalk to the rear of the conservatory and take the lawn or driveway to Martin Drive. Go south (left) on Martin Drive (WP 3), which parallels the river. As you cross over Martin Drive to the sidewalk, you will be walking beside Hinkle Magnolia Garden and following the ADT, leading to Covington, Kentucky. You will pass by Bettman Fountain as you near the end of the garden.

Next you will come upon a large brick building with gargoyles on its smokestacks that served as the pumping station for the reservoir (WP 3). The date on the building reads 1889; it was designed, as was the water tower, to enhance the beauty of the park landscape. The reservoir was under Mirror Lake, and you will walk by the site of the old retaining wall on your right as you continue south on Martin Drive.

Eventually, turn right (west) from Martin Drive onto Parkside Place (WP 4). At 1021 Parkside is the Cincinnati Art Club, whose mission is to promote the knowledge and the love of art through education. It is the second-oldest art club in the country. Cincinnati is well known for its cultural heritage, largely attributed to Germanic influences on the city. As you walk away from the river you can also see a few of the Mount Adams courtyards as well as interesting views of the city below, including the arched Cincinnati Museum Center at Union Terminal, with its three museums.

As Parkside dead-ends into Louden Street, walk up the concrete steps (WP 5) on your right to Mount Adams Drive. The Cincinnati Playhouse in the Park, at the top of the stairs, has 10 different productions each season. Turn to your left and continue walking a winding road north past a swimming pool and fantastic lookout over the river. Descend to Art Museum Drive and turn right (WP 6). The Cincinnati Art Museum, on the hill, is a Romanesque building faced in limestone that houses world-renowned collections spanning more than 500 years. Children under 18 are admitted free.

Walk down the steps (WP 7) to a plaque explaining the history of the original reservoir and then walk to the sidewalk encircling Mirror Lake. Take a turn around this large reflecting pool and investigate the arched gazebo (WP 8) made of bronze and stone. This popular structure, completed in 1904, is the symbol used for Eden Park on street signs in the area.

To the right of the gazebo find the Hinkle Floral Trail to Krohn Conservatory. It parallels Eden Park Drive and Mirror Lake. On the Hinkle Floral Trail, you will see the rear of the old pumping station.

Across the street from the conservatory are 48 steps that will take you to the top of the hill. Near the top, go off to the left to visit the Presidents' Grove (WP 9), where a tree has been planted for each American president. The white oak that honors George Washington was transplanted from an area near his tomb. The interpretive sign at the center of the grove has a list and a map showing each president's tree.

Now, walk toward the water tower. The tower, visible to most people in the area, rises 172 feet above its base in Eden Park. Disguised as a

German castle, it reminded the many early German American residents of their homeland along the Rhine.

Walk to the right past the tower (WP 10) and over the Melan arch bridge to the stairs and return to the parking area. As you near the bridge, notice the Vietnam War memorial off to your left.

FEATURED HIKE 2
FORT ANCIENT STATE MEMORIAL

DISTANCE 4 miles, if you park at the Little Miami Scenic Trail (LMST) public parking area, off SR 350.

TIME With a 1-hour visit to the museum, you should plan to be in the area for at least 4 hours.

DIFFICULTY Moderately easy, except for the 250-foot climb on the River Connector Trail. Wooden steps on the Connector Trail include a bench for resting, which eases the ascent. Hikers can avoid this climb by driving to the North Overlook parking area, inside the memorial. If you use the Connector Trail, be sure to take enough money to pay as you enter the park. If you have a card showing you are a member of Ohio History Connection, the visit is free.

There is a Hiker on the Go map for this section of the Buckeye Trail.

Fort Ancient is on SR 350 near Lebanon, Ohio. Signs from I-71 (from the south or north) will direct you to the park. The hike begins at the public parking lot (WP 1) on the Little Miami River, to the west of Morgan's Canoe Livery. (Do not park in their lot unless you plan to use their services.) The walls of Fort Ancient appear above this site. The gold lines on the map indicate the traces of the actual earthen walls.

Walk east (right) from the parking lot to the LMST, just east of the canoe livery. Turn right and walk south along the Little Miami River. You are now on the Buckeye Trail but you will not see any blue blazes. The park authorities discourage blazing and it is really not needed on such a well-defined blacktop trail. Signage along the way will tell you that you are on the BT as well as the North Country Trail (NCT).

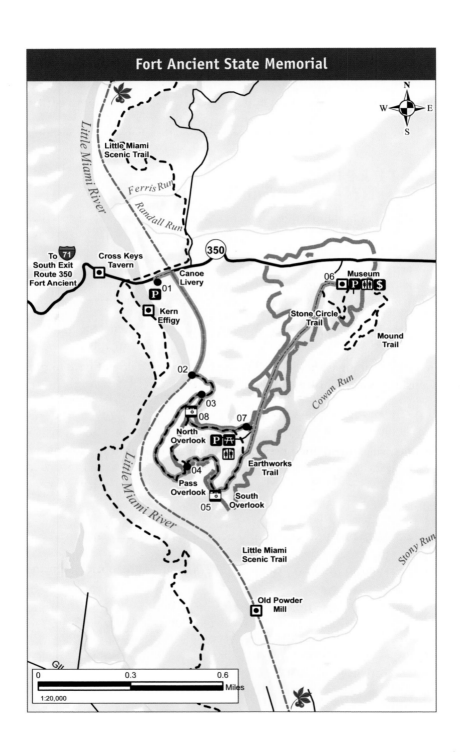

In spring and summer wildflowers abound along the river. In May look for the drooping yellow flower of bellwort, which likes the limestone soils found in this area. Also, in May through June look for the small pale-blue fringed flowers of Miami mist, which thrives in the rich moist woods and wet meadows along the LMST.

The woods along the trail are second growth; where you are walking was once a railroad bed. The whistle marker still seen on the left side of the trail reminded the engineer to blow the train's whistle to alert traffic on SR 350. Note the low spots along the left side, which are often filled with water. These man-made wetlands were caused by borrowing earth to elevate the railroad. BT trail builders also use borrow pits to elevate the trail, a process called turnpiking. The trail will pass much older borrow pits later at Fort Ancient.

Our next stop is the River Connector Trail (WP 2). Bryan McCreary reconstructed this trail in 1996 for an Eagle Scout project. You will see other Eagle Scout projects, bridges and boardwalks, on the Terrace Trail, later in the hike. As you turn left onto the Connector Trail, the fees for visiting Fort Ancient are posted and should be paid at the park entrance, which you will pass later. Ohio History Connection members or Fort Ancient season pass holders with membership cards do not have to pay. Consult www.ohiohistory.org for current rates.

Turn left onto the River Connector Trail (WP 2) to ascend to Fort Ancient. The trees on the steep slopes here have not been harvested, resulting in a mature oak-and-maple forest. Soon you will encounter the wooden steps mentioned previously. About 70 feet from the top of the ridge you will arrive at the Terrace Trail (WP 3). Turn left and follow a half-mile trail that offers a walk beside the earthworks and a look at some rare wildflowers.

The Terrace Trail has interpretive signs on tree identification, and you are challenged to find the trees described. The Terrace Trail has been greatly improved by the work of Eagle Scouts. The Terrace Trail will end after a climb to the Pass Overlook (WP 4), one of the openings in the fortification. From the Pass Overlook bear right (north) on the Earthworks Trail, which parallels the earthworks inside the earthen walls of the South Fort. Soon you will arrive at an opening in the woods and you will follow a mowed path to the South Overlook (WP 5). In winter, you will see the Little Miami River.

Next, walk north to the South Fort picnic area and facilities in the lovely open area of the park, enlivened in fall by the yellows and oranges of maple and oak. The Hopewell civilization, not the Fort Ancient group, actually built the mounds (as they did those at Fort Hill; see chap. 3). Although their actual purpose can only be surmised, the mounds were certainly ceremonial, not fortifications, so the appellation fort is not accurate. Some believe that several of the 67 openings in the earthen walls trace the movements of the sun and moon. If you stand near certain mounds you can see the sun rising over specific openings on the summer and winter solstices (fig. 5.8). The moon's cycles may be followed in the same manner. In other Hopewell mound formations at Newark and Chillicothe, the circular enclosures that connect to octagonal mounds track the rising and setting of the moon through an 18.6-year cycle. Between the

Figure 5.8 Ancient solstice (Courtesy of Ohio
History Connection)

Hopewell occupation of the site and the coming of the Fort Ancient culture—the people originally thought to be the mound builders—some 500 years passed. By then, corn (maize) had been imported from the southern climes, where it was first derived from a Mexican grass, and larger villages sprang up due to an increase in the food supply. Visit the museum to learn more about these fascinating cultures.

Follow the paved park road north from the South Fort through the narrower Middle Fort. Continue north through the North Fort to the park entrance and pay admission (unless you are a member of Ohio History Connection). From the entrance, walk east to the museum (WP 6). Spend at least an hour there to learn the history of Native Americans from 13,000 b.c. to the advent of the long-knives from Europe, around 1600. Some outstanding features:

- A re-creation of a prehistoric Indian garden, containing lamb's-quarters, squash, maygrass, sunflower, goosefoot, and knotweed.
- A rectangular lodge (15 x 21 feet) built of native materials.
- When Worlds Collide, an exhibit depicting the impact of the Europeans on Native American life. The information on the Iroquois and their westward expansion during the Beaver Wars is especially enlightening.
- A 24-foot birchbark canoe made in 1870.
- Tecumseh's tomahawk-pipe.

The gift shop has many reference works concerning Native Americans. Especially recommended are Fort Ancient by Jack Blosser (site manager) and Robert Glotzhober and People of the Mounds by Bradley Lepper.

When you leave the museum, visit the mound to the east of the toll-booth at the entrance to the site. An interpretive sign there shows some of the alignments of the sun during the summer and winter solstices. The summer solstice alignment occurs at sunrise through the first gateway arch to the north of SR 350. To view the winter solstice alignment use the smaller stone mound to the left of the entrance road, on SR 350. The winter solstice sunrise is seen through two openings to the south of SR 350. The Hopewell did have a calendar to mark the changing seasons.

You will now return to the South Fort picnic area. Across from the parking area, find a trailhead (WP 7) to the Earthworks Trail that will lead to the North Overlook. Continue following the Earthworks Trail as it goes west. Along the way notice borrow pits on your right that were created during construction of these ancient Hopewell earthworks. Several species of mole salamanders depend on the temporary ponds in these pits. These amphibians live underground most of the year, but in late winter they briefly emerge to mate and lay eggs in the borrow-pit ponds.

Looking due north from the North Overlook (WP 8), the focal point is the massive Jeremiah Morrow Bridge on I-71 (fig. 5.9), spanning the Little Miami River. You can imagine the Buckeye Trail, following the riverbank on the LMST trail and continuing north under I-71.

Go to your right from the North Overlook and retrace your footsteps to the River Connector Trail and the LMST. To return to your car, be sure to turn right at the bottom of the River Connector Trail.

After returning to your car, if you are still perky, visit the Kern Effigy. Walk from the parking lot, turn left (west) and cross the SR 350 bridge over the Little Miami River. At the end of the guardrail on the left-hand side of the road will be a BTA white-blazed side trail. Before it was moved to the Little Miami Scenic Trail, the BT followed this side trail. You will be walking on property owned by the YMCA's Camp Kern. Kern Effigy no. 1 will be discovered within 5 minutes of walking south. Once excavated, the limestone flagstones revealed the effigy of a rattlesnake constructed around

Figure 5.9 View from North Overlook, Fort Ancient

A.D. 1200. On the summer equinox a shadow is cast in exact alignment with the 29-foot formation. (For more information on serpent effigies, see chap. 3, Serpent Mound.)

FEATURED HIKE 3
GLEN HELEN AND CLIFTON GORGE

DISTANCE Glen Helen 1 mile, Clifton Gorge 2.5 (both are out-and-back hikes).

TIME At least 4 hours for both, including car travel. You might plan additional time to lunch at Clifton Mill.

DIFFICULTY Moderately easy. There are steps at most locations where you climb or descend.

GLEN HELEN NATURE PRESERVE

To find Glen Helen Nature Preserve, go to Yellow Springs, north of Dayton on SR 68. At the center of town, turn left onto Corry Street. The parking lot is located across from Antioch College on the east side of the bike path/Little Miami Scenic Trail. In the mid-1800s to the early 1900s, the city of Yellow Springs was a popular tourist spot where visitors came for the healing waters of the springs.

The Buckeye Trail follows the bike path that runs beside Glen Helen. Before your hike, visit the Nature Store at the north end of the parking lot. The store carries a fascinating selection of field guides, bird-watching items, and bird-feeding supplies. The store is open seven days a week. You can pick up a map of Glen Helen that will detail the more than 30 different trails on the site. Use the map to spread your wings.

There is a $2 parking fee at the parking area of Glen Helen. Deposit the fee in a slotted collection box. It is a good idea to apply mosquito repellant. Unlike State Nature Preserves, at Glen Helen you may take your dog, if on short leash.

Start the hike at the kiosk and walk down a graveled walking path (WP 1). Go past a memorial to Arthur Morgan, who was instrumental in organizing the TVA under Franklin Roosevelt and whose engineering company planned and built a series of dry-dam reservoirs in the area to prevent a recurrence of the catastrophic 1913 Dayton flood.

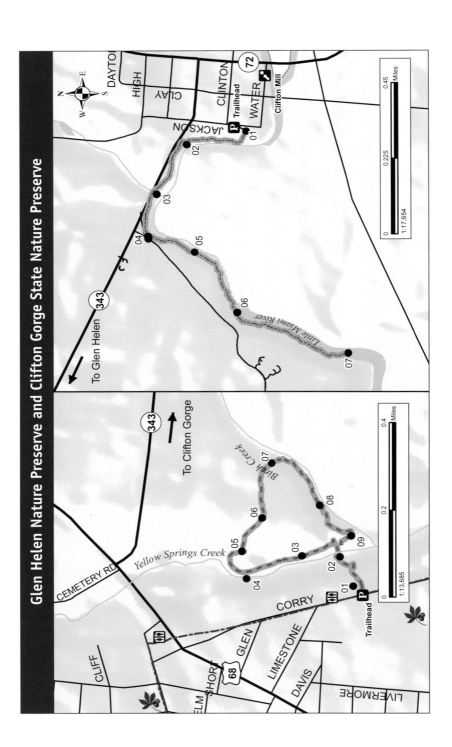

Glen Helen Nature Preserve and Clifton Gorge State Nature Preserve

At the stone stairs, you will pass Trailside Museum. The museum is open at irregular hours, but if it is open, all are welcome to view the exhibits. This hike often uses stone steps to get the hiker up and down the steep cliffs.

We will be following the Inman Trail. It is highlighted in red on the Glen Helen map, but there will be no trail markers along the way. After descending the steps, cross a wooden bridge (WP 2) over Yellow Springs Creek. Just after the bridge, go to the left and take the trail less traveled. Soon you will come to a wooden boardwalk through a low area. There is an extension off the boardwalk (WP 3) for Pompey's Pillar, a dolomite slump block that has broken away from the cliff and has eroded into a dramatic stone pillar. The pillar is rumored to be moving downhill. When will it topple?

WP 4 is the travertine grotto to your right and the dam on your left. Walk down to the bridge to get a good view of the remnants of the dam, which was built in the early 1900s and served as a recreational site for visitors and the community. The travertine grotto is a mound of calcium carbonate that was precipitated from the waters of the Yellow Spring, on the hill above. You will continue your hike by walking a gentle slope up the mound to the Yellow Spring, near the crest of the ridge. Stay to your right as you go up.

WP 5 is the Yellow Spring (fig. 5.10). The spring carries 60 gallons of water to the surface each minute. In the mid-1800s, the community of Yellow Springs had a hotel and people would venture to the pool of water at the springs for water therapy. The yellow color of the rocks surrounding the spring is due to the iron in the water. After the springs, go left up the wide path, passing a side trail to the right. Continue straight ahead and notice to the right a Hopewell mound (WP 6). The shallow mound is difficult to distinguish in summer because of the foliage. The mound is on the National Register of Historic Places. It was excavated in the 1950s and again in 1971 and determined to be a burial mound. This mound, known as Orators Mound, was used in the 1800s as a dais for speeches. Henry Clay and Daniel Webster were known to have addressed crowds of people from atop this mound. Abraham Lincoln is quoted as saying of Henry Clay, a United States senator, "he is my ideal of a great man."

Continuing on, you will begin to hear falling water. Before getting to the falls, there will be a memorial to the founder's daughter, Helen. In 1929, Hugh Taylor Birch donated 530 acres of land to Antioch College as a tribute to his daughter, who loved the glen, hence Glen Helen. Go straight ahead on a slight descent to a rail fence and the viewing area for the Cascades (WP 7). The water drops off a 50-foot cliff, hits a flat area,

Figure 5.10 Yellow Spring (David Fischer)

and then cascades over three smaller falls. You can take a walk above the falls to the bridge crossing Birch Creek, but the view below the falls is the most impressive.

Follow the trail to the right of the falls and stay close to the creek and fence. The trail gets narrower and is "rooty," but as long as you are next to the creek, you are on the correct path. At (WP 8) ascend and walk a short distance from the creek. On top of the ridge, bear to your left and take a set of stairs going down.

At the bottom of the steps (WP 9), look to your left and see a set of stepping stones that cross the creek. This is not the direction back to the car, but it is just fun to walk the stones. To finish the hike, go right and head back to the car. At the next intersection, take a left and go over the creek and use the stone stairs to go up to the parking lot.

CLIFTON GORGE STATE NATURE PRESERVE

Clifton Gorge State Nature Preserve possesses a magnificent dolomite gorge cut through by the brawling headwaters of the Little Miami River.

From Yellow Springs drive to the state preserve by taking SR 343 (east) from U.S. 68 just north of Yellow Springs. Before you get to the village of Clifton, consider stopping at the John Bryan State Park to get maps and information for the area. The Park Office is located on SR 370, off of SR 343.

To get to Clifton, continue east on SR 343. From SR 343 turn right immediately as you enter Clifton, onto Jackson Street. There is parking at the end of Jackson.

Start the hike at the kiosk at the northwest corner of the parking lot on a wide gravel walking path (WP 1). The first 855 feet of this hike is handicap accessible. The gorge you are entering eventually butts up against the watershed that separates the basin of the Little Miami from that of the Great Miami River. To travel north from here, Native Americans and early explorers had to climb to the gorge rim to portage their canoes.

There are interpretive signs at all the scenic overlooks. At the first, the Kennard Outwash is explained as an ancient glacial outwash river that created the Little Miami River. The canyon cut here by glacier meltwater is the reason Clifton Gorge is a National Natural Landmark. Be extremely cautious on this trail and use only the four overlooks provided to observe the action of the water that has created the abstract panorama below.

The falls of the Little Miami appear next, and soon after this you arrive at the Patterson Mill Overlook (WP 2). A cotton and wool mill was built right over the rushing water of the gorge. A flood in 1876 destroyed its dam and the building. Clifton was known for its many mills during the early 1800s. Clifton Mill (fig. 5.11), located in Clifton, just one block from the parking area, has been restored as a working gristmill.

The aromatic white cedar growing in the gorge can be seen from the Pool Overlook (WP 3). Looking to the left from the overlook, you will see Devil's Gorge, the spot where Cornelius Darnell, a member of Daniel Boone's salt-making party, supposedly leaped across the gorge in 1778 to successfully evade his Indian captors. He must have been quite an athlete. As you leave this area, you will walk close to SR 343 but behind a concrete wall—very safe. At the Bear's Den Interpretive Center (WP 4) you will find a set of stairs that will take you down to the North Gorge Trail.

The stairs descend next to the cliffs that form the north rim of Clifton Gorge. The dolomite cliffs on your left are an excellent example of the bedrock of the Silurian Period (see appendix 1). You will see easily eroded shale that characteristically forms slopes, and limestone-and-dolomite cliffs. Snow trillium blooms quite early here in the gorge, while snow still covers the ground. You will see more interpretive signs that tell of the

Figure 5.11 Clifton Mill

geology, history, and biota of the gorge. Notice the mill road, which was used to transport products from a former paper mill, leading down from the top of the gorge. Waterfalls tumble down the cliff sides along the way. The sound of their rushing waters creates a sense of tranquility.

As you walk along the river, the cliffs recede further to your right and the flora and fauna of the steep slopes will catch your eye. Notable trees include the cliff-loving northern white cedar (American arbor vitae), whose roots are specially adapted to tap the plentiful water in the dolomite. The chinquapin oak, whose leaves and fruit resemble its larger cousin the chestnut, also likes the shale midsection of the gorge.

Wildflowers to look for include the potentially threatened snow trillium and the round- and sharp-lobed hepaticas, with their three-lobed liver-shaped leaves and white to pink or lavender flowers. Along the sides of the dolomite slump blocks you might see the walking fern, with its small arrowhead-shaped leaves. Also seen is the curious rattlesnake fern, with a fertile stalk originating from a base of lacy blades, like the rattles on the tail end of its namesake.

In the summer months you may see small birds known as flycatchers. The Acadian flycatcher and the eastern wood pewee both are grayish brown with dusky to white breasts (the former species with a light eye ring) and perch high in treetops. The rare black-and-white warbler creeps along limbs like a nuthatch. Among the finches, the indigo bunting—a migrant from the tropics—nests here. This bird's feathers actually contain no pigment, but the diffraction of light through them changes the wavelengths to a striking blue. The male sings over 200 songs per hour while perched at his post advertising for a mate.

Steamboat Rock (WP 5) is a slump block that fell from the towering cliffs and ended up in the river. Can your imagination produce a reason for the name? A storyboard at this site explains the varying layers of rock in this area. Dolomite, a very hard rock, rests atop fragile shale. As the shale erodes, the dolomite is toppled and falls off the cliff.

Shortly you will come upon the Blue Hole (WP 6) (fig. 5.12). This is a calm area of the river that has been memorialized with a famous painting by Robert S. Duncanson, an African American from the mid-1800s. It can be found in the Cincinnati Museum of Art.

The outward leg of this hike ends at the beginning of the Cincinnati-Pittsburgh Stagecoach Trail (WP 7), which leads into a picnic area in John Bryan State Park (1.3 miles). This trail is quite wide and easy to walk, and

Figure 5.12 Blue Hole (Marissa Fretz)

one can easily imagine its use by a stagecoach. To get back to your car, retrace your steps.

If you choose to explore further, maps are available at the Park Office at John Bryant State Park off SR 343, between Clifton and Yellow Springs.

LOCAL CONTACTS

- Caesar Creek Lake Visitor Center. http://caesarcreekstatepark.com.
- Clifton Mill. www.cliftonmill.com.
- Eden Park. www.cincinnatiparks.com.
- Greene County Park District. www.greenecountyohio.org/parks.
- Hiker on the Go map for Fort Ancient. www.buckeyetrail.org.
- John Bryan State Park. http://parks.ohiodnr.gov/johnbryan.
- Ohio History Connection. www.ohiohistory.org.

WAYPOINT ID'S

WAYPOINT ID	DESCRIPTION	LATITUDE	LONGITUDE
	EDEN PARK		
1	Twin Lake Overlook	39.11704000	−84.48720800
2	Navigation Monument	39.11642700	−84.48825700
3	Martin Drive	39.11448500	−84.49067800
4	Martin & Parkside Pl	39.11076800	−84.49304500
5	Concrete steps	39.11057200	−84.49726600
6	Art Museum Drive	39.11255300	−84.49732400
7	Steps to Mirror Lake	39.11449900	−84.49530600
8	Gazebo	39.11425100	−84.49355100
9	President's Grove	39.11609700	−84.49110300
10	Water tower	39.11724600	−84.49048000
	FORT ANCIENT		
1	Public Parking ST Rt 350	39.40686700	−84.09996700
2	Entrance to Fort Ancient	39.40230600	−84.09779000
3	Terrace Trail	39.40135700	−84.09718200
4	Pass Overlook	39.39782900	−84.09797000
5	South Overlook	39.39645800	−84.09625000
6	Museum	39.40694100	−84.08871800

WAYPOINT ID	DESCRIPTION	LATITUDE	LONGITUDE
7	Trailhead to North Overlook	39.39981900	−84.09443000
8	North Overlook	39.40050500	−84.09783800
GLEN HELEN			
1	Kiosk at parking area	39.80090400	−83.88547600
2	Wooden bridge	39.80135400	−83.88421600
3	Pompey's Pillar	39.80257100	−83.88419700
4	Travertine grotto and dam	39.80434400	−83.88522700
5	Yellow Springs	39.80450500	−83.88405200
6	Hopewell Mound	39.80387900	−83.88258000
7	Cascade Falls	39.80358700	−83.88022600
8	Stairs down from ridge	39.80202800	−83.88201500
9	Stepping stones	39.80099600	−83.88330100
CLIFTON GORGE			
1	Kiosk	39.79506200	−83.82854800
2	Patterson Mill overlook	39.79752200	−83.82934600
3	White cedar overlook	39.79874100	−83.83215300
4	Stairs down to river	39.79908000	−83.83450900
5	Steamboat Rock	39.79713500	−83.83535900
6	Blue Hole	39.79533300	−83.83874000
7	Stage Coach Trail	39.79068800	−83.84095600

Canal Boats to Trains and Bicycles to Planes

BTA SECTION MAPS Troy, St. Marys, Delphos.

COUNTIES TRAVERSED Greene, Montgomery, Miami, Shelby, Auglaize, Allen. The town of Delphos also includes the border of Van Wert (pronounced "wart") County.

DISTANCE COVERED 145 miles.

OVERVIEW

In this chapter we will continue our travels to the north, along the western side of Ohio. The area is generally flat as the result of several periods of glaciation. Flat, that is, except for the end moraines crossing east to west along the way—features caused by the Wisconsinan glacier, which retreated

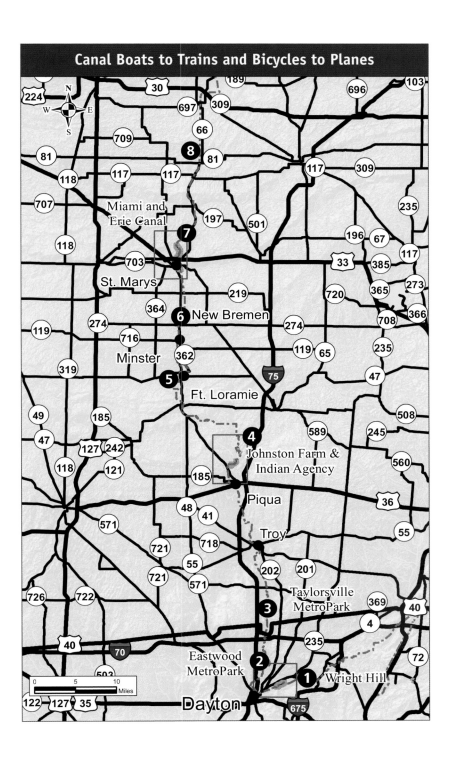
Canal Boats to Trains and Bicycles to Planes

from the area 14,000 years ago. As the glacier melted it deposited great hills of clay, sand, gravel, and boulders that were accumulated as its front traveled down from the north.

Much later, this became a land of planes, trains, bicycles, and canal boats, where you will find places and artifacts forming a concise history of transportation. The Buckeye Trail—with a general north-to-south orientation in this chapter—was first used by prehistoric animals, then by American Indians, and later by early pioneers. These historic trails followed rivers that provided more efficient travel by canoe, but early travelers often had to portage over summits that separated watersheds. The Miami and Erie Canal system, built early in the nineteenth century, utilized the same stream-valley paths and required huge lakes, mechanical locks, and large excavations, called deep cuts, in order to move bulky canal boats from Toledo to Cincinnati.

From the 1830s to the 1860s trains began to compete with the canal systems in Ohio. Tracks were often laid parallel to canal corridors, maintaining the orientation of transportation systems to rivers and other streams. Trains could deliver goods and services more efficiently than canal boats, which could not even work during the winter months when the canals were frozen, or during periods of flooding. In fact, the extreme flooding of 1913 marked the demise of canal transportation. It is often argued that railroads still deliver the most goods with greater efficiency than any other land-based transportation system, but better highways and the interstate system have made the personal automobile and truck transportation more competitive.

It is interesting to note that today's rails-to-trails are due largely to the demise of the railroads. In the Miami Valley, which includes the city of Dayton, there exists 330 miles of such trails offering citizens an opportunity to get outdoors and exercise.

The modern safety bicycle appeared in the 1880s, shortly after railroads decorated the landscape. It rapidly became a significant part of the transportation system, with 4 million bicyclists by the early twentieth century. One of the nation's largest bicycle museums is found in New Bremen. To the south, Dayton is the birthplace of aviation and the home of the Wright brothers, who manufactured bicycles and used this technology in the world's first successful powered flight.

Close to the BT in Dayton are 4 separate sites that together make up the Dayton Aviation Heritage National Historical Park. One of the sites, Huffman Prairie Flying Field, where the Wright brothers flew some of their first planes, may be seen from an overlook at the site's Interpretive Center.

The park entrance is off Kaufman Avenue (Point 1), just before it intersects with Springfield Street and SR 444. At the top of the hill, there is a beautiful park area with a cluster of 6 Adena mounds. The Interpretive Center is operated by the U.S. Air Force, in cooperation with the National Park Service. Also at this park is a 17-foot pink-granite obelisk dedicated to Wilbur and Orville Wright and the many others they taught to fly (fig. 6.1).

The overlook to the north of the memorial has an interpretive kiosk. Busy SR 444 and the Conrail tracks are viewed below. Huffman Dam is visible beyond SR 444. To the right of the dam is the Huffman Prairie Flying Field. A memorial pylon on the site should be visible. The Wright brothers and their many disciples used an electric interurban railway, predecessor of Dayton's present RTA, to travel to and from the nation's first airfield. Vestiges of this rail corridor are still seen along the bike trail across Springfield Street.

To actually visit this early airfield you must drive to Gate 16A at Wright-Patterson Air Force Base (WPAFB) and receive a visitor's pass. The gate is east of the Wright Memorial, off SR 444. This flying field is where many early leaders in aviation were trained. A replica of the original 1905 hangar is there. The foundation of the building, once lost to

Figure 6.1 Wright Memorial

posterity, was rediscovered in 1991. An interpretive walking tour of the prairie airfield reveals a lepidopterist's paradise; 28 moth species have been collected here. A new species of moth, *Glyphidocera wrightorum*, has been collected only in this prairie. Birds that may be spotted at Huffman Dam are the western grebe, osprey, bald eagle, and white-winged scoter.

While in the area, a visit to the National Museum of the United States Air Force, the oldest and largest air power museum in the world, is a must. The NMUSAF (Point 2) is just around the corner from the Huffman Prairie Flying Field Interpretive Center. The entrance is on Springfield Street, at Gate 28B. It is one of the most popular museums in the United States, with over a million visitors per year. Parking and the museum visit are free. You will find more than 300 aircraft and missiles arranged chronologically from the days of Kitty Hawk to the Space Age. You will see World War I aircraft and modern stealth fighters. The Presidential Gallery projects an aura of power. Some displays are interactive and you can even sit in a cockpit. For a fee, the IMAX theater offers movies on a six-story screen supported by a six-channel sound system.

After passing the museum, the BT wanders into Eastwood MetroPark (Point 2) and our first Featured Hike. From Eastwood, the BT ventures south to Deeds Point MetroPark. Highlights of this park are the statue to the Wright Brothers and the Five Rivers Fountain of Lights (fig. 6.2), which are lit in the evening. The view of downtown Dayton across the river is outstanding. After Deeds Point, the BT heads north out of the city.

The other three sites of the Dayton aviation park are near the BT's turn northward, in the heart of historic Dayton. Two of these sites will be found from West Third Street. The restored Wright Cycle Company (fig. 6.2) is found at 22 South Williams Street and nearby, at 219 North Paul Laurence Dunbar Street (previously North Summit Street), is the Dunbar House. This Italianate, turn-of-the-century structure houses a museum memorializing this great writer's life.

The BT encounters U.S. 40, or the Old National Road, in the Taylorsville Reserve area (Point 3). The historic National Road originally connected Baltimore and Vandalia, Illinois. The Buckeye Trail crosses the National Road two times in its journey around the state. Primitive forms of transportation, such as stagecoaches and Conestoga wagons, were the first to use our country's earliest federally funded interstate.

The blue blazes cross the Great Miami River on Taylorsville Dam, built in the 1920s. Arthur Morgan was the engineer who planned and implemented the Miami Conservancy District, which resulted in five large dams being built from 1918 to 1922. Huffman Dam, seen on the first

Figure 6.2 Fountain of Lights (Laura Loges)

Featured Hike, and Taylorsville Dam were two of those dams, designed to protect the people of the Miami Valley from floods like that of 1913.

The ghost town Tadmor is found in Taylorsville MetroPark. The town was vacated after the devastating flood of 1913, which killed 360 people and caused untold others to evacuate the Miami Valley. To visit Tadmor, you must walk 1.3 miles north on the BT, which follows the towpath of the Miami and Erie Canal. A paved bike trail parallels the blue blazes and the canal. Parking and a trailhead can be found on the west side of Taylorsville Dam.

Vestiges of 4 transportation systems, with some on-site interpretations by way of signage, exist in Tadmor (fig. 6.3). The original National Road was built to pass straight through the village using a covered bridge over the Miami River. (U.S. 40 today uses the dam to form a large U around Taylorsville Reserve.) The other three transportation systems are the Dayton and Michigan Railroad, which ran north and south; the Miami and Erie Canal, which the former railroad paralleled; and the Miami River itself, one of the earliest forms of transportation to the area. Don't be startled if you hear a train seemingly bearing down on you at Tadmor or while walking along the trail—the modern B&O Railroad is just to the west.

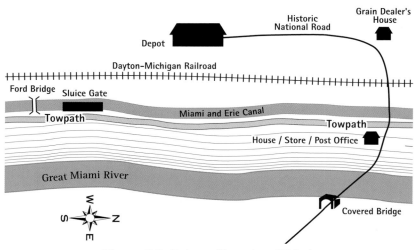

Figure 6.3 Tadmor (Jonathan White)

There is also a white-blazed side trail from the BT at Tadmor that follows the Great Miami River and makes an interesting loop hike. (Allow at least 2 hours for the leisurely 3.3-mile loop.) Birding is excellent at Taylorsville MetroPark. Along the river great blue, as well as the smaller green, herons can be found. At the canal, watch for vireos, small songbirds with hooked bills. (*Vireo* is Latin for "I am green.") You can distinguish vireos from warblers because vireos sit still for a minute or two after perching, while warblers move continuously.

Our next stop on the BT is the Johnston Farm and Indian Agency Historical Site (Point 4), where Indian agent John Johnston established a farm in 1804 from which he shipped apples and other farm products via the canal. Our second Featured Hike, part 1, begins at the museum on the Johnston farm, where you can also take a ride on a canal boat (fig. 6.4), and ends at the site of the now demolished Loramie Mill. Lock 8 will be seen along the way.

The Loramie Summit begins in the village of Lockington and ends in the village of New Bremen. This 21-mile plateau of water required locks south and north of the summit to raise boats 513 feet from Cincinnati and then to lower them 395 feet to Toledo. Native Americans crossing this area connecting the Auglaize Trail and the Miami Trail had to portage their canoes from the south-flowing Miami River to the north-flowing Auglaize. For these early travelers, this summit may have loomed as formidably as the continental divide for Native Americans in the West.

Figure 6.4 Canal boat *General Harrison*
(Courtesy of Ohio History Connection)

Along the Loramie Summit the blue blazes visit the town of Fort Loramie (Point 5), where a historical marker delineates the Treaty of Greenville line. This political border, established in 1795 by treaty with the major Indian tribes in Ohio, allowed the lands south of the line to be settled peacefully. Many of today's roads, as well as township and even county lines, follow this historic boundary that runs from Fort Loramie northeast to the eastern side of the BT, which leads through Fort Laurens, in Bolivar (chap. 11). Pilots of small aircraft say they can yet follow this historic line by noting the direction of field borders and fencerows.

Visit the BT at a park located in Fort Loramie where several historical markers are located, including a canal mile marker explaining that you are 116 miles from Cincinnati. From the park, cross SR 66, passing the Wilderness Trail Museum and St. Michael's Cathedral, built in 1881. From here the BT heads east to Lake Loramie, built in 1824 as a reservoir for the Miami and Erie Canal. Lake Loramie State Park offers more than 8 miles of trails, including the BT. The area is named after Peter Loramie, a French-Canadian Jesuit priest who later became a trader to the more than 400 Indian families living in the area. Loramie was considered an enemy of the American settlers, and his trading post was destroyed in 1782, forcing him to flee west with his Shawnee friends.

Ohio's first designated state trail originated at Lake Loramie. The original Miami and Erie Canal Towpath Trail was 44 miles long. Now 55 miles long, the trail stitches together the Piqua Historical Area, Lake Loramie, Minster, New Bremen, St. Marys, and Delphos. Both the BT and the North Country Trail (NCT) share this trail, which follows the historic canal.

Minster, the next canal town on the BT, is in an area known as the Land of the Cross-Tipped Churches (fig. 6.5). New Bremen, just to the north, is an energetic Midwestern village of neatly detailed homes. In a lovely park the blue blazes march along the canal to Lock 1S, at the northern end of the Loramie Summit.

The Bicycle Museum of America (Point 6), just off the park on West Monroe Street, is the nation's largest museum devoted to the bicycle and traces the evolution of the two-wheeler from 1816 to the present (fig. 6.6).

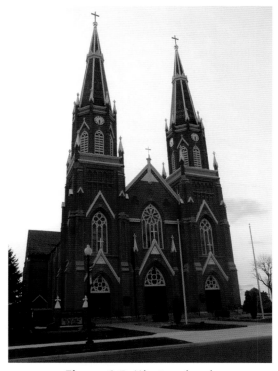

Figure 6.5 Minster church
(Andy "Captain Blue" Niekamp)

Figure 6.6 Bicycle Museum of America poster
(The Bicycle Museum of America)

A tour is recommended, followed by a tasty meal at the grill next door, where bikes hang from the ceiling.

The third Featured Hike takes place at St. Marys (Point 7), the next canal town to the north. St. Marys was first known as Girty's Town, after the notorious renegades Simon Girty and his brother Jim, who operated a trading post on the St. Marys River. Simon, adopted by the Seneca in 1755, when he was 15, spoke at least three Indian languages and sided with them in their efforts to stop the settlers' migration into the Ohio country.

Simon was perceived as so evil that mothers on the frontier would warn wayward children that Girty would get them if they didn't straighten out. Lt. James Girty deserted from the Continental Army to join his brother to support the British in efforts to prevent American independence.

Grand Lake St. Marys, east of St. Marys, was the largest man-made lake in the world until the completion of Hoover Dam, in 1936. Grand Lake was built as a reservoir for waters to feed the canal system. The work was begun in 1837, claimed many lives (including the author's great-grandfather), and was completed in 1841.

Deep Cut (Point 8), a National Historic Landmark, is essentially a ditch dug to cross an east-to-west glacial moraine (a geological feature mentioned in the Overview). The cut eliminated the need to build more expensive locks that required a lock tender and maintenance. The mile-and-a-quarter excavation through tough blue clay reached a depth of 52 feet. An interpretive sign at Deep Cut Historical Park, along SR 66, reminds us of the human cost of such an enormous project.

The Lincoln Highway crosses the BT at Delphos. Planning for the construction of this coast-to-coast highway began in 1913, and it became a 3,389-mile roadway connecting Times Square in New York to Lincoln Park in San Francisco. It is now U.S. 30 in the East and Midwest.

In the Delphos section the BT ends at the village of Junction, where Indiana's Wabash and Erie Canal intersected the Miami and Erie Canal. The juncture of the old canal prisms (beds) is barely visible. The blue blazes continue north in the Delphos section to Defiance, where the next chapter begins.

FEATURED HIKE 1
EASTWOOD METROPARK AND NATIONAL MUSEUM OF THE USAF

DISTANCE 2.5 miles in park, 1 mile round-trip to museum.

TIME About 1 hour for park hike.

DIFFICULTY Easy.

To begin the hike, take the Eastwood MetroPark entrance that is south of the Mad River on Harshman Road, between SR 4 and Springfield Street. The address is 1385 Harshman Road, Dayton, Ohio 45431. Eastwood is one of the Five Rivers MetroParks. Pets are permitted, if on leash. The park area has picnic tables, restrooms, a children's play area, and scenic

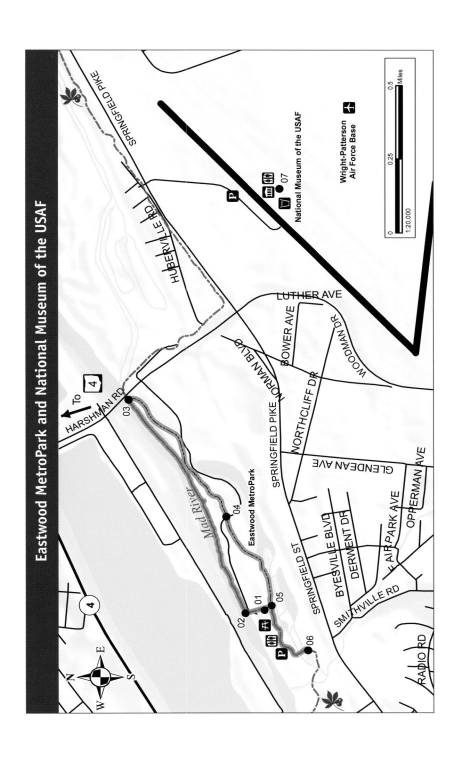

Eastwood MetroPark and National Museum of the USAF

walkways. On the other side of the Mad River, the north portion of the park is a 185-acre recreational lake. Canoeing and kayaking are popular on the river, and there is a convenient launching area on the river at the park entrance on the south side of the river.

Our first Featured Hike will begin from the parking lot, which is at the far southwestern end of the park. This parking area is located between the lagoon and the river and has the playground equipment. The lagoon and Eastwood Lake serve as part of a recharge system for Dayton groundwater. Dayton is the largest groundwater user in the state. The lagoon is a remnant of the original riverbed. In 1914 the river was moved and channeled to "tame" the river and control flooding. Currently efforts are underway to naturalize the present riverbed to provide better wildlife habitat and more exciting boating experiences.

Go to the east corner of the parking lot, where you will find a service road for canoe and kayak launching. The blue blazes are painted on the pavement (WP 1). Look toward the river and find the blue blazes on a utility pole. Walk toward the pole and across the lawn and park road to a sign announcing the entrance to the NCT and the BT. Go down the steps to a footpath that goes to your right (WP 2). You will be following a footpath next to the Mad River. There are numerous paths made by fishers and others wanting to get closer to the river. The path is shaded by many sycamore trees. Even in relatively dry periods, there are vernal (ephemeral) pools to the right of the trail. Come prepared with mosquito repellent.

Because of the closeness to the water, the air is melodious with the sounds of many birds. In midday, even during summer, you will hear catbirds, wrens, robins, song sparrows, field sparrows, cardinals, and many varieties of warbler. Birds in the park also include blue herons, belted kingfishers, cedar waxwings, Baltimore orioles, and bald eagles. Since 2009 a pair of eagles has been nesting near the park. In 2013 they reared two eaglets. If you are a serious birder or simply a wannabe, put this spot on your list.

You will not see blue blazes on this trail, even though it is the Buckeye Trail. When you get to the end of this footpath and intersect the bike path, you will again see blue blazes. Notice that they go to the left, toward the Air Force Museum. We will go to the right on the bike path (WP 3). As the bike path heads back to the parking area, you will pass two prairie habitats. These habitats are on a regularly scheduled burning maintenance program to encourage the prairie flowers and discourage shrubby growth. A few of the summer flowers are bergamot, coneflower, teasel, and black-eyed Susan. The grassland openings are former prairies that retain the rich prairie soil and lend themselves to prairie restoration.

At WP 4, the bike path crosses the park road and passes closer to the lagoon. As you continue on, you may want to leave the bike path and walk closer to the water. The lagoon area is now much shadier than the bike path. Also, the bike path is very popular with bikers and walking on the lagoon edge will be more pleasant. There are 4 islands in the lagoon that are connected by bridges (fig. 6.7). To access them, walk to the far end of the lagoon, where a bridge crosses over the lagoon water's outlet to the Mad River. Then, walk east and begin crossing the bridges. Fun!

At WP 5 you will intersect the Buckeye Trail and see the parking lot. Your hike is over, unless you want to continue to walk the Buckeye Trail straight ahead as it leaves Eastwood MetroPark (WP 6) and continues on to Deeds Point in Dayton. At Deeds Point, 3 miles ahead, you will find statues of Wilbur and Orville Wright. These statues hold court over the confluence of the Mad and the Great Miami Rivers. The Five Rivers Fountain of Lights, a water display, operates seasonally and is illuminated at night.

If you decide to include the National Museum of the United States Air Force on your hike, at WP 3 turn left on the bike path and go under Harshman Road. Follow the bike path to a stoplight on Springfield Pike. You may cross at this light to enter the museum property. Features of this museum are found in the Overview for this chapter.

Figure 6.7 Bridge at Eastwood MetroPark (Five Rivers MetroParks)

FEATURED HIKE 2
JOHNSTON FARM AND INDIAN AGENCY HISTORIC SITE AND THE LOCKS AT LOCKINGTON

DISTANCE/TIME 3 miles (round-trip) for a hike from Johnston Farm to Lock 7 and 1 hour for the visit to Lockington.

DIFFICULTY Walking along the canal's towpath or the heel-path (the berm on the other side of the canal) is quite easy.

JOHNSTON FARM AND INDIAN AGENCY HISTORIC SITE

Piqua is the nearest city to the site of this Featured Hike. From I-75 take U.S. 36 into this historic canal town. The name Piqua might have come from the legend of a man created from the ashes of a large fire: "He rose like a phoenix to lead the Pekowi [Piqua] division of the Shawnee."

The museum at Johnston Farm is the recommended point of departure. There is a fee to enter this Ohio History Connection site. Use the Internet to see when they are open. If you are visiting during a time when the park is not open, see the last paragraph for parking and using the Buckeye Trail from Hardin Road. To reach the historical area, take SR 66 northwest from Piqua to Hardin Road (about 3 miles from U.S. 36). After turning right on Hardin (C-110), there are historical markers along the side of the road with small parking areas. One marker introduces the village of Pickawillany, or Upper Piqua (1 mile to the northeast), site of an important early trading post in the 1740s. Another memorial along Hardin Road is dedicated to Col. John Johnston, whose farmhouse dates from 1815 and may be toured (fig. 6.8). The third memorial is dedicated to local Union volunteers in the Civil War effort who were mustered into the infantry on these historic grounds.

In the museum you will learn about the village's destruction by the French and of the horrible death of la Demoiselle (or Memeskia), the Miami chief who founded the village and courted the English settlers. The English presence there led to French attacks that ultimately led to the French and Indian War.

The major Eastern Woodland Indian groups and their cultures are showcased in the museum—Delaware (also known as Lenape), Huron, Mingo (Iroquois), Shawnee, and Wyandot. Canal boat history is also featured and you will learn about the locks you will visit later. The restored canal at the museum offers rides—in season—on the *General Harrison,* a

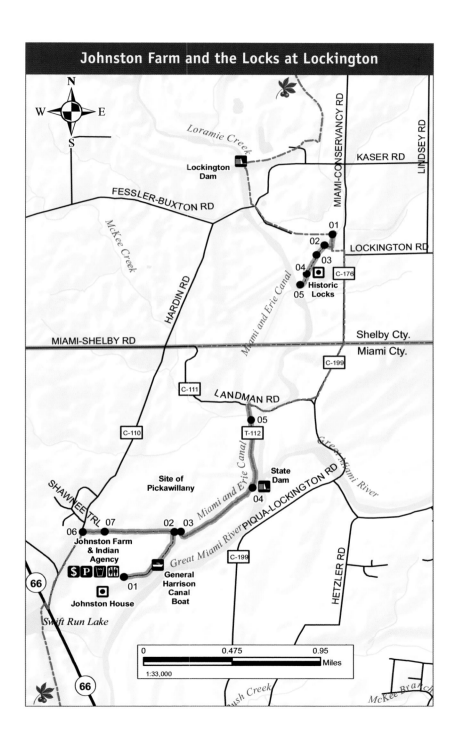

Johnston Farm and the Locks at Lockington

Figure 6.8 Johnston farmhouse (Miami and Erie Canal Corridor)

replica of a mule-drawn canal boat (see fig. 6.4). Riding a canal boat is like stepping back in time—to the early 1800s—when life moved at a much slower pace.

The Johnston farm is endowed with several innovations for the early 1800s, including a cider house with a cupola that was vented in the summer to keep the cider cool and a springhouse with a lively stream dancing through. The water's constant 50° temperature enabled better food storage through both the summer and winter. The original barn was built in 1808 with log-pin construction. Johnston was also patriarch of this frontier community. He helped keep the Native Americans out of the War of 1812 and was later appointed as a federal Indian agent. Respected for his fair dealings with the local tribes, Johnston was one of a very few champions of the "Indian cause" at that time.

WP 1 is the parking lot of the Johnston Farm. The farmhouse and the museum may be toured before or after the hike. To begin the hike, walk toward the museum on the sidewalk. Leave the sidewalk and walk to the field just north of the building. Do not go down the driveway to the loading ramp for the *General Harrison*. Instead, walk along the field toward the wooded area ahead and follow the tree line. You will soon come to a gravel service road and see the blue blaze on the bridge (WP 2). Turn to the right and follow the blue blazes up a slight rise. The blue blazes will turn off to the right (WP 3) and into woods to proceed to the canal. To see the site of Pickawillany go straight ahead. The open field was the area of the main village and is now being farmed. This site is very close to the Great Miami River, but up high enough to allow the Native American settlement to elude flooding.

The trail meanders through the immature woods and the canal will be visible on the right. This hike on canal lands is quite different from previous visits to canals. There will be very little foot traffic to intrude upon your visit. There will be no bicycles approaching from the rear. Shortly, the trail becomes a one-person-at-a-time bridge and crosses a small breach in the heelpath (berm). This breach caused this low area to the left to flood and created a quiet pond for waterfowl. The trail continues on with water on both sides of the path.

At WP 4 the trail passes Lock 8, which is known as the State Lock, because the State Dam was just downstream on the Great Miami River, after the confluence of Loramie Creek and the Great Miami River. The General Harrison makes a turn at this lock during its tour on the canal. The hike continues on past Lock 8 and follows a dry canal prism. The trail is nicely shaded and it is a gentle walk. The off-road trail will end at Landman Road where the Loramie Mill once stood (WP 5).

If you choose to visit during a time when the museum is not open, you may park just past the museum entrance at a gated area just off Hardin Road (WP 6). This is on the Buckeye Trail and you will follow the blue blazes. Walk beside a hedgerow on a service road and past a runway. Shortly, you will turn into the hedgerow (WP 7) and walk through an arbor to the service road bridge (WP 2).

LOCKS AT LOCKINGTON

After visiting the Johnston Farm, return to Hardin Road and turn right (north). Turn right on Landman Road (C-111). Just before you cross Loramie Creek, you will see blue blazes along the road. In 0.4 mile turn north on Piqua-Lockington Road (C-199). The road name changes at the Shelby County line to Miami Conservancy Road (C-176). After entering the village of Lockington and passing East Lockington Road, the BT turns left (west) on Museum Trail, County Road 111, and the Lockington Locks. A parking area is found just west of the locks. Children should be watched closely on this walk.

Begin your hike at Lock 1 (WP 1), an Ohio History Connection site maintained by the Piqua Historical Area. After reading the historical sign, face south to view the line of locks from Lock 1 South. You are standing at the highest point of the Miami and Erie Canal system. The locks were numbered from the summit level out in both directions, so there is a Lock 1 South, as well as a Lock 1 North. In the playground to the north you can see the prism of the Sydney Feeder Canal, which came in from the northeast. It supplied water to the summit level from Lewistown Reservoir, which is now Indian Lake.

Lock 1 is known as the Big Lock because its lift was the greatest of the locks in this area. The lock began to deteriorate in 1913, when, after the devastating flood, regular use of the canal was stopped. In 2013 restoration of this lock was begun with a price tag exceeding 2.5 million dollars. All the stones were moved and catalogued before repair of the canal prism. The stones were then reassembled and the project completed in 2014.

Looking to your right (west) over the parking area, you will see the house of the lock tender, the official who controlled traffic through the locks and collected tolls. Apparently, lock tending could be a stressful occupation. A lock tender at Lock 10, south of Piqua, was involved in a rock fight with one group of canal boaters who thought they had the right to use lock equipment without permission. Finally, the tender produced a shotgun and fired a round at the boaters. The boat captain, not intimidated, grabbed the gun from the tender and laid open his scalp with a mighty blow.

Looking to your left (east), you will see a house with one corner shaved off. The house was modified for the canal right-of-way because its owner supposedly tired of mules rubbing against his house! The brick home to your left as you begin to walk down the towpath was the Red Garter Saloon and Inn which, local lore tells, served as a house of ill repute.

On the way south to Lock 2 (WP 2) you will see a large turning basin to the right (west). This was used to hold boats until it was their turn to proceed through the locks. There was also a dry dock for a canal boat repair facility off the basin. Lock 2 is the best preserved of the five locks at Lockington.

An old mill straddled Lock 3 (WP 3). The canal water furnished the power used to grind grain. Notice the exposed timbers at the north end of the chamber. The depth of this lock is at least 30 feet.

While the grassy areas between the walls of Locks 4 and 5 are tempting, the precariousness of the stone walls make it dangerous to walk between the walls (WP 4). The square cut to the left of the millrace at Lock 4—and as you look north into the chamber of the lock—is known as a slip, or tumble. Tumbles adjusted water levels in the locks as they raised the boats. The entrance to the Piqua Hydraulic Canal came in from the southwest. Hydraulic canals supplied water and water power to industries such as the 25 copper shops in Piqua. Part of this canal still holds water. Swift Run Lake, near SR 66 and Hardin Road, was part of that system.

From Lock 5 (WP 4, fig. 6.9) look back along the walk just completed to best view the 67-foot hill, for which the locks were created in order to raise boats. Just as marvelous to comprehend is the aqueduct built to get the boats over Loramie Creek. The original aqueduct had three spans of timbers resting on stone piers. At WP 5, across Loramie Creek to the south, are some of the remaining pier structures. Lock 6 is on the other side of the creek. The creek can be deep at this point and it is not advisable to ford it. As you return north, notice the depressions along the towpath paralleling some of the locks. These depressions signal rotting timbers under the ground supporting the locks. Replacement of this wooden superstructure would require complete disassembly of the lock and rebuilding, as was done on Lock 1.

Figure 6.9 Locks at Lockington (MECCA)

For those driving to Lockington, an easy return to I-75 is to take Piqua-Lockington Road south to County Road 25A. Turn left and go 1 mile to exit 83.

FEATURED HIKE 3
THE MIAMI AND ERIE CANAL TOWPATH TRAIL, ST. MARYS

DISTANCE 8 miles out and back.

TIME 4 hours, with time to relax and enjoy the area. Also see alternate hikes at the end of this Featured Hike.

DIFFICULTY Easy. The canal towpath and the surrounding landscape are flat.

For this recommended hike, park at the parking lot for Geiger Park, located on Greenville Road, east of SR 66 (south of the St. Marys business district). With nearly 9,000 residents, St. Marys is one of the most prosperous of the canal towns in this region. Earlier residents were the Shawnee, who established Kettletown here because of its strategic location on the St. Marys River. Connecting with the Maumee River in Indiana, this smaller river forms a natural link between the Great Lakes and the Ohio River. The blue blazes lead to the mighty Maumee in the following chapter.

Tecumseh and his brother, the Prophet, along with Blue Jacket and Chief Logan were among the famous people who lived and visited here in the late 1700s. The savage extirpation of Native Americans from Ohio is illustrated by the following timeline

- 1795 Treaty of Greenville—Indians forced north of treaty line and into St. Marys area
- 1818 Treaty of St. Marys—Indians placed on three reservations—the Shawnee on 120 square miles centered in the Wapakoneta area—other tribes placed at Lewistown and Hog Creek Reservations
- 1832 Treaty with Indians to purchase all reservation land in Ohio, resulted in the 1,100 surviving Native Americans being exiled to the West

To begin the hike, visit the confluence (WP 1) of the Miami and Erie Canal, the St. Marys River, and the feeder canal from Grand Lake St. Marys, across the street. This is the site of a canal aqueduct that carried

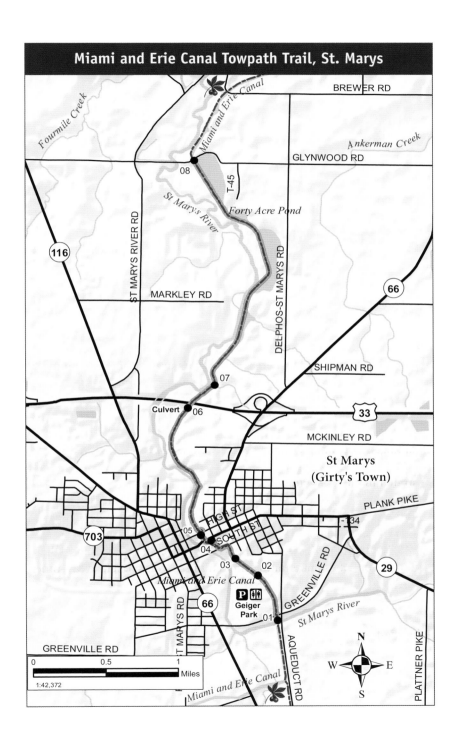

Miami and Erie Canal Towpath Trail, St. Marys

BREWER RD

Fourmile Creek

Miami and Erie Canal

Ankerman Creek

GLYNWOOD RD

08

St Mary's River

T-45

Forty Acre Pond

116

ST MARYS RIVER RD

DELPHOS-ST MARYS RD

66

MARKLEY RD

SHIPMAN RD

07

Culvert 06

33

MCKINLEY RD

St Marys
(Girty's Town)

PLANK PIKE

T-134

703

HIGH ST

05 SOUTH ST

04

03   02

29

GREENVILLE RD

Miami and Erie Canal

P 🚻
Geiger
Park

66

T MARYS RD

St Marys River

01

GREENVILLE RD

AQUEDUCT RD

PLATTNER PIKE

Miami and Erie Canal

N
W   E
S

0   0.5   1
Miles

1:42,372

water for the canal across the St. Marys River. The trail returns to the park and follows the canal. At WP 2 there is a canal boat turnaround area. Walk under a railroad overpass (WP 3) and leave Geiger Park. Turn left on South Street and walk to Memorial Park, in the center of town. If you want to start your hike here, you can park behind the library, on the corner of South and Chestnut, in a spacious lot.

Visit the Memorial Covered Bridge (1992), which crosses the surprisingly narrow St. Marys River. Also view the full-size replica (1989) of the *Belle of St. Marys* (WP 4, fig. 6.10) floating in the old canal. The entire park, with its clock tower and grotto, offers a respite after the earlier walk along the canal. Notice the doors of the buildings facing the canal where the Belle is located. See how they are at boat level for ease of loading and unloading materials from the boats. Walking past the *Belle,* you will cross under Spring Street and follow the walkway to Lock 13 (WP 5, fig. 6.11).

Lock 13 was unearthed when the St. Marys Woolen Mill was torn down. The factory was built over the top of the old canal and the prism was used as a cistern to wash blankets and mix dyes. When the building

Figure 6.10 *Belle of St. Marys*

Figure 6.11 Lock 13 (MECCA)

was removed, it was discovered that Lock 13 was concrete. Concrete locks were replacing wooden locks by the 1900s, about the time when Lock 13 was modified. (Concrete was known as artificial stone early in the 20th century.)

The trail passes this lock and continues on the canal path. You will be walking between the Miami and Erie Canal and the St. Marys River. The walk on this path is open and you can easily imagine the mules towing the canal boats along the route at 3 or 4 miles per hour during the heat of summer. A trip from Cincinnati to Toledo, say, took 5 days and 4 nights. There were no screens on the cabin windows and mosquitoes were plentiful along the canal. Stops at 9 a.m. and 2 p.m. allowed for picnicking along the banks and attention to other bodily needs. Back in the boat, there was an omnipresent odor, along with flies, emanating from the stable in the middle of the boat, where the spare team of mules that towed the boat for 6 hours at a time rested between shifts. From time to time a small cannon was fired to alert the lock tender of the boat's approach.

In 1 mile, the trail will reach a culvert that crosses under U.S. 33 (WP 6). The Buckeye Trail continues to the other side of U.S. 33, where it will wind through a grove of trees. At WP 7, 2 miles into the hike, the trail passes another turnaround for the boats. As you walk along the canal towpath, notice how flat the land is, with little glacial moraine. The large farms in this, the North Central Tillplain Ecoregion, are its main income producers. This fertile, almost treeless landscape was once part of a huge forested wilderness extending from the Allegheny Mountains of Pennsylvania into the prairies of Illinois. Only 6 percent of the original forest remains in this ecoregion.

The hike from Greenville Road to Forty Acre Pond (WP 8) is 4 miles. Forty Acre Pond was created when the St. Marys River was relocated for the creation of the canal. The pond was used as a turnaround point for the canal boats and the water was used to stabilize the water in the canal system. After Forty Acre Pond, the Buckeye Trail continues north along the canal route.

After returning to your car, drive SR 66 north for about 6 miles to Bloody Bridge, which crosses the canal on the left side of the highway. A small parking lot is here and a historical marker that tells the story of Bloody Bridge:

> *During the canal years of the 1850's a rivalry grew between Bill Jones and Jack Billings for the love of Minnie Warren. This became hatred by Bill because Minnie chose Jack. On a fall night in 1854, returning from a party, Minnie and Jack were surprised on the bridge by Bill, armed with an ax. With one swing, Bill severed Jack's head. Seeing this, Minnie screamed and fell from the bridge into a watery grave. Bill disappeared, and when a skeleton was found years later in a nearby well, people asked was it suicide or justice.*
>
> —Erected by Auglaize County Historical Society 1976

After your visit to Bloody Bridge, drive north to visit Deep Cut at the roadside park on SR 66. In about 0.7 miles you can spot the well-preserved aqueduct that spans Six-Mile Creek. The quaint village of Kossuth is next, where you will begin to see evidence of glacial-end moraine to the north, consisting of hummocky ridges higher than the adjacent terrain. Deep Cut's trench, described above in the Overview, passes through this moraine.

Many excellent hikes may be planned along the BT's lovely canal towpath and the Miami and Erie Canal Towpath Trail. If you have two cars, spotting one and driving to the other trailhead permits a longer one-way hike. One-way hikes with adequate trailhead parking nearby are Deep Cut to Bloody Bridge (5.3 miles); Lock 14 (on Lock 14 Road, off SR 66) to

Forty Acre Pond (a broad basin used to turn canal boats) (4.25 miles); and Forty Acre Pond south to St. Marys, at the aqueduct (4 miles). Contact the St. Marys Area Chamber of Commerce for more information on the popular Walk with Nature hikes scheduled in October.

LOCAL CONTACTS

- Bicycle Museum of America. www.bicyclemuseum.com.
- Dayton Aviation Heritage National Historical Park. www.nps.gov.
- Five Rivers MetroParks. www.metroparks.org.
- Johnston Farm and Indian Agency Historic Site. www.ohiohistory.org.
- Miami Erie Canal Corridor Association(MECCA). www.meccainc.org.
- National Museum of the U.S. Air Force. www.nationalmuseum.af.mil.
- St. Marys Area Chamber of Commerce. www.stmarysohio.org.

WAYPOINT ID'S

WAYPOINT ID	DESCRIPTION	LATITUDE	LONGITUDE
	EASTWOOD		
1	Parking lot	39.78156900	−84.13679000
2	Bottom of steps on river walk	39.78248400	−84.13700300
3	Jct footpath and bike path	39.78818100	−84.12368800
4	Bike path crosses park road	39.78346700	−84.13094400
5	Junction bike path and BT	39.78124500	−84.13647600
6	Kiosk	39.77949800	−84.13925600
7	National Museum of the USAF	39.78110000	−84.11010000
	JOHNSTON FARM		
1	Parking lot	40.18054000	−84.25524800
2	Bridge on service road	40.18421500	−84.25022100
3	BT enters woods	40.18426000	−84.24957500
4	Lock 8	40.18785800	−84.24239600
5	Former site Loramie Mill	40.19326400	−84.24265400
6	Parking on Hardin Road	40.18408500	−84.25951800
7	Hedgerow	40.18415000	−84.25733400

WAYPOINT ID	DESCRIPTION	LATITUDE	LONGITUDE
	LOCKINGTON		
1	Lock 1	40.20835000	−84.23475500
2	Lock 2	40.20746900	−84.23556000
3	Lock 3	40.20667500	−84.23635800
4	Locks 4 & 5	40.20512900	−84.23730700
5	Aqueduct remnants	40.20423400	−84.23793900
	ST. MARYS		
1	Geiger Park	40.53549100	−84.37779300
2	Canal boat turn around	40.54004100	−84.38046200
3	RR overpass	40.54170600	−84.38352400
4	Belle of St. Marys	40.54350500	−84.38671000
5	Lock 13	40.54407600	−84.38809100
6	Tunnel under ST RT 33	40.55712800	−84.39009900
7	Canal boat turn around	40.55950900	−84.38664700
8	Forty Acre Pond	40.58280600	−84.38985100

The Great Black Swamp

BTA SECTION MAPS Defiance, Pemberville.

COUNTIES TRAVERSED Paulding, Defiance, Henry, Lucas, Wood, Sandusky.

DISTANCE COVERED 110 miles.

OVERVIEW

Unless you live in northwestern Ohio, you will probably not understand the title of this chapter. The name Great Black Swamp describes an area that appears no longer as a swamp, but as an immense garden. The fertile land in this area has been drained and cleared to yield the largest per-acre agricultural crop in Ohio. The former swamp was 30 to 40 miles wide and

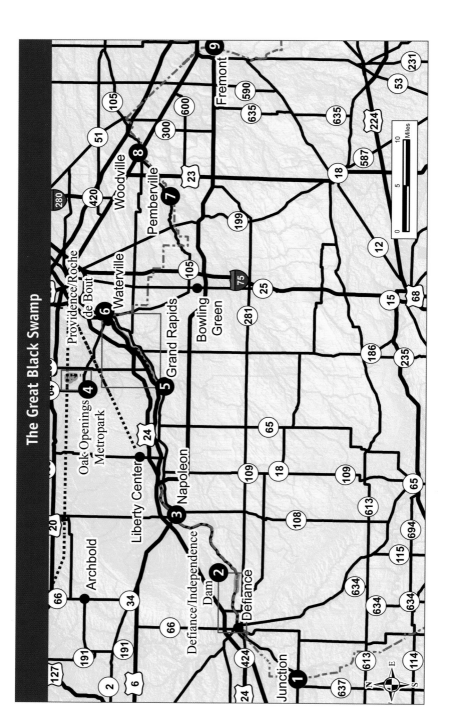

The Great Black Swamp

120 miles long, stretching from the Sandusky River (which passes through Fremont) in the east to near Fort Wayne, Indiana, in the west. It was a formidable barrier to the early settlement of this area as well as to travelers to Toledo or points northwest.

Early travelers described the approach to the haze-overlaid swamp as "an immense blue wall of trees stretching across the horizon." There is no way for today's traveler to experience the Great Black Swamp of the early 1800s. Today the closest you can come is to visit Goll Woods State Nature Preserve north of the BT but quite close to the route of the North Country Trail. Here you will see some of the largest, oldest, and rarest trees in Ohio: giant burr oaks up to 400 years old, trees that once covered the state. The best time to visit is early spring or late fall, before or after the mosquito invasion. The fall foliage at Goll Woods is fantastic, especially at the overlook over the Tiffin River.

What created this Great Black Swamp, a land most people considered uninhabitable before it was drained? Glacier action is responsible for most of it. As the last glacier melted, it created moraines or hills that acted like earthen dams to hold the water over an area that was once the bottom of a lake much larger than the present Lake Erie. The low-lying ground between the moraines and Lake Erie could not drain efficiently, and the result was standing water most of the year. The trees grew huge and the standing water supported snakes, mosquitoes, and other water-loving critters. The hardships endured by early settlers were unimaginable, including chills and fever brought on by what they called the ague. They did not know that mosquitoes, and not "bad" swamp air, transmitted the disease known today as malaria. Early farmers had to return to the cabin in the afternoon in order to "lay down and take their shake."

Ditches and "enough tile to reach from the earth to the moon" finally drained the swamp in the late 1800s. The drainage tile was produced in Ohio's factories from clay and shale abundant in northwestern Ohio and with the expertise of settlers from the lowlands of Holland and northern Germany. Today the land has been engineered for efficient agriculture. Even with the removal of this freshwater, the Great Lakes provide one-fifth of the world's freshwater and contain 95 percent of the freshwater in the U.S.

The blue blazes lead north from the once rip-roaring village of Junction, where the Wabash and Erie Canal from Indiana joined the Miami and Erie Canal, which we followed north in the last chapter (Point 1 on the Overview Map). North and east from here the combined canals were 60 feet wide rather than the standard 40 feet. This wider canal was known as the Twin Canal. The Buckeye Trail and the canal bed follow the Auglaize River northwest to Defiance and the Maumee River. Defiance College, a liberal arts college in the heart of town, requires that every student, regardless of major, serve as a community volunteer.

The Maumee, a State Scenic River, once was crystal clear, according to the diaries of early settlers. Later clouded by pollution, its water is now slowly responding to environmental measures, and aquatic life is increasing: 67 rare animal species and 191 rare plants live in this watershed. Environmental cleanup is important for all the streams feeding into Lake Erie. Each carries its share of waste from agricultural fertilizers, urban and suburban sprawl, and industrial processes.

The story of the strange and delicate mayfly is instructive. Long reviled before it was almost extirpated, the insects are also known as Canadian soldiers. (I have heard that some Canadians call them American soldiers.) The mayfly was disliked because the adults, which emerged from nymphs that fed off the lake bottom, swarmed when mating and then died. (The nymphs live two years underwater, but the adults, lacking mouthparts, live only a few days after mating.) Their bodies choked streets and sidewalks for a few days in the spring.

The insect's near demise in 1953 was due to lack of oxygen in the lake bottom—a depletion caused by industrial and agricultural waste and raw sewage from the surrounding watershed. This harbinger of Lake Erie's bad health led to improvements in lake conservation efforts, but environmental disasters still occur: in 1983 the blue pike was declared extinct by the U.S. Fish and Wildlife Service.

The blue blazes cross the Maumee River in Defiance to Pontiac Park, the beginning of our first Featured Hike (Point 2). The hike in Defiance explores the former site of Fort Defiance, on the south side of the Maumee and at the confluence of the Auglaize (fig. 7.1). The walk will give you some perspective on the defeat of Ohio's Native Americans. Johnny Appleseed, as well, will be remembered on our return to Pontiac Park, on the north side of the river. The blue blazes leave Pontiac Park and follow SR 424 to Independence Dam State Park (Point 2; fig. 7.2), along the wide Maumee and the Twin Canal. Independence Park, a 6-mile strip of land, is sometimes no more than 30 yards wide. There are 40 primitive campsites at the campground. Hikers will enjoy walking between the historic Miami and Erie Canal and the mighty Maumee. The village of Florida, just east of Independence Dam State Park and on SR 424, was the location of a much earlier American Indian population center, Snaketown. The BT continues east to pass through the Meyerholtz Wildlife Area and on into

Figure 7.1 Fort Defiance

Napoleon (Point 3), with the Henry County Courthouse, completed in 1882. Graceful arches above the windows and doors highlight the Romanesque Revival building.

The blue blazes continue on the north side of the river to Waterville. This trail is followed by the North Country Trail (NCT; see chap. 11), until it leaves the BT by heading north on SR 109 to find the Wabash Cannonball Trail at Liberty Center. This 67-mile dirt-and-cinder rail-trail connects the village of Liberty Center with the city of Maumee (see the southwestern diagonal on the Overview Map). The east-west segment of the Wabash Cannonball Trail passes through Oak Openings Preserve Metropark (Point 4), the site of our second Featured Hike. As you drive to Oak Openings, note the seemingly endless farm fields supported by small towns with grain elevators piercing the skyline.

Oak Openings, a Toledo Metropark, is home to Ohio's only living (moving) sand dunes, which mark an edge of Lake Warren, one of the several ancient lakeshores created by the glaciers (see the Lake Plain in

Figure 7.2 Independence Dam (Andy "Captain Blue" Niekamp)

appendix 2). The last glacier, thousands of feet thick, melted 14,000 years ago. The waters receded, forming present-day Lake Erie. During the melting process many lake terraces were formed, resulting in sand ridges, dunes, and sandbars now covered by oaks and known as oak savannas. The oak savanna area in northwestern Ohio is huge, covering 150 square miles, and even extends into Michigan, but most of it is endangered by development. The oak savanna in the park—low vegetation under a thick tree canopy—is home to more than a third of Ohio's endangered species. This type of ecosystem has vanished over much of the rest of the world.

From SR 109, the blue blazes continue on to Providence Metropark, in Grand Rapids (Point 5). The Maumee Trail, used by Blue Jacket and other American Indian leaders and located mostly on the north side of the river, came through here. At that time (1794) the river was shallow and choked with the fallen trees of the Black Swamp. It is thought that at least one small skirmish occurred in this area before the decisive Battle of Fallen Timbers, which took place upriver, at Maumee.

Here also you might be walking in the footsteps of Tecumseh, a young warrior in 1794. He returned to battle against the long-knives as a great Shawnee war chief in 1811. This final uprising of the Eastern Woodland Indians led to his death at the Battle of the Thames, in Canada in 1813, leaving the Native Americans of northwestern Ohio with little real leadership.

Today, Providence Dam has created 20 miles of broad and navigable water on the Maumee. The primitive campground at Mary Jane Thurston State Park, in a wooded setting, appeals to hikers and nature lovers. The BT uses the park's half-mile Gilead Side Cut Trail, which leads to Grand Rapids. The reconstructed lock at the "side cut" once allowed canal boats to dock at this tastefully restored town of quaint shops and great restaurants. In spring the rapids below Providence Dam are a great attraction, as the swollen river roars downhill to Lake Erie.

The trails along the Maumee were also used by African Americans fleeing to safety under the British flag in Canada. The rapids at Grand Rapids were a favorite place to cross the Maumee. Here conductors of the Underground Railroad had to fend off those who made their living by catching and returning escaped slaves to the South. One documented story tells of an Underground Railroader shooting the horse out from under a slave catcher who was pursuing a group of escaped slaves near the rapids.

The bridge on SR 578 in Grand Rapids crosses the river to U.S. 24—the Anthony Wayne Trail. West of the bridge is the village of Providence, once known as Mount Gilead. That village was wiped out by the cholera epidemic of 1852. The solution to this problem in the Black Swamp was inadvertently found when the swamp was drained. The shallowly dug wells went dry, forcing residents to dig deep wells that provided water not polluted by runoff from barnyards and outhouses.

Our third Featured Hike begins at Providence Metropark (Point 5, fig. 7.3), the southernmost in Toledo's Metropark system, and ends in Waterville at the rock in the river known as Roche de Bout (Point 6). The blue blazes leave the Maumee at Waterville to head east into Wood County, named for Lt. Col. Eleazar Wood, an engineer who built Fort Meigs. Although the fort lies about 6 miles north of the blue blazes, near Perrysburg, a visit is recommended, for it played an important role in the War of 1812. The now reconstructed fort once guarded the head of a series of rapids on the Maumee that ended at Roche de Bout in Farnsworth Metropark (fig. 7.4). The British, with their Indian forces, attacked this key position many times to no avail. Without the fort, Oliver Hazard Perry's celebrated victory on Lake Erie may not have been possible, and Gen. William Henry Harrison probably would not have invaded Canada to end the War of 1812.

The BT leads eastward from Waterville toward Pemberville (Point 7) in the Black Swamp, which is the name of the map for this section of the

Figure 7.3 Providence Metropark (Toledo Metroparks)

Figure 7.4 Farnsworth Metropark (Toledo Metroparks)

Buckeye Trail. Pemberville, like other cities and towns founded in the Black Swamp area, was situated on the banks of a river—in this case, the Portage River. The section map's log recommends Beeker's General Store as "an interesting time capsule." There is also a bike trail to walk in the area where bald eagles often nest.

The blue blazes next cross over U.S. 20 at Woodville (Point 8). U.S. 20 follows the original route taken by the historic Maumee and Western Reserve Turnpike. Impressive milestone markers—carved in 1842 from native limestone—mark the turnpike, one of the first roads through the Black Swamp. Woodville is known as the Lime Center of the World for its immense limestone quarries and associated industries (see appendix 1 for Silurian deposits). At the Woodville Historical Museum, 107 East Main Street, artifacts from Sandusky County's first 150 years include rare-plant fossils found in local quarries.

From Woodville, the Buckeye Trail continues east toward Fremont.

FEATURED HIKE 1
FORT DEFIANCE AND INDEPENDENCE DAM STATE PARK

> **DISTANCE** 1 mile in Defiance, 3 miles at Independence Dam. Both hikes are out and back.

> **TIME** Easily done in half a day, with time for exploring and for contemplation of monuments and plaques.

> **DIFFICULTY** Easy.

FORT DEFIANCE

Begin at Pontiac Park in Defiance (WP 1), at the intersection of North Clinton Street (SR 66) and East River Drive (SR 424). This hike will follow the blue blazes of the Buckeye Trail. The park was named for Ottawa war chief Pontiac, born at the confluence of the Auglaize and Maumee Rivers and famous for leading an American Indian uprising in 1763. Pontiac's Conspiracy was an early rebellion by several tribes against the unfair trade practices of the British invaders.

In the center of the park is a monument showing a cross-section of the trunk of the French Indian Apple Tree (WP 2, fig. 7.5) of record dimensions: 9 feet in diameter, 45 feet high, with a canopy spread of 60 feet. The tree died in 1887, at 217 years of age. In his journal of 1761,

Fort Defiance and Independence Dam State Park

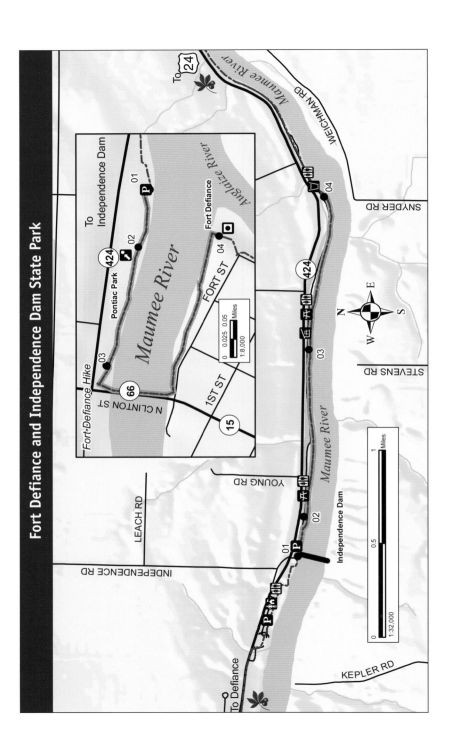

Major Robert Rogers, leader of the famed Rogers' Rangers, recorded: "We found wild apples along the west end of Lake Erie."

Anyone standing under this particular tree in 1794 would have witnessed the construction of Fort Defiance (see fig. 7.1) as a safe haven for forays against the Indians who were in league with the British. Built by the troops of General "Mad" Anthony Wayne to secure northwestern Ohio from the American Indians and their British allies, Fort Defiance probably got its name from the claim of one of Wayne's lieutenants that it could "defy the English, Indians, and all the devils in hell." Soon after the fort was built, Wayne's troops defeated the American Indian tribes aligned with the Western Confederacy—which included the Shawnee, Miami, and Delaware—at the Battle of Fallen Timbers. The result was the Treaty of Greenville, which removed the unwanted American Indians from Ohio lands east of the Cuyahoga River and south of a line stretching from present-day Greenville to Fort Laurens. (In chapter 6 we crossed the Greenville Treaty line in Fort Loramie, and the BT visits Fort Laurens in chapter 11.)

The Buckeye Trail passes a fountain (WP 3) at the west end of the park before reaching the bridge at Clinton Street (SR 66). The trail then crosses the bridge to Fort Street and follows the sidewalk along the Maumee River

Figure 7.5 Apple tree monument, Pontiac Park

to Fort Defiance Park (WP 4). All (U.S.) land north to Canada was sur-
veyed on a baseline running from the fort's flagstaff. The hillock defenses
are all that remain of the fort. If you climb to the center of the fort area,
you will be impressed with how small the fortification was. There are
interpretive signs at the site that present interesting facts.

Beside the fortification is a plaque dedicated to Johnny Logan (born
Spemica Lawba), a Native American from the Shawnee Nation. Johnny
Logan was captured by an American officer, Captain Benjamin Logan,
when he was in his early teens and raised as an Englishman until he was
returned to his native family because of treaty agreements. In 1812 he
joined the American forces against the British. Upon his death that year,
his courage and loyalty earned him full military honors at his burial on
the grounds of Fort Defiance.

After returning to Pontiac Park, walk to the east of the park (away
from the bridge) on River Road (SR 424) to view a monument to John
Chapman—Johnny Appleseed. Chapman (1774–1845) spent his life collecting apple seeds from cider presses and planting them in woodland
nurseries that he cleared and fenced with logs and piles of brush. The
seedlings were then sold to settlers near the nurseries.

This site along the Maumee was one of his nurseries (1811–28), an
area famous for large, fruitful French Indian apple trees planted by French
traders and missionaries. John Chapman had other nursery sites along the
BT, just downriver near Florida, Ohio, and his largest nursery in the area
was a mile west, along the Tiffin River. Apples provided early settlers with
vital nourishment during the winter. They were preserved as applesauce
and apple butter and were used to make cider. Hard cider was a great
"attitude-adjuster" that lifted the spirits of winterbound pioneers. Johnny
Appleseed's early contributions may be why Ohio now ranks 10th in the
U.S. in apple exports.

INDEPENDENCE DAM STATE PARK

The second part of this hike is at Independence Dam State Park. The park
offers access to the canal towpath, unbroken for 7 miles. This hike will go
out and back along the Maumee River.

As you drive into the Independence Dam site from SR 424 and enter
the park, you will cross over the site of Lock 13 of the Miami and Erie
Canal. A visitor can park near the lock and investigate or park at the dam
and walk back.

Park your car at the dam (WP 1), which is a popular fishing spot. The
cement dam was built in 1924 to replace a wooden dam created to make

"still water" for the canal boats. The park was dedicated in 1949 to provide recreational activities around the dam. The hike leaves the dam and goes east along the Maumee River. Shortly, the trail will pass a Civilian Conservation Corps picnic shelter (WP 2) with a large fireplace, built during the Depression (1934). Along the riverbanks the trees are mature sycamore, beech, maple, and black locust. The walk is very shaded and pleasant. In spring and summer, jewelweed, spring beauties, and violets are abundant. The mature trees and easy source of water offer friendly habitat to the Louisiana waterthrush and the yellow-throated warbler.

WP 3, one mile from the dam, is the site of Fort Starvation. Men from Kentucky came north to fight in the Indian Wars. They left Kentucky in summer and ended up on the banks of the Maumee in December. They had only summer clothing and inadequate food. Their shelter was simple huts that they constructed hurriedly at the onset of cold weather. Hundreds of these men died from exposure and starvation and were buried in the area. The plaque at this side commemorates their struggle. Where is the plaque for the native people who were forced from their homes and died of hunger and starvation?

The Indians who were defeated were not savages, as some might believe, but mainly farmers and hunters settled in log cabins similar to those of the European pioneers. Their gardens were said to "afford almost every species . . . of vegetable in the greatest abundance." This doomed confederacy, with sophisticated leadership in 1793, pleaded in vain with American officials to let them remain in peace:

> *Consider Brothers that our only demand is the peaceable possession of a small part of our once great Country. Look back and view the lands from whence we have been driven to this spot, we can retreat no further, because the country behind hardly affords food for its present inhabitants. And we have therefore resolved, to leave our bones in this small space, to which we are now confined.*
>
> —*R. Douglas Hurt,* The Ohio Frontier

At WP 4, 1.75 miles from the dam, the fence across the drive says, Walking only. The area beyond was at one time a campground. From this point you could choose to continue for up to 5 more miles of off-road trail or return to your car. The next mile is paved roadway and after that a footpath, which eventually takes you to the village of Florida. The Maumee River is a favorite eagle nesting site. When there are eagles nesting, parts of the trail may be closed.

FEATURED HIKE 2
OAK OPENINGS METROPARK

DISTANCE 3-mile loop

TIME 2 hours

DIFFICULTY Easy. The relatively flat land and well-maintained trails combine to offer a relaxing walk in the woods.

To drive to Oak Openings Preserve Metropark, take SR 295 north from U.S. 24 northeast of Grand Rapids. Take the first left into the Metropark after passing SR 64. This road, Oak Openings Parkway, will take you past a lodge to a left turn into the parking lot at pristine Mallard Lake (see the map of Featured Hike 2). Obtain a map at the kiosk in front of the Buehner Center. There are restrooms available here. Begin the hike on the west side of the parking lot in front of the Buehner Center. This is the trailhead for numerous trails in the park. This hike begins on the red-blazed Sand Dunes Trail (WP 1).

Almost immediately, there is a divergence of trails. Stay with the red trail going through a quiet evergreen forest. Notice how the trail is sandy. If you have hiked in the state of Florida, this will bring back memories. The soil of Oak Openings Preserve Metropark is largely composed of sand laid down thousands of years ago by ancient lakes that covered the state of Michigan and northern Ohio. The sands of at least 12 ancient lakeshores are found throughout the Black Swamp area, which formed as the glacial ice retreated and before present-day Lake Erie was finally established.

As part of the Great Lakes Ecoregion, which covers portions of eight states and one Canadian province, the ecosystems of Oak Openings vary from prairie openings and sand dunes to thick overhead canopies of the oak savanna. The diverse habitats host such rare species as the brilliant-orange wood lily and the largish lark sparrow. The fox snake and Blanding's turtle, commonly found here, are not found anywhere else in Ohio. The larvae of the frosted elfin and the endangered Karner blue butterflies depend on the wild lupine for their survival. From April through July, this plant has a columnar group of flowers ranging from blue to pink to white. The widely spaced mature oak trees protect the wild lupine as well as an understory of tall prairie grasses. Today's remaining oak savannas are imperiled, and the rare plants and animals that depend on this

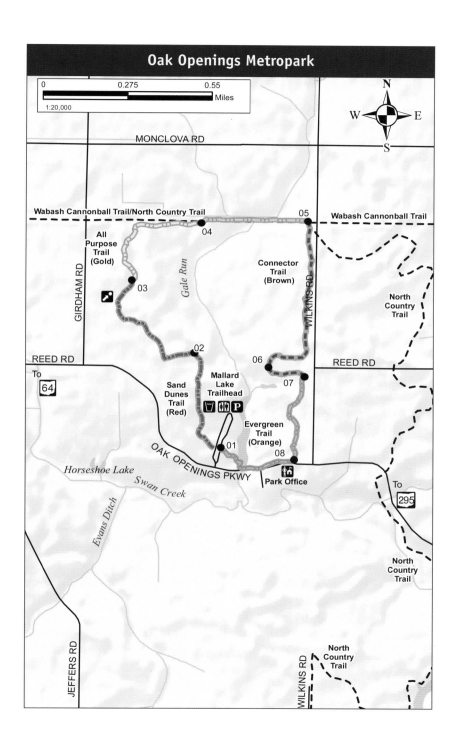

Oak Openings Metropark

0   0.275   0.55
Miles
1:20,000

N
W E
S

MONCLOVA RD

Wabash Cannonball Trail/North Country Trail

Wabash Cannonball Trail

05

04

All
Purpose
Trail
(Gold)

Connector
Trail
(Brown)

03

Gale Run

North
Country
Trail

GIRDHAM RD

WILKINS RD

02

REED RD

06

REED RD

To
64

Sand
Dunes
Trail
(Red)

Mallard
Lake
Trailhead

07

North
Country
Trail

P

Evergreen
Trail
(Orange)

01

08

OAK OPENINGS PKWY

Horseshoe Lake

Park Office

To
295

Swan Creek

Evans Ditch

North
Country
Trail

JEFFERS RD

WILKINS RD

North
Country
Trail

habitat are being lost. This makes Oak Openings one of the most important in the state.

About a quarter mile into the hike, the trail crosses the abandoned portion of Reed Road. Very shortly, at WP 2, the red trail coming from the parking lot meets the Sand Dunes Trail loop. You will want to turn left to visit the dunes. When the red trail intersects the All Purpose Trail (gold), turn right and then immediately go left with the red blazes. Note the ferns growing in the open areas below the canopy of tall, widely spaced oaks. A fern identification book would be useful on this hike. The Metropark staff use controlled burning to maintain the delicate environment. The burns do not harm the oaks but do reinvigorate dormant seeds.

The first sand dunes will soon appear to the left (fig. 7.6). You might wish to leave the trail here to explore the dunes, with their strikingly fine, yellowish sand. According to the park brochure, "the Sand Dunes Trail passes through the largest of the open sand dunes and allows visitors to see how the sand is spilling over to the east and southeast smothering vegetation, thereby proving sand dunes actually move. Some of the park's rarest plant species can be found near the dunes." Return to the red-blazed Sand Dunes Trail and, at WP 3, intersect with the All Purpose Trail. The red trail will cross over the All Purpose Trail and return south to the parking lot.

Figure 7.6 Sand at Oak Openings

Our hike will turn left (northeast) on the all-purpose trail, which goes through a denser wooded area with shrubby undergrowth. At WP 4, our hike turns left on the blue-blazed Fern and Lakes Trail to reach the Wabash Cannonball Trail. The North Country Trail uses this trail on its route from the Maumee to Michigan. The hike goes right (east) on this broad trail that follows the historic Wabash Railroad bed (later, it became the Norfolk and Western Railway). The Wabash Cannonball Trail brochure asks, "Did the famed Wabash Cannonball Engine run on these lines? On a hot shimmery, summer day, look down the trail and listen for the jingle . . ."

Four backpackers could easily walk abreast on this wide trail. A wide range of colorful wildflowers, thistles, sumac, and cattails abounds in the wetland borrow pits on either side of the railroad bed. During the summer, fritillaries swallowtails, and angle wings are profuse (one, the thistle butterfly, or painted lady, is orange on black with white spots).

At WP 5, 1.5 miles into the hike, you leave the WCT on the paved brown connector trail. This trail parallels Wilkins Road and will be passing through woodlands. At WP 6 you cross the remnants of Reed Road and bear left. At WP 7, leave the paved connector trail and go right on the orange Evergreen Trail. The trail goes through a conifer forest with very mature scotch and red pine. The park brochure explains that many of the scotch pines are dying of old age and will not be replaced, as they are not native to the area. The forest floor is covered in pine straw and the downed timbers provide habitat for lichens and mosses. The orange trail will cross a service road.

At WP 8 follow the orange trail back to Mallard Lake. Go over the bridge, following the lake to your right and climb the stairs to the parking area at the Buehner Center.

FEATURED HIKE 3
PROVIDENCE METROPARK TO ROCHE DE BOUT

DISTANCE Almost 10 miles (one way).

TIME At least 4 hours to hike one way. Bicyclists could easily ride the 20-mile out-and-back trip in half a day. Most hikers will require two cars.

DIFFICULTY Easy, along the level crushed stone of the canal towpath.

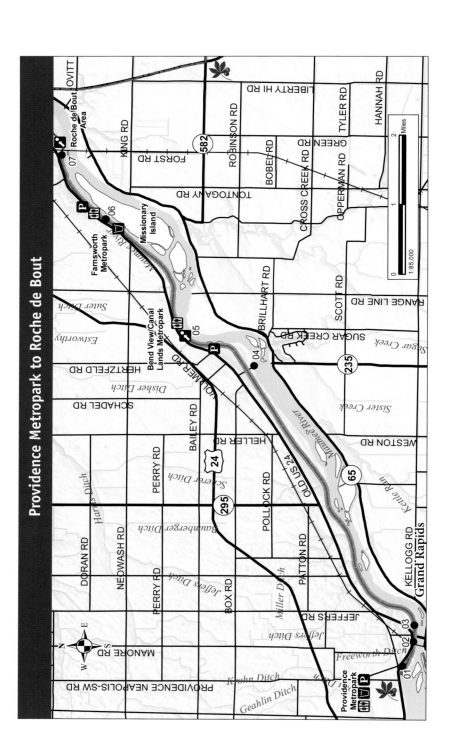

Providence Metropark to Roche de Bout

The hike begins at Providence Metropark parking lot, near Grand Rapids on U.S. 424. If using two cars, park one car there and the second at Farnsworth Metropark in Waterville.

Providence Metropark is the beginning point for our tour along the old twin-canal system. From the parking lot (WP 1), the trail crosses the bridge spanning the canal. Brochures are available at the restrooms located just before the bridge. The centerpiece of this park, Providence Dam, was first built in 1838, rebuilt in 1908, and renovated in 1996. The water below the dam is very shallow and visitors may walk on the rocks, fish, and play in the water. The stone shelter house was built in 1941 by the Works Progress Administration.

Locate the trailhead along the canal and begin to hike east along the towpath (fig. 7.7) between the canal and the river. In less than 5 minutes find the restored water-powered Isaac Ludwig Mill (WP 2), with its geared elevator used to lift cargo from canal boat level to mill level. The mill was constructed in 1847. A tour shows how a water-powered saw works and how grain was once milled. A general store next to the mill offers snacks and interesting gifts and collectables.

Figure 7.7 Canal Towpath

Next along the towpath, at Kimball's Landing (WP 3), a working canal boat drawn by mules offers a 50-minute ride to Ludwig Mill and back. The ride takes you through Lock 44. This is the only lock in Ohio where you can experience a "lock-through," where the water level in the lock will be lowered and raised to match the level of the water in the canal. For this short trip, no stable is needed on the boat for spare mules, but earlier canal passengers were treated to their company for several days. At the mill, there is a sign that displays the mileages to cities to be visited. Cincinnati is shown as 220 miles ahead and St. Marys as 90 miles.

While in this area you might hear a Blackburnian warbler. An interpretive sign at the dock tells of forest loss thousands of miles to the south that affect this species and other neotropical migrants that use the flyway over northwestern Ohio. Many natural areas that are protected along the Maumee offer respite to migrants as they navigate north.

As the trail leaves Providence, it turns from manicured path to footpath that is well maintained by walkers and bikers. The trail is mostly shaded by tall hardwood trees. The closeness of the river offers chances to see waterfowl and the rippling flow of the river accompanies the sound of your boots. In spring be prepared to see and hear the warblers as they fly through. Chickadees, blue jays, and robins are ever present. Flooding of the Maumee replenishes the soils and provides lush habitat for native flowers. The lushness of the areas near the trail supports many kinds of fungi.

After 5 miles, the trail will pass across old Otsego Road (WP 4) leading to the shallow ford that early settlers and Native Americans used to cross the Maumee. The trail then continues on to Bend View, the next Metropark (WP 5). The bend in the river is created by sheer 30-foot bluffs where the towpath and the blue blazes turn more to the northeast. The river overlook here is memorable. There are a number of projects completed by the CCC. The picnic pavilion is most inviting, but carrying a picnic lunch into the area is not. Bend View is 6.5 miles from the Providence trailhead.

In another 2 miles is Farnsworth Metropark (see fig. 7.4), offering a great picnic area, restrooms, and playgrounds. Camp Deposit (WP 6) was built here by General "Mad" Anthony Wayne as a citadel to keep his supply chain intact before the Battle of Fallen Timbers. Several large islands in the river form Missionary Island Wildlife Area, which features prehistoric American Indian sites. The towpath trail ends in Farnsworth Metropark.

At the far north end of Farnsworth Metropark is the Waterville Electric Bridge, built in 1908 for the crossing of the interurban. At that time it was one of the longest reinforced-concrete railroad bridges in the world. It

Figure 7.8 Roche de Bout (Toledo Metroparks)

passes over an island of rock known as Roche de Bout (WP 7, fig. 7.8), once used as an American Indian council site. The rock was reduced by a third when the bridge was built. Roche (pronounced "roash") is French for rock and Bout ("boo") means the end of a passageway or trail (in this case, the end of the rapids that once extended from Fort Meigs to Waterville). The rock is also known as Roche de Boeuf. Since Boeuf (sounds like "book," with an f replacing the k) means beef or ox, to early French explorers the rock must have looked like a bull or buffalo, and Buffalo Rock is another name for it.

A council of war chiefs, including Little Turtle and Blue Jacket, gathered here in the summer of 1794 to plan their strategy against the American forces led by Mad Anthony Wayne. The Native Americans were eventually defeated at the Battle of Fallen Timbers. Two warriors representing opposing sides in this battle would later fight each other in the War of 1812: one was a young lieutenant, William Henry Harrison, the other a young Indian named Tecumseh.

LOCAL CONTACTS

- Independence Dam State Park. http://parks.ohiodnr.gov/independencedam.
- Pontiac Park. www.visitdefianceohio.com.
- Toledo Metroparks (parks in Featured Hikes 2 and 3). www.metroparkstoledo.com.
- Wabash Cannonball Trail. www.wabashcannonballtrail.org.
- Waterville Historical Society. www.waterville.org.

WAYPOINT ID'S

WAYPOINT ID	DESCRIPTION	LATITUDE	LONGITUDE
	FORT DEFIANCE		
1	Pontiac Park parking	41.28917000	−84.35568800
2	Apple Tree	41.28907500	−84.35715500
3	Fountain	41.28963300	−84.36026900
4	Fort Defiance	41.28761800	−84.35687300
	INDEPENDENCE DAM		
1	Independence Dam	41.29279000	−84.28396300
2	Picnic shelter	41.29205600	−84.26247700
3	Site of Fort Starvation	41.29113900	−84.24653400
4	Gate	41.29218000	−84.27979000
	OAK OPENINGS		
1	Parking lot	41.54535300	−83.84513200
2	Left turn to visit dunes	41.54981500	−83.84699800
3	Jct Red and All Purpose	41.55331200	−83.85098800
4	Jct WCB and All Purpose	41.55619900	−83.84671700
5	Jct Brown and WCB	41.55632300	−83.84012800
6	Abandoned Reed Road	41.54918100	−83.84232200
7	Jct Evergreen and Brown	41.54473100	−83.84061200
8	Right turn on Orange Trail	41.54473100	−83.84061200
	PROVIDENCE METROPARK		
1	Providence Metropark	41.41764200	−83.86889800
2	Ludwig Mill	41.41550500	−83.86211900
3	Kimball's Landing	41.41538400	−83.85750600
4	Old Otsego Road	41.44846300	−83.78725000
5	Bend View Metropark	41.463194	−83.778412
6	Farnsworth Metropark	41.47874600	−83.74714400
7	Roche de Bout	41.48778000	−83.72947800

The Watershed Trail

BTA SECTION MAPS Pemberville, Norwalk, Medina.

COUNTIES TRAVERSED Sandusky, Seneca, Huron, Lorain, Medina.

DISTANCE COVERED 116 miles.

OVERVIEW

Fremont (just north of Point 1) was named in honor of John Charles Frémont, noted explorer and U.S. presidential candidate. The city on the Sandusky River was once known as Lower Sandusky. Fremont marks the eastern border of the Great Black Swamp and the beginning of this chapter's Overview.

The Watershed Trail

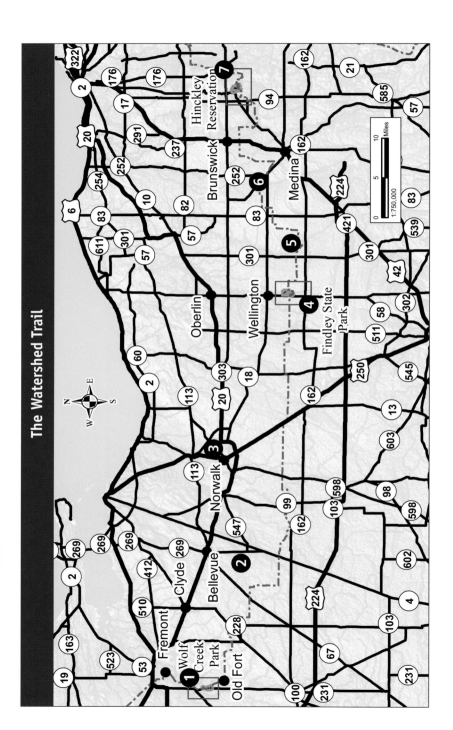

One of the interesting historic sites in Ohio is the Rutherford B. Hayes Presidential Center in Fremont. The impressive Victorian home of our 19th president, with its welcoming veranda, was built in 1916 and sits on 25 wooded acres. The docents here offer superb guided tours, and the nation's first presidential museum and library is also housed here.

Fremont also has Ballville Dam, which creates a reservoir in the Sandusky River. Biologists and archeologists are interested in what fish migrated from Lake Erie into the upper reaches of the Sandusky before the dam was built. From bones in centuries-old Indian refuse pits, or middens, researchers are identifying species no longer living in the Sandusky, including the sturgeon and the eastern longnose sucker. Unlike the Maumee, which offers 9 river miles for spawning walleye, the Sandusky River offers only 2 miles. If Fremont builds an underground reservoir, the dam might be eliminated, and some of the fish formerly found in the beautiful Sandusky might just make a comeback.

Ohio's major watersheds are the Lake Erie basin and the Ohio River basin (fig. 8.1). Water that falls on the side of the Lake Erie basin will end up in the Atlantic Ocean, water on the Ohio River basin side will flow to the Gulf of Mexico. This watershed divide roughly separates the state into thirds from north to south, the northern part being the Lake Erie basin. The principal rivers the BT crosses in this northern watershed are the

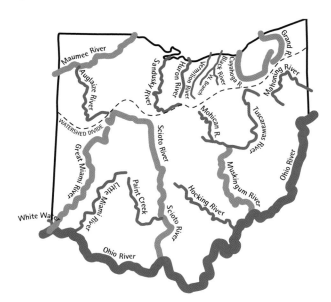

Figure 8.1 Watershed Trail

Maumee (chap. 7), the Sandusky (where this chapter begins), the Vermilion, and the two branches of the Black. The Cuyahoga and Grand Rivers are encountered in later chapters.

The Watershed Trail, a trail used by American Indians, paralleled this major Ohio watershed eastward from the Norwalk area, where it joined the Mahoning Trail in the Cleveland area. Early British and American soldiers and explorers, such as Maj. Robert Rogers of the famed Rogers' Rangers (circa 1760), also used the Watershed Trail, for it—along with the Great Trail—offered the only link from Fort Pitt to Detroit. State Routes 162 and 18 were built on this early trail. The blue blazes closely follow, or at least parallel, these roads and the ancient trail as they lead eastward to the Cuyahoga Valley to connect with the blue blazes that form the big loop around the state at Brecksville Reservation.

Mull Covered Bridge, built in 1851, is found just west of Wolf Creek Park (first Featured Hike) (Point 1) on Gilmore Road (T-9). The Buckeye Trail leaves Wolf Creek Park through a cemetery that holds the remains of veterans of the War of 1812 (fig. 8.2). Soon after leaving Gilmore Road,

Figure 8.2 Hill Cemetery

the blue blazes enter Seneca County as they pass through the village of Old Fort, just east of SR 53. Old Fort was the site of Fort Seneca, where General Harrison first heard of Perry's victory over the British in the battle for Lake Erie.

Seneca Caverns (Point 2), an Ohio Natural Landmark, is 5 miles north of the BT just after it crosses SR 18 in Seneca County. In this rare form of cavern known as a fracture cavern, you can observe jigsaw fits between limestone pieces on the roof and on the floor. A fee is charged for the 1-hour tour. You will need to bend and stretch a great deal in order to traverse the numerous carved-out and often slippery steps and perhaps even crawl to pass through narrow limestone passageways.

Preserved close to its natural state, the caverns' limestone holds fossil evidence including brachiopods, abundant elsewhere in Ohio, and some rarer sightings, such as horn corals and the head of an armored fish that may have been 12 feet long. Bring your own flashlight, for a flashlight-wielding tourist discovered this last fossil in 1991, and future findings are probable. The northern long-eared bat is one species inhabiting the caverns. This bat is currently under consideration for listing as an endangered species.

The land surrounding the caverns is karst terrain (see chaps. 3 and 4). This area, the Bellevue-Castalia area, is believed to contain the most sinkholes in Ohio. There are also mysterious streams disappearing underground, only to reappear miles away. Seneca Caverns is in a recharge area, where water goes underground. You will see the Old Mist'ry River, over 100 feet underground. Divers have failed to find its bottom, even after diving 100 feet deeper. This same water has been traced to the Blue Hole, now privately owned, as well as to several other springs in an area 14 miles to the north. Known as discharge areas, these springs are fed from the same aquifer found in the bottom of the caverns. The volume of water flowing from the Blue Hole must have been a source of amazement to early Native Americans. Seven million gallons flow from the earth daily, enough water to supply a city of 75,000 people. The water level in the cave fluctuates from drought years like 1973, when the river was down to the 13th level, to flood years like 1969, when the water was up to the first level.

The recharge areas around the Blue Hole are extensive in this area's karst formations. For example, Green Springs, 2 miles north of the BT and 8 miles west of Seneca Caverns on SR 19, claims to have one of the largest white-sulfur springs in the world. The water from these notable springs has also been traced to the Blue Hole. East of Green Springs, along Old Military Road (T-195), the blue blazes pass a monument to veterans of the War of 1812. This monument is a fitting tribute, for if they had not fought and died for us we might yet be subservient to a European power.

The BT in this chapter now crosses from the older Silurian, karst-forming bedrock to the younger bedrock of the Devonian and Mississippian geologic systems (see appendix 1). This means that the sweet limestone soils of western Ohio give way to more acidic sandstone soils. In terms of trees, the hiker might see more oaks at first but later will move into the original beech-maple forest to the east. There are many exceptions to this generalization. Oak and hickory will always dominate the drier parts of the beech-maple forest and beech will be found in the moist but well-drained soils to the west.

North of the blue blazes in Huron County is the city of Norwalk, with its Firelands Museum (Point 3). The Firelands area, approximately defined by Huron and Erie Counties, were lands reserved in 1792 to compensate American patriots whose homes were burned by the British during the Revolutionary War. The Firelands are the westernmost lands of the Connecticut Western Reserve's 3.2 million acres in northern Ohio (see chap. 9). Due to the wildness of the area and the danger of Indian attacks, settlement was almost nonexistent in the Firelands before the War of 1812 and quite slow until after 1825. Considering that the patriots of 1792 were compensated with these lands, most of those compensated were at least 33 years older by the time they actually acquired the land.

The house containing the Firelands Museum was built soon after settlement began (1836) and was later moved to its present location. The house contains three floors and 10,000 exhibits, including a period dining room with antique china. A gun room holds one of the largest collections in the country, with hundreds of guns—including five- and eight-barrel derringers and even a cannon—dating back to the 1600s. The huge Indian artifact collection contains stone implements used for killing and skinning such large extinct animals as mastodon, mammoth, and bison. There is also a walking tour guide to the West Main Street Historic District, described in the 1967 Ohio Historic Survey as "the best individual street of homes (in terms of variety of architecture) in Ohio."

Our second Featured Hike is in Findley State Park (Point 4), 2 miles south of Wellington, with 10 miles of hiking trails and at least 1 mile of mountain bike trail. The BT utilizes 2 miles of trail as it crosses the park from SR 58 on the western side to Hawley Road on the east. Findley Lake was formed in 1956 when Wellington Creek, a tributary of the Black River, was dammed. The entire family will enjoy the campground, naturalist programs, and swimming and canoeing.

Nearby Wellington was once second in the nation in the production of cheese. The town hall, built in 1885, is said to be in the Romanesque style, but its onion-topped clock tower and Moorish dormers make it look like something from Turkey. Wellington is also the home of Archibald Willard (built in 1855), whose painting "The Spirit of '76," with its familiar trio of fife and drum players, celebrates the signing of the Declaration of Independence. The Spirit of '76 Museum here honors Willard's memory.

Twelve miles north of Findley State Park is Oberlin, in Lorain County. The Allen Memorial Art Museum (admission free) on SR 58 offers tours of a house designed by Frank Lloyd Wright—one of his Usonian homes, intended for moderately priced living. For a self-guided walking tour of this intriguing community visit the Chamber of Commerce at 20 E. College Street (east of SR 58).

Oberlin College, founded in 1833, continues to be an important innovator. Oberlin shocked society by being the first coeducational college in the United States. It was also the first college to refuse to discriminate against African Americans. The influence of the college firmly committed the Oberlin area to the antislavery movement in the early 1800s, and the city was openly, not secretly, an important part of the Underground Railroad. The college's Conservatory of Music, founded in 1865, is the nation's oldest continuously operating conservatory.

The excellent docents at the Oberlin Heritage Center give a deeper understanding of the values of the citizens of Oberlin from 1833 to the 1930s (see Local Contacts). Tours begin at the Monroe House, home of James Monroe, the famous abolitionist. The home was first occupied by Gen. Giles W. Shurtleff, leader of Ohio's first African American regiment in the Civil War. The one-room Little Red Schoolhouse next door, built in the pioneer era (1836), is the oldest building in Oberlin. Local primary students still attend school here in May to learn more of their heritage. The third house on the tour was the home of chemistry professor Frank Jewett. The attached woodshed houses equipment like that used by one of his students, Charles Martin Hall, to develop the process for commercially manufacturing aluminum.

During the tour at the Monroe House you will also hear the story of John Price, a runaway slave who lived in Oberlin. Trapped by two slave hunters in 1858, he was spirited off to a hotel in Wellington. Some residents returning to Oberlin along the road to Wellington (now SR 58) saw Price and his captors. Hundreds of angry armed citizens took every conveyance and even walked to Wellington to rescue him. To their credit, no one was injured, and John Price returned to safety in Oberlin. Under the

Fugitive Slave Law, originally passed in 1793 and revived in the Compromise of 1850, several leading citizens of Oberlin were put on trial for interfering with the recovery of a slave but were exonerated. A photo seen during the tour shows the Oberlin-Wellington rescuers with the sheriff outside the Cuyahoga County Jail in 1859.

Returning to the blue blazes, as the BT leads east from Findley State Park it crosses the east branch of the Black River near the Spencer Lake Wildlife Area (Point 5), where it crosses a quarter-mile causeway. From Spencer Lake the blue blazes pass the entrance to Letha House Park, a Medina Metropark, just north of Spencer Lake Road (C-45). The half-mile trail there reveals the beauty of the Black River floodplain, with its prominent rock outcroppings.

From here the BT leads north to pass several farm businesses offering tours, including several alpaca farms and Greenfield Gardens. The BT next arrives at the trailhead for the Lester Rail Trail (Point 6, fig. 8.3), dedicated in 1997. This 3.25-mile crushed-limestone trail passes through woods and fields typical of the area. Horses are not allowed but bicycles are welcome. The BT utilizes 2.9 miles of the rail trail to Abbeyville Road, where it turns north. There are parking and facilities at the Lester Road end.

The blue blazes now approach the Allegheny Escarpment near Brunswick, in Medina County, and enter the Allegheny Plateau (see appendix 2).

Figure 8.3 Lester Rail Trail (Andy "Captain Blue" Niekamp)

This portion of the plateau in Ohio that is glaciated is best described as a land of rounded hills and broad valleys containing numerous wetlands, such as glacial lakes, bogs, and fens. In chapters 3 and 4, the blazes traversed this same plateau, but because it is unglaciated, the terrain is rugged with steep hills and deep valleys.

This entire countryside was once covered by a huge forest with trees so large there was little or no underbrush and settlers could drive wagons and sleds through the woods. To clear the land for crops, the trees in a large area were cut halfway through. Later, when there was a suitable wind, trees to windward were felled. These trees crashed into the partially severed trees downwind, which then fell like dominoes. Huge hunts for "dangerous predators" were organized, and one at Hinckley was well documented. The game was driven to a central point and slaughtered. Included in the dead were 17 wolves, 21 bears, 300 deer, and uncounted smaller animals.

Just south of the blue blazes, modern Medina (once known as Mecca), still retains its New England town square, so typical of the communities in the Western Reserve. The A. I. Root Company, founded in 1869 to build beehives, is still in business. Great-grandson John Root carries on the business—now making candles.

As they approach Hinckley Reservation, the blue blazes next visit the Cleveland Hiking Club's Camp Onwego, on Kellogg Road (T-80). The CHC, founded in 1919, bought the property adjacent to the reservation in the 1930s. An interurban was used to get to the park and Camp Onwego in the early years. The CHC has been of enormous importance to the Buckeye Trail (see chap. 13).

The third Featured Hike takes place at Hinckley Reservation (Point 7), our next stop on the BT. This is the southernmost of Cleveland's Metroparks and is famous for the annual return of the buzzards (actually turkey vultures) on March 15. The high rocky areas in the Hinckley area offer natural nesting spots for these carrion eaters (fig. 8.4). Hinckley Reservation also has a 90-acre lake surrounded by picnic areas and many long trails, including the BT. Rock climbing is a popular sport on Whipp's Ledges, 350 feet above Hinckley Lake (see fig. 8.10). The vultures sail over these exposed rocks, which are typical of the Allegheny Plateau.

Hinckley Reservation is one of 14 reservations created by Cleveland Metroparks. Known as Cleveland's Emerald Necklace, the reservations encircle this large population center. It is difficult to believe that within minutes of the city's busy streets exist 19,000 acres of the natural world, with connecting parkways, that make you feel as if you have stepped back into another era. There are waterfalls, pristine gorges, and scenic vistas.

Figure 8.4 Turkey vulture
(Cleveland Metroparks)

Follow the blue blazes east from Hinckley Reservation to find a humorous bull-warning sign (fig. 8.5), as you travel on to Brecksville Reservation.

The BT at Brecksville Reservation is where the big loop—explored since the beginning of *Follow the Blue Blazes*—meets the northeastern Little Loop (see map of the BT, fig. 1.1). We will continue our explorations in the next chapter, "Connecticut's Western Reserve: Big Loop to Little Loop."

Figure 8.5 Bull warning sign (Andy "Captain Blue" Niekamp)

FEATURED HIKE 1
WOLF CREEK PARK

DISTANCE About 1.5 miles.

TIME 1 hour.

DIFFICULTY Easy. Wide trails follow the flat to gently rolling floodplain of the Sandusky River.

Wolf Creek Park is 9 miles south of Fremont on SR 53. There are two entrances off the east side of SR 53: the northern entrance has the picnic area, restrooms, and canoe access. If you visit the north entrance, note the large glacial erratics along the park road. The southern entrance takes you to the campground. To start the hike, enter the park at the southern entrance and park at the first parking lot (WP 1). You will be walking the Nature Trail and the Buckeye Trail on this hike. Walk the entrance road toward the highway and turn left on a mowed meadow trail. You will see blue blazes for the Buckeye Trail on the post supporting a interpretive sign about the meadow. The nature trail has interpretive signs about every 50 feet. You will see that the blue blazes immediately go off to the right to visit Hill cemetery. The cemetery (see fig. 8.2) is worth a visit. It has many old stones and some for veterans of the War of 1812, a war fought and won largely in this area and on nearby Lake Erie. Especially sad is the number of children and young people remembered here.

For this hike, continue on the Nature Trail through the meadow and enter a copse of roughleaf dogwood and sumac. The roughleaf dogwood has clusters of small white flowers in the spring and the fruit in the fall is white berries. Look for the interpretive sign explaining the sumac and other native shrubs.

After a short walk in the woods and crossing a bridge, the trail will come to a bench with a good view of the Sandusky River, a State Scenic River (WP 2). The rapids during low water reveal exposed limestone and dolomite deposits. The cities built along the two major rapids on this river were identified as Upper Sandusky and Lower Sandusky (now Fremont). Of course, the 80-mile river was a major thoroughfare for the Wyandot, Seneca, and Delaware (Leni-Lenape), who lived along its banks. An interpretive sign at this site provides history of the river.

After leaving the river, the trail will descend to a creek and bridge before exiting the woods at the campground access road. Around the

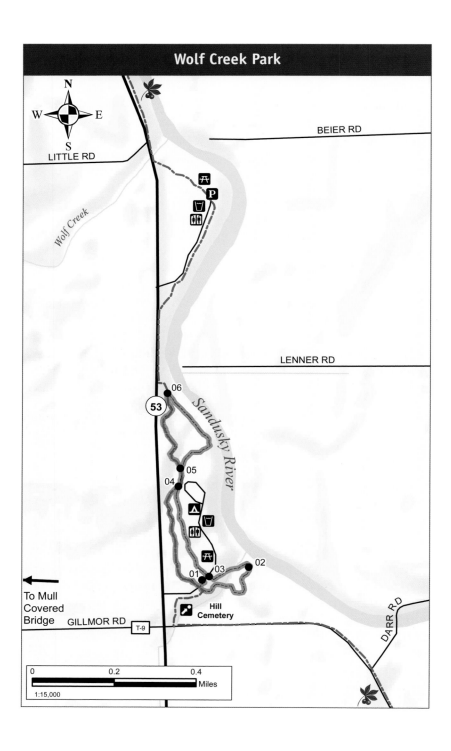

Wolf Creek Park

creekbeds, in the spring, you can expect to see pink spring beauties, yellow trout lilies, Dutchman's breeches, and bloodroot. Another sign tells of bald eagles along the river.

At the campground access road (WP 3, fig. 8.6), continue straight ahead. The trail rambles through woods and then a meadow. The meadows are brilliant in the fall with the yellow and purple asters. In the summer, listen for the field sparrows' descending trills and raucous blue jays. The warm sunshine is welcome on a cool spring day. After the meadow, the trail passes quite close to the campground and intersects the Buckeye Trail (WP 4). Continue straight ahead for a short distance and then leave the BT and go to the right (WP 5).

This part of the trail is in the floodplain for the Sandusky River. Hikers will be walking quite close to the river and can enjoy the sight and the sounds of the moving water. They may get to hear and see a kingfisher hunting just above the waters.

At WP 6, the Nature Trail intersects with the BT, which comes down from the park's northern entrance. This hike turns left and goes south with the blue blazes to head back toward the campground parking lot. A hiker could follow the BT north and walk to the northern part of the park. This would include a quarter-mile walk along busy SR 53. The red-white-and-blue markers you will see are for a liquefied petroleum gas (LPG)

Figure 8.6 Wolf Creek campground road (Jeanne Dieterich)

pipeline. Over 3,350 miles of LPG pipeline, as well as over 57,000 miles of natural-gas pipeline, crisscross Ohio. Pipelines reduce the need for truck transport, but they can also rupture, causing great environmental damage. In 1993 a pipeline burst in Indiana, spilling 30,000 gallons of diesel fuel into the Fish Creek watershed, a tributary of the St. Joseph River in northeastern Ohio's Williams County. Fish Creek is the last known stream with the endangered white cat's paw pearly mussel. The Wolf Creek pipeline runs northwest to Toledo. To the east it goes to the Cuyahoga River in Cleveland. On the walk north, the trail is marked with the blue blazes.

Upon returning from the optional northern adventure, at WP 6, the trail continues following the blue blazes south. The blue blazes are painted on the posts for the interpretive signs for the Nature Trail. The hardest part of walking the Nature Trail is stumbling on the walnuts. A sign on this section of the trail provides information on this prolific tree. Another tree that is highlighted is the tulip tree, a species used by Native Americans for dugout canoes. More signs describe other trees: honey locust, with its characteristic large thorns and big bean pods; sugar maple, whose winged seeds were called squawkers because children used them as whistles; and white ash, used for baseball bats. The park is an information treasure hunt for all ages.

When the trail reaches WP 4, at the edge of the campground, bear to the right and stay with the blue blazes. Shortly, the trail reaches the campground access road and the parking lot.

FEATURED HIKE 2
FINDLEY STATE PARK

DISTANCE 3 miles.

TIME 2 hours to leisurely visit the sites.

DIFFICULTY Easy. Flat except for a few ups and downs into and out of wetland areas.

There is a Hiker on the Go map for this section of the Buckeye Trail.

Findley State Park is just south of Wellington on SR 58. You can get to SR 58 from SR 2 in Lorain or from I-71 in Medina to SR 18, which leads west to Wellington. Find the main park entrance 2 miles south of Wellington.

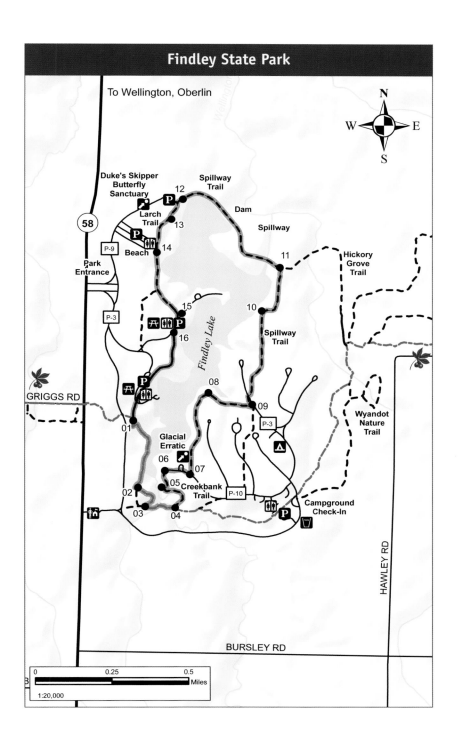

At the entrance, bear right on the entrance road to follow Park Road 3 south to the access road for the Park Office, or you can enter at the park service road from SR 58. Obtain information and literature for the park at the Park Office. Return to Park Road 3 and drive north to the parking lot for Disc Golf. Restrooms are available just north of the area, through the woods at a major parking lot. The BT enters the park from Griggs Road (C-43) and the Wellington Wildlife Area, to the west. It crosses Park Road 3 at the Disc Golf area and follows the Hickory Grove Trail to exit the park on the east at Hawley Road (T-44). This hike begins at the southeastern edge of the parking lot (WP 1, fig. 8.7). The blue blazes mark the entrance to the trail and a sign announces the Buckeye Trail.

This park was abandoned farmland as recently as 1956, and most of the trees are small. They include white and red oak, shagbark hickory (for which the trail may have been named), black cherry, eastern hophornbeam (or ironwood), and American beech. The leaves of the northern red oak turn a brilliant red in the fall. A few larger trees, especially the large

Figure 8.7 Trail in Findley

beeches, were not cut when the area was farmed. The spring trilliums are abundant.

The lake is on the left as the trail meanders through a young pine forest. There are blue blazes on the trees. The trail is clear from many footsteps, but the adjacent forest floor is covered in pine straw. There is much poison ivy, whose three leaves in the fall are brilliant yellow. Because of the foot traffic, the poison ivy does not impinge upon the trail.

At WP 2 the Buckeye Trail goes off to the left, but the All Purpose Trail continues straight ahead. After leaving the All Purpose Trail, you will encounter numerous twists and turns. Be sure to keep the blue blazes in sight. At WP 3 the BT will encounter a trail coming in from the Park Office. Stay to the left and follow the blue blazes crossing a small bridge and going up a slight rise to a stand of hemlock.

Soon the trail crosses Wellington Creek, the source of water for the lake (WP 4). This stream beckons you to stop and reflect for a while. At the end of this large bridge with handrails, the trail makes an immediate left and follows the Creekbank Trail. Leave the blue blazes, which lead straight ahead.

The Creekbank Trail is very narrow and prone to overgrowth. It follows the creek closely to end up in a campground area. To the left of the trail, closer to the water, there are sycamores and a grove of pawpaw. Early settlers used sycamore bark to treat measles, coughs, and colds, and the fruit of the pawpaw was used for jellies. WP 5 is an intersection with a trail heading toward the water. You want to make a right and shortly come to a parking area (WP 6) for a canoe ramp.

Follow the road (Park Road 10) to the right. The trail will pass a glacial erratic, a large stone scored by a long trip south with the glacier 10,000 years ago. This stone—formed from igneous (nonsedimentary) material, found far to the north—is evidence that glaciers moved down from Canada to cover this land. Just past this point, take the Lake Trail (WP 7) to the left. The Lake Trail is at least three persons wide and easy to walk. It will be meandering behind the campgrounds, and portable toilets are occasionally available. When it comes upon an intersection with another trail (WP 8), this hike makes a right and goes away from the water. At the back end of the camping area, it goes to the left and proceeds on a very wide trail. Shortly it will go down a steep slope and then come back up to Park Road 3. This is the end of the Lake Trail (WP 9).

To the left and across the road is the Spillway Trail. The Spillway Trail leads through deciduous woodland, with very few pine trees. At WP 10 there is a scenic overlook with a bench. After leaving the woods (WP 11), come upon the spillway floodplain and an intersection of three trails, the Hickory Grove, Spillway, and Thorn Mountain Bike Trails. Make a sharp left and follow the footpath through the meadow across the spillway. The spillway acts like a relief valve for the lake during times of flooding. There are bluebird boxes in the open area here. The park is actually quite close to the active Norfolk and Western Railroad, to the north, and trains might be heard.

Cross the mowed meadow and go up a rise into the woods. Follow a path that leads a short distance through a wooded area with tulip trees to the earthen dam forming the lake. The dam backs up the waters of Wellington Creek, which flows north from the dam to the west branch of the Black River and eventually to Lake Erie. This point should be 2 miles and about 1 hour into the hike. Metal boxes for wood duck stand along the lakeshore here. The concrete floodgate out in the lake is used to periodically drain some of the lake water to remove silt and perform necessary maintenance to the beach and other shore areas.

After crossing the grassy embankment, see the Thorn Mountain Bike Trail intersection (WP 12). Go straight ahead and shortly, follow the footpath to the left on the Larch Trail. The Larch Trail edges the Dukes' Skipper Butterfly Sanctuary. Skippers are small and noted for their erratic flight. Your chances of spotting this butterfly are small; it is a rare species and the adult feeds at night. Scientists are interested in the Dukes' Skipper for they can track its migration pattern from the Gulf Coast region since the end of the Ice Age. This knowledge may someday show how other species populated Ohio since the retreat of the glaciers, which left little vegetation on Ohio's landscape. The Dukes' Skipper is protected and should not be collected, but there are many other butterflies in the area to fulfill the desires of most lepidopterists.

At WP 13 there will be a split in the trail. Either trail can be taken, as both will end up at the beach area. WP 14 includes both the concession area and restroom facilities during the season. Follow the paved roadway in front of the concession stand and just past the playground find the Larch Tail going into a wooded area. The tamarack, or eastern larch, is deciduous; it sheds its needles in winter. The blue-green needles grow in brushlike clusters, the egg-shaped cone is one-half to three-quarters inches long, and the bark is reddish-brown and rough. This is the southernmost range for these huge trees; most are found in Canada.

Upon reaching the parking lot for Picnic Point (WP 15, fig. 8.8), wander out to the point and enjoy this tranquil lake, which allows only electric motors. The restrooms here are clean and spacious and open most of the year. This area is popular with families who come to picnic and throw a line in the water. Fishermen have been asked to return all grass carp (white amur) to the lake unharmed. The lake was stocked with this fish in order to control aquatic vegetation, thereby improving the fishing for varieties that can be taken home

To continue south on the Larch Trail, walk to the far end, or road entrance, of the parking lot and turn left (WP 16). Very shortly, the trail will enter the large disc golf area—with picnic tables, much parking, and restroom facilities—you may have visited before beginning the hike. Walk the length of the parking area and cross the access road that leads to the boat ramp. At this end of the parking area, there is a bridge that will lead to the other picnic area for disc golf and to your car.

Figure 8.8 Findley Lake

FEATURED HIKE 3
HINCKLEY RESERVATION

DISTANCE About 3.5 miles.

TIME At least 3 hours for time to enjoy the park, and refreshments and shopping at the Hinckley Lake Boathouse and Store.

DIFFICULTY Moderately easy. The trails around the lake are undulating.

Hinckley Reservation is just east of Medina. From State Road (C-44) enter the park on West Drive. Ample parking will be found at Johnson's Picnic Area on West Drive. The BT comes into the park from the southwest on the All Purpose Trail at the parking lot.

Hinckley Reservation is famous for the annual spring migration of large carrion-eating birds that are probably attracted to the ledges in the area. Mistakenly called buzzards, the birds are actually turkey vultures (see fig. 8.4). The similar black vulture, usually found further south in Ohio, is slightly smaller than the turkey vulture and when soaring is distinguished by its white wing tips and short, broad tail. The turkey vulture has a more slender tail and the adult has a red head.

After parking (WP 1), follow the blue blazes north toward the marina (fig. 8.9) on the All Purpose Trail (purple jogger). Just before the shelter in the picnic area, the Buckeye Trail (WP 2) leaves the All Purpose Trail and goes to the right around the south end of the lake. This hike will follow the All Purpose Trail north, around the west shore of the lake. This is a loop hike and will return to the parking lot by way of the Buckeye Trail.

The All Purpose Trail will pass the Hinckley Lake Boathouse and Store. Here you may rent paddleboats, canoes, and rowboats in season. Only electric and muscle-powered boats are allowed, making the lake a tranquil place to walk beside. After visiting the store, continue north along the Blue Heron Trail, just behind the store. A blue-heron blaze marks the trailhead (WP 3). The trail is graveled and arm's width wide to make walking easy. The trail is blazed in light blue, just like the BT.

The lakeside trail is undulating and wooded. During summer heat, this is a shaded respite. There are a number of benches along the lakeside—a place for quiet reflection. At WP 4, follow the trail to the right and stay close to the lake.

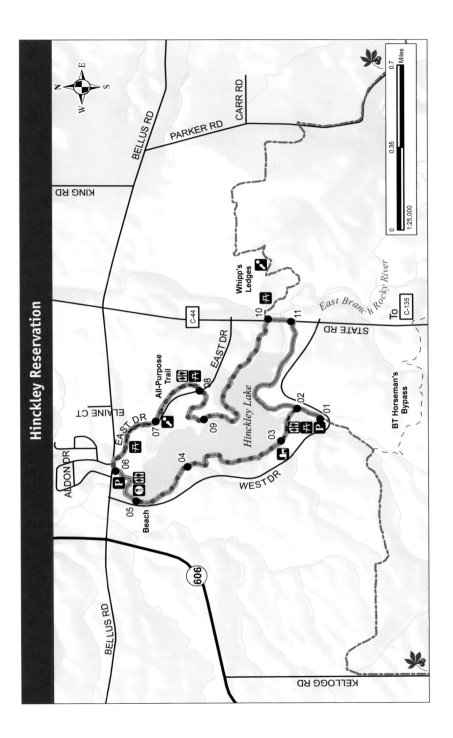

Figure 8.9 Hinckley Lake Marina

It will take about half an hour to reach the dam. Take the steps down (WP 5) to the beach area, unless you have a dog with you. If you have a dog, you will have to skirt around the beach. The falls over the dam drop into a pool that forms a swimming area with a sandy beach. After crossing the spillway, hikers can visit the restroom facilities up the steps or proceed directly to the parking lot. Look for the All Purpose Trail (paved trail with green stripes) at the northwest corner of the lot.

WP 6 is the intersection of the All Purpose Trail from the parking lot and the trail as it comes from the west along Bellus Road.

Follow the All Purpose Trail to the east (right) and walk toward East Drive. After you cross East Drive, go to the right and walk up a grade to the East Drive Overlook (WP 7). This has a bird's-eye view of the lake to your right.

Next, the All Purpose Trail will pass a ball field and cross over a bow bridge leading to a second ball field and restrooms. Cross East Drive at the ball field entrance (WP 8) and walk into the parking area for Indian Point Picnic Area. Walk to the back of the picnic area and at the restrooms find the signs for the Heron Trail. Descend on the trail to the lakeside and make a left.

This portion of the Heron Trail (WP 9) is less traveled than the western portion. There are interpretive signs along the trail that identify and describe various species of trees. There will be great opportunities to find wildflowers in the spring and their fruits in the fall. The lake is shallow, and herons and egrets are spotted as they stand guard over their territory. Of course, many varieties of wildfowl call Hinckley Lake home.

WP 10 is the intersection of the Heron Trail, the Buckeye Trail, and the All Purpose Trail. Across the road, see the entrance to Whipp's Ledges. Take time for a visit now or later. From the Heron Trail, go right on the All Purpose Trail and the BT's blue blazes. Just after crossing the bridge, follow the BT's blue blazes off to the right on a wide footpath (WP 11). In about a quarter mile, the hike will again intersect the All Purpose Trail in Johnson's picnic area. Take a left and find your car.

If you did not visit Whipp's Ledges (fig. 8.10) during your hike, drive to its entrance off State Road. Note the picnic shelter built by the WPA in

Figure 8.10 Whipp's Ledges
(Cleveland Metroparks)

1938 of sandstone that was probably quarried nearby. Take the wooden steps from the picnic shelter up to two diverging trails at the top. The trails form a loop through the ledge area. These ledges, formed of Sharon conglomerate some 350 million years ago, rise 350 feet above the lake. The quartz stones imbedded in the sandstone are known as lucky stones, or pudding stones. Note that these white stones are formed into strata, the levels of which represent the passing of thousands, if not tens of thousands, of years. The 1880s graffiti marks the passage of more recent time. At least some of the dates are authentic, and residents of the Cleveland area have told me that a few of Cleveland's roads carry the same names as those recorded here.

Weekend visitors will almost surely see action at this popular rappelling and climbing area. To take part in this strenuous sport you need a permit from the Cleveland Metroparks (see Local Contacts). The blue blazes found in the ledges area lead over the top of the ledges and then east to Summit County.

Next, visit the Worden Heritage Homestead and Worden's Ledges, found on Ledge Road, just west of the intersection of Ledge Road and State Road (south of Whipp's Ledges). After parking, find the graveled horse trail (H-12) to the west of the homestead's outbuildings. Take the horse trail to the right (north), which takes you downhill to sandstone ledges. Soon you will see the Raccoon Trail slanting off to the right. Along this trail is a series of folk art carvings made in the 1940s by Noble Stuart, including a sphinx 8 feet long.

In chapter 9 we will explore more of the wild areas of the Emerald Necklace around the port city of Cleveland. Perhaps you will learn to appreciate the efforts of those early planners who unselfishly provided for the conservation of our natural resources.

LOCAL CONTACTS

- Hinckley Reservation. www.clevelandmetroparks.com.
- Findley State Park. http://parks.ohiodnr.gov/findley.
- Firelands Museum. www.firelandsmuseum.org.
- Hiker on the Go map for Findley State Park. www.buckeyetrail.org.
- Medina County Convention and Visitors Bureau. www.visitmedinacounty.com.
- Medina County Park District. www.medinacountyparks.com.

• Oberlin Heritage Center. www.oberlinheritagecenter.org.
• Seneca Caverns. www.senecacavernsohio.com.
• Wolf Creek Park. www.lovemyparks.com.

WAYPOINT ID'S

WAYPOINT ID	DESCRIPTION	LATITUDE	LONGITUDE
	WOLF CREEK		
1	Campground parking area	41.26449300	−83.16619300
2	River overlook	41.26497000	−83.16400600
3	Campground access road	41.26462100	−83.16586500
4	Jct Nature and BT Trails	41.26789400	−83.16735100
5	Right turn from BT	41.26855100	−83.16727500
6	North on BT	41.27128400	−83.16790900
	FINDLEY		
1	Disc parking area	41.12758000	−82.21624400
2	BT leaves All Purpose Trail	41.12427300	−82.21602600
3	Left turn	41.12335100	−82.21558600
4	Creek Bank Trail	41.12328200	−82.21371100
5	Right turn	41.12428600	−82.21455400
6	Parking for canoe ramp	41.12508400	−82.21434800
7	Lake Trail	41.12489900	−82.21278500
8	Right turn away from lake	41.12884100	−82.21161000
9	End of Lake Trail	41.12826900	−82.20887500
10	Scenic overlook with bench	41.13283700	−82.20826500
11	Spillway flood plain	41.13497600	−82.20712100
12	Jct Spillway and Mt Bike	41.13835300	−82.21315900
13	Two-way split in trail	41.13736800	−82.21388700
14	Concession stand	41.13572600	−82.21480600
15	Picnic Point parking	41.13272700	−82.21324300
16	Larch Trail at Picnic Point	41.13176400	−82.21375500
	HINCKLEY		
1	Parking lot	41.21552500	−81.71463000
2	Jct All Purpose and BT	41.21687900	−81.71376800
3	Lake Store	41.21785100	−81.71634000
4	Split in trail	41.22338400	−81.71833000
5	Steps to beach	41.22644100	−81.72103800
6	Parking lot	41.22763000	−81.71859400

WAYPOINT ID	DESCRIPTION	LATITUDE	LONGITUDE
7	East Dr Scenic Overlook	41.22523100	−81.71466000
8	Indian Point Picnic Area	41.22262200	−81.71226300
9	Heron Trail	41.22238800	−81.71456400
10	Jct BT and Heron	41.21852000	−81.70655200
11	Jct BT and All Purpose	41.21717700	−81.70677500

Connecticut's Western Reserve: Big Loop to Little Loop

BTA SECTION MAPS Akron, Bedford.

COUNTIES TRAVERSED Lake, Geauga, Cuyahoga, Summit, Stark.

DISTANCE COVERED 123 miles.

OVERVIEW

This chapter begins at Brecksville Reservation (Point 1 in the Overview Map, fig. 9.1), where the 1,000-mile Big Loop from the west meets the 200-mile Little Loop in northeastern Ohio. The reservation is part of Cleveland's Emerald Necklace, described in chapter 8. In this chapter we will visit other reservations in the necklace as we follow the BT north toward Lake Erie. But first, the blue blazes lead south toward Akron.

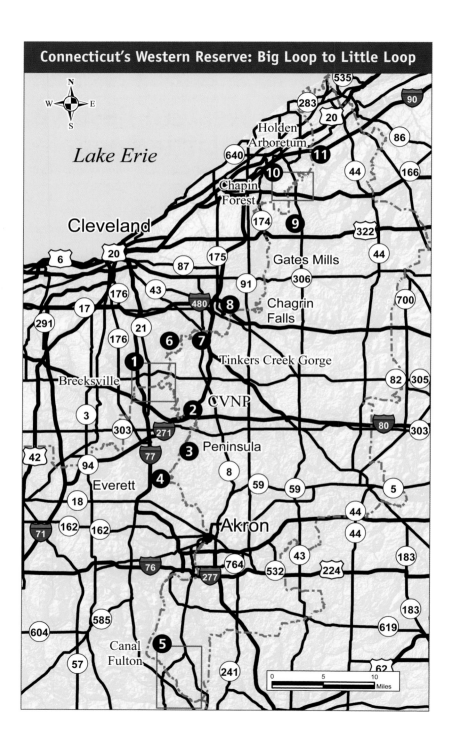

Connecticut's Western Reserve: Big Loop to Little Loop

Figure 9.1 Deer Lick Cave at Brecksville (Cleveland Metroparks)

No one knows for sure why the Little Loop exists. Two groups in northeastern Ohio wanted the trail to pass through their area. One group was led by a state senator from Akron. Ralph Regula fought to have the BT go through Akron by following the Ohio and Erie Canal. Not only was Congressman Regula a friend of the BTA, but this trail location also helped in his efforts to keep the canal lands in the public domain. The other group, composed of BTA volunteers, preferred the rural area east of Akron. Both groups were satisfied and the Little Loop was completed and blazed. Upon completion, the founders of the BTA were pleased to have a continuous trail from Lake Erie to the Ohio River. The dedication of the BT's "Lake to the River Trail" took place at Mogadore Reservoir (see chap. 10) on October 10, 1970.

The BT's Little Loop conforms to the Cuyahoga River's U shape in northeastern Ohio (fig. 9.2). The glacier that created Lake Erie 10,000 years ago caused this abrupt turn in the river. (The Lake Erie watershed was described in chap. 8 and shown in fig. 8.1.) The tremendous force of the glaciers shifted the beginning point, or headwaters, of the 100-mile river to the east and north of Burton, in Geauga County. From that eastern beginning point, the waters of the upper Cuyahoga flow south to the Akron area. (In chap. 10 we will follow the Upper Cuyahoga, a state-designated Scenic River.) The river then turns abruptly north to pass by

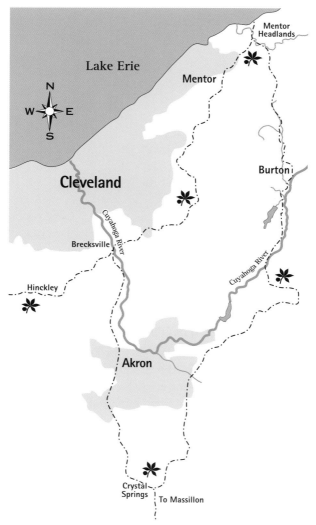

Figure 9.2 Little Loop and Cuyahoga River (Jonathan White)

the Brecksville area and end in Lake Erie at the Flats, in downtown Cleveland. The Buckeye Trail generally follows the Lower Cuyahoga, from Akron to Lake Erie (in this chapter). The estuary of the Cuyahoga in Cleveland burst into flame in 1969, prompting federal legislation designed "to restore the chemical, physical, and biological integrity of our nation's surface water."

Iroquois called the Cuyahoga Ya-sha-hia, or "crooked river." Potentially warring tribes in the area agreed that the river should be neutral territory, so their people could travel safely from Lake Erie to the area that is now Akron, where they could portage to the south-flowing Tuscarawas River. Once on the Tuscarawas, they connected with the mighty Muskingum near Zanesville to get to the Ohio and Mississippi Rivers.

This entire area surrounding the river is part of the Allegheny Plateau, where the scrubbing action of the glacier filled valleys with glacial debris and changed old drainage patterns like that of the Cuyahoga, which once flowed south into what was the earlier course of the Ohio River. Other geological features in this area (and the mucks, in chap. 10) indicate the glacier's presence on the Allegheny Plateau. Experienced hikers of the BT have noted the difference between the land in the glaciated Allegheny Plateau, in the northeast, and the unglaciated Plateau, in southeastern Ohio (see chaps. 11 and 12).

Most of the Little Loop travels through the Connecticut Western Reserve. If you extend a line west from the bottom of Connecticut (approx. 41° latitude), after passing through Pennsylvania, the line defines the region to the north that Connecticut laid claim to by a charter signed by King Charles II of England in 1662. The western edge of the reserve, 120 miles from the Pennsylvania line, is the Firelands (chap. 8). Connecticut's sale of the Western Reserve lands resulted in a perpetual fund, the interest from which helps support the state's schools.

While visiting the Western Reserve, look for villages reflecting the design of old New England villages. Typical is a centrally located and once communal square with a New England–style steepled church. (Native Americans might have cleared the land that later formed many of these central squares.) From diaries left by some of these early villagers, we know that their lives revolved around home, farm, family, and neighbors. They had to be self-sufficient and led much slower lives than we do today. A visit to Hale Farm and Village, described below, will remind you of these early settlers.

This chapter's Overview branches in two directions. The BT in the Akron section, from Brecksville Reservation south, will be described first. After reaching the village of Crystal Springs (see Overview Map), the bottom of the Little Loop, we will return to Brecksville Reservation to describe the Bedford section. This BT section map covers the trail's course north from Brecksville Reservation to its junction with the eastern part of the Little Loop, in Lake County.

As we travel south from Brecksville Reservation, the location of our first Featured Hike, we encounter a 33,000-acre national park that follows

22 miles of the Lower Cuyahoga River. Cuyahoga Valley National Park (CVNP) (fig. 9.3) was formed in 1974 to protect the river and its green spaces from the urban sprawl threatening to overwhelm it.

The blue blazes also pass near such natural attractions as Blue Hen Falls (Point 2), 7 miles south of Brecksville in a forested segment between Columbia Road (C-125) and Boston Mills Road (C-32). This falls has two levels and is only a 20-foot drop, but it is a favorite for waterfall seekers. Buttermilk Falls is a quarter mile downstream. (A waterfall is formed where a layer of rock that resists erosion overlays rock that erodes more easily.) The waterfalls in the Cuyahoga Valley are delightful.

After the waterfalls, the blue blazes connect with the 20-mile Ohio and Erie Canal Towpath Trail, a centerpiece of the CVNP. Along the OECTT you may visit many sites that played a part in the history of Ohio's canals. The trail's crushed-limestone surface passes through meadows, forests, and wetlands. Wildlife that you would not expect in this highly

Figure 9.3 Cuyahoga Valley National Park (Andrew Bashaw)

populated area is plentiful. Even coyotes have been seen in the valley. The OECTT is a large part of the 110-mile Ohio and Erie Canal National Heritage Corridor, which follows the Ohio and Erie Canal from Cleveland to New Philadelphia. The blue blazes are found along much of this corridor.

The BT joins the OECTT (the BT is not blazed along the OECTT) along Boston Mills Road, just north of I-271. An interactive museum with exhibits on how to build a canal boat is found at the Boston Store, near the trailhead. The BT wanders back and forth across the OECTT as it leads south. The two trails are complementary; the OECTT is flatter and more comfortable, and the BT is less crowded. The OECTT leads you to historic sites along the trail, while the BT offers a more pristine natural environment. Together they offer lovely loop hikes.

At Peninsula, further south, the Ohio and Erie Canal once crossed the Cuyahoga River on a major aqueduct. Restaurants and galleries here are visited by the Cuyahoga Valley Scenic Railroad, which runs between Cleveland and Canton. Parking is available on the BT just north of SR 303, between the railroad and the river, where canal relics may be viewed. (Just east of here on SR 303 is a CVNP visitor center—the Happy Days Visitor Center.)

The two trails lead south to Deep Lock Quarry Metropark (Point 3), one of the Summit County Metroparks. Historically, Deep Lock Quarry furnished stone to rebuild canal locks and millstones for grinding grain. Lock 28 has survived here. It was one of a staircase of locks used to raise canal boats 395 feet to the level of Summit Lake in Akron. As at Deep Cut, on the Miami and Erie Canal (chap. 6), the workers who built the locks and quarried the stone faced many hardships inconceivable today. As recently as 1913 the area was stripped of vegetation. Now shrubs and trees, including the Ohio buckeye, are plentiful. The shallow swamp in the quarry harbors reptiles and amphibians. Narrow-leaved cattail and rosepink grows at the wetland's edges.

The BT leaves the OECTT at the restored village of Everett, near Hunt Farm, where local agricultural history may be learned. From here, and after passing through a restored covered bridge, the blue blazes pass by Hale Farm and Village (Point 4), a museum of the Western Reserve Historical Society. This is a must stop for those with children or those who enjoy living history. Actors at the village of Wheatfield will take you back in time to 1848. If you mention cars or other features of 21st-century life they might give you a blank stare and remind you that "James Polk is our 11th president and Ohio is the 5th largest state in the Union." They will also show you their homes and crafts, tell you how the crops are doing, and brag about their glassmaking furnace or glasswork. You will also realize how intensely early settlers followed the political affairs of their new country.

A visit to Akron, known as the Portage City, convinces one that the city is and has always been about transportation. Here you can walk or drive the portaging trails between the Cuyahoga and Tuscarawas Rivers, travel along the canal that ended the need for carrying canoes, and visit museums to learn how automobile tires evolved in the Rubber Capital of the World. The Goodyear Company started manufacturing bicycle tires in 1898. During your visit to the city you may even see a Goodyear blimp hovering on the horizon. B. F. Goodrich and Firestone (now Bridgestone/Firestone) were also founded here, but these companies moved their headquarters south in the 1970s. Akron now aspires to become a leading polymer center. New tourist attractions have also been constructed to entice visitors (see Local Contacts).

The BT enters Akron from the north and passes Portage Path as it follows the OECTT into the downtown. Portage Path served as the pathway for the Indians as they traveled from the Cuyahoga to the Tuscarawas. It was the only portage required on a journey from the Great Lakes to the Gulf of Mexico.

Less than a mile west of the BT in downtown Akron and south on Portage Path is Stan Hywet Hall and Gardens, the magnificent home of Franklin and Gertrude Seiberling, completed in 1915. Franklin was a cofounder of Goodyear Tire and Rubber. His wife was an artist and a lover of gardening and nature. Guests at Hywet (pronounced "haw wit") have included Helen Keller, Will Rogers, and the Trapp family of *Sound of Music* fame, as well as Presidents Taft, Hoover, Coolidge, and George H. W. Bush.

One of the finest examples of Tudor Revival architecture, the 65-room home has many large windows, ample fireplaces, steep roofs, flattened arches, and an impressive tower with battlements. Carved wooden panels hide telephones as well as radiators that provide central heating. Tours are available of the castle and magnificent gardens,

The blue blazes in Akron's downtown follow the OECTT through Cascades Locks Park (fig. 9.4), which includes Locks 10 through 16 and is supported by a unique nonprofit, the Cascade Locks Park Association. The trail passes by the Mustill Store, a reconstruction of a general store that served the community at Lock 15 in the 1800s. Lock 2 Park in Akron has a full-scale skeleton of a canal boat that you may walk through to experience the size and nature of the decks of these boats. It is behind the Canal Park Stadium on Main Street. The beautifully designed stadium is the home of the Akron RubberDucks, a class AA affiliate of the Cleveland Indians.

Figure 9.4 Akron Towpath (Tim Houk)

At the Ohio Women's Rights Convention in Akron in 1851, former slave and ardent feminist Sojourner Truth (the former Isabella Baumfree) gave a historic speech to an audience that included a group of sanctimonious preachers (all male, of course) that had crashed the affair. A bronze plaque commemorating her famous "Ain't I a Woman?" speech is on the Sojourner Truth Building, at 37 North High Street, next to the Y-bridge in downtown Akron and just a couple of blocks from the OECTT.

Following the OECTT south through the Akron area will allow you to continue to explore the Ohio-Erie canal system along Summit Lake, so named because it once was the canal's summit. A floating towpath was used to pull the canal boats along the shore opposite the BT. The summit for the historic canal is now the rerouted Tuscarawas River, which you will join further south. A walk along the old canal is possible south of Nesmith Lake, which is just below I-277 and SR 224 on SR 93. In canal days Young's Tavern was Young's Hotel. Here, at the present-day canal summit, you can see waters dividing and flowing north to Cleveland via the canal and south to the Ohio River via the Tuscarawas.

To learn more about the Ohio and Erie Canal, follow the BT to Canal Fulton, a town in Stark County, for our second Featured Hike (Point 5, fig. 9.5). Visiting this now quiet community, you will scarcely believe it was a wild canal town whose main intersection was called Brimstone Corners.

Figure 9.5 Canal Fulton

The southern juncture of the BT's Little Loop is at the village of Crystal Springs. Here the reader will have to reverse course, for we now return to Brecksville Reservation (where the chapter began) to travel northeast toward Lake Erie.

From the Station Road Bridge Trailhead near Brecksville Reservation, the BT connects once again with the Ohio and Erie Canal Towpath Trail (OECTT), where there are no blue blazes. The historic Frazee-Hynton House within Cuyahoga Valley National Park is found 3 miles north, directly across Canal Road from the OECTT (Point 6). It is reputed to be the second-oldest existing brick residence in the region (1826). Excavations have helped determine the history of the home and of the people who once lived there.

The BT leaves the OECTT and the Ohio and Erie Canal at Sagamore Road. From here a series of hiking trails and suburban roads leads you northeast to Bedford Reservation and an overlook from which you can view spectacular Bridal Veil Falls (Point 7). Spring is the best time to experience the power of the falls, but in winter ice formations offer abstract compositions for the photographer. For the day hiker, I recommend first parking at the Bridal Veil Falls parking lot along Gorge Parkway, which follows Tinkers Creek Gorge. From here, take the BT north or south to enjoy out-and-back hikes of 4 to 6 miles on footpaths that offer great views of the gorge and its Berea sandstone cliffs.

As the blue blazes turn from northeast to north they next visit South Chagrin Reservation near Chagrin Falls (Point 8). In this park is a huge piece of Berea sandstone known as Squaw Rock. Engraved on this massive rock are bas-relief carvings by Henry Church Jr., including an Indian "squaw," a serpent and panther, a quiver of arrows, a skeleton, an American flag, and a papoose. Some believe that Church was portraying the oppression of the Native Americans. To find Squaw Rock, first find the Squaw Rock Picnic Area off Chagrin River Road. From the west side of the picnic area find the path down to the Chagrin River. Turn right (south) to follow the trail along the river and you will not miss the famous rock. To return to the parking area, take the trail near the rock up to the top of the gorge. Turn right and the blue blazes will return you to the parking lot.

Henry Church Jr. was a blacksmith and avant-garde folk artist in the late 1800s whose works are now nationally recognized. His work was definitely not for the people of his time, for when Henry carved his own tombstone—a huge lion with glass eyes—the town fathers judged it inappropriate for local cemeteries. After threatening them with living forever, he was finally allowed to place it in Evergreen Hill Cemetery, where it can be found today.

North Chagrin Reservation (Point 9) is the last Cleveland Metropark visited by the blue blazes. The BT then leads to Chapin Forest (Point 10), a Lake County reservation, and the site of our third Featured Hike. While in this area, tour the Kirtland Temple, dedicated in 1836. This is one of the most impressive structures in the Western Reserve, and I found on my tour that children are as fascinated as their parents. When Mormon prophet Joseph Smith stopped here on his way west from New York, he personally supervised the communal construction of this complex mix of Greek Revival, Georgian, Gothic Revival, and Federalist architectural styles. The church sits on a high bluff overlooking the valley of the East Branch of the Chagrin River.

From Kirtland the BT passes the Holden Arboretum (Point 11). From the planting of the first tree, in 1931, the collection—reported to be the largest in the U.S.—has grown to 5,400 species. The BT in this chapter ends in Lake County. The next chapter will follow the blue blazes from the northern terminus, at Lake Erie, to the Little Loop's terminus, at Crystal Springs.

FEATURED HIKE 1
BRECKSVILLE RESERVATION

DISTANCE 4 miles.

TIME Allow at least 4 hours.

DIFFICULTY Moderately difficult. Some steep climbs.

There is a Hiker on the Go map for this section of the Buckeye Trail.

To find Brecksville Reservation, take I-77 N to SR 82 East. Just after the junction of SR 21, in midtown Brecksville, enter the reservation on Chippewa Creek Drive. Before you begin the hike, you may want to visit Chippewa Creek Gorge Scenic Overlook, just to your left. A short distance further on the right is a memorial to Harriet L. Keeler (1846–1921), teacher, educational administrator, community leader, and author. Of her eleven books, seven were about the outdoors. Her 300-acre Memorial Woods, located within the reservation, is dedicated to the restoration of native trees, shrubs, and wildflowers. Just after the Keeler memorial is the Brecksville Nature Center.

Here you can obtain maps, brochures, and answers to your questions about the reservation. The Works Progress Administration built the Brecksville Nature Center, Cleveland Metroparks' oldest building, in 1939. The Berea sandstone in its foundation was locally quarried. The American chestnut used in the building was from trees that had already died from a blight that was introduced to North America in 1904 and reached Ohio in the 1930s. Only suckers from the stumps still live. Perhaps someday these shoots will be able to resist the scourge transmitted by a leaf-hopping insect and we will again see these 100-foot hardwoods that inspired Longfellow to immortalize "the spreading chestnut-tree."

Near the Nature Center is a tallgrass prairie. Original prairies were wet in spring but suffered drought in autumn. Fires often started naturally, but Native Americans started them as well to drive game. They also knew that prairie plants, especially grasses, thrived after fire and the new forage attracted elk and buffalo. Without annual burnings, succession would occur, bringing edge plants into the open areas. Eventually these plants and their hardwood successors would eliminate the prairie environment. Here in profusion are big bluestem and Indiangrass, true prairie sunflowers, prairie dock, mountain mint, and wild bergamot, along with

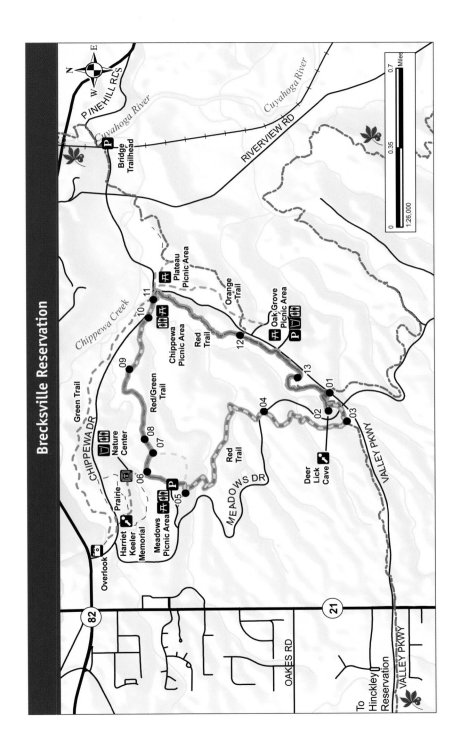

Brecksville Reservation

the less common prairie (or gray-headed) coneflower, Ohio spiderwort, and common (or autumn) sneezeweed. Also found is foxglove beardtongue, with its white, five-lobed flowers that have a tuft of hair on one stamen. The park staff regularly has controlled burns of this prairie.

After leaving the parking area for the Nature Center, the next road to your right will be Valley Parkway. Instead of heading directly to the hike, why not follow Chippewa Creek Drive to the Station Road Trail Head. Here you will find the train station, a stop for the Cuyahoga Valley Scenic Railroad (fig. 9.6). The trailhead is in Cuyahoga Valley National Park and the Cuyahoga Valley Scenic Railroad train may be boarded here. This train visits two of the sites mentioned in the Overview: Hale Farm and Stan Hywet Hall. The Buckeye Trail enters the park here from the north.

After a visit to this area, back track to Valley Parkway. Follow this park road for about 1 mile and you will come upon a sign announcing an entrance to the Buckeye Trail and then a sign that says Deer Lick Cave. You may park at either area—both are near this hike.

Start your hike at the entrance to the Buckeye Trail sign (WP 1) and notice the triple blazes on a tree just ahead. This blazing announces the Buckeye Trail is going to be going in three directions just ahead: the north

Figure 9.6 Brecksville train station (Richard Lutz)

spur to Lake Erie, the south portion to the Ohio River, and the westward portion to western Ohio and the Great Black Swamp (chap. 7).

After this point, stop and read the interpretive sign about the Buckeye Trail and then go west following the blue blazes (westward portion of the BT) to Deer Lick Cave. At the first intersection go to your right and follow the blue blazes. At WP 2 you are at Deer Lick Cave (see fig. 9.1). Keep following the blue alongside a peaceful creek and waterfall up and out of the ravine. At the top of the ravine, turn right and follow red and blue blazes. Continue across Meadows Drive and then turn right and follow red and yellow (WP 3). This is a bridle trail, primarily for horse traffic, but is quite pleasant to walk. We leave the Buckeye Trail as it continues westward to Hinkley Reservation.

The nature of the hike after the Meadows Drive crossing is walking along ridge tops for a time and then walking down into gorges and back up. The ups and downs of this portion of the hike are no more than 70 or 80 feet. There are numerous switchbacks that make the hike easier. In winter, look for the robin-size loggerhead shrike, a songbird with a distinctive hooked bill and hawklike behavior. Lacking the talons of the hawk, the shrike has adapted by impaling prey on the thorns of trees or on a barbed-wire fence. Unfortunately, the shrike's numbers are diminishing and no one knows why. Sometimes you may be led to a shrike because smaller songbirds are mobbing it. *Mobbing* is the term used to describe the gathering of similar species of birds to ward off a predator's attack.

At WP 4, cross Meadows a second time and continue to follow the red and the yellow. Pass through several more deep gorges with Berea sandstone outcroppings. As you pass through the gorges, note that the varied sandstone formations appear on the same levels in different locations. Sandstone is a sedimentary rock mostly formed from sands of ancient seas. Since this quartz-laden rock is less easily eroded than other sedimentary rocks, layers of sandstone are often exposed by the elements. Sandstone contains fossil evidence, most strikingly that of large fish. Don't look for evidence of dinosaurs, however. These deposits were formed 200 million years before brontosaurus.

Continue to follow the well-defined bridle trail, regardless of the temptations of intersecting footpaths.

At WP 5 the red trail leaves the yellow and red. If you want to visit the Nature Center you should go left on the red trail and pass through the Meadows Picnic Area. Enter the woods, following red, and go to WP 6, where you will take the steps down and back up to the Nature Center.

Upon return to WP 6, bear left on the green trail to later intersect the yellow bridle trail.

If you are skipping the Nature Center, continue on the yellow trail around the perimeter of a meadow. This is interesting because if offers quite a difference of habitat from the deep woods. This meadow is mowed to stop succession. Many varieties of plants: daisy, knotweed, cornflower, small shrubs and thistle will be found. Try to hear the different bird sounds: robin, field sparrow, blue jay, catbird. At WP 7, the yellow intersects with the green and red trails. From here follow yellow, green, and red.

Shortly, at WP 8, the red and green go off to the right. Follow this trail for foot traffic. This trail is on a ridge and is relatively easy walking. Notice the sarsaparilla growing along the trail. It is a perennial woody vine that may reach fifty feet in length. It has small flowers and black, blue, or red berrylike fruits. The root (which has been used for centuries as herbal medicine) is long and tuberous, and has a spicy-sweet and pleasant taste when processed; but before processing the roots are bitter, sticky, and have a strong odor. Sarsaparilla is also used in soft-drink making. This spicy, pleasant-smelling root is what originally gave root beer its distinct taste, and it is also responsible for root beer's foaming qualities. Just before the trail's descent, notice a stunning view off to the left. A creek meanders through the valley area. The deer have browsed the steep hillsides to such and extent, it seems to be manicured. Even in the full leaves of summer the view is great. At WP 9 the red and green intersect with the yellow. Go to the right following the red, green and yellow.

WP 10 is an easy ford on a creek and the trail goes straight ahead on red and yellow. WP 11 is Chippewa Picnic Area with restrooms. Just before Valley Parkway, follow the red to the right and ascend a steep slope. This is a 150-foot climb and there are no switchbacks to ease the ascent. There are beech, maple, and other hardwoods on the top of the ridge.

The Buckeye Trail intersects the hike at WP 12. This section of the BT has come south from Lake Erie. You will follow the blue blazes and red trail now for the rest of the hike. Shortly, you will come upon a double blue blaze. The top blaze points up a hill to the left. The Buckeye Trail is unique because it warns the hiker of a change in direction with the use of the double blaze.

At WP 13, the red trail goes straight ahead and the blue blazes go off to the right for a short trip to a steep-gorge view. Follow the blue blazes. The red trail is a shortcut to get you to your car sooner, but you would miss the gorge view.

After this quick trip to the ravine edge, return to the road and the hike is over.

FEATURED HIKE 2
CANAL FULTON

DISTANCE 5-mile round-trip along the towpath.

TIME Less than 3 hours.

DIFFICULTY Easy.

Take SR 93 south from I-277 in Akron or north from U.S. 30 near Massillon. Park your car in the ample parking lot just south of SR 93 in downtown Canal Fulton. The Canal Fulton Heritage Society's Old Canal Days Museum is on the corner of SR 93 and the entrance to the Ohio and Erie Corridor parking lot. In the museum you will learn the history of the canal and the village that nurtured and benefited from it.

Here you will also see a replica being built from plans of the *St. Helena,* a working canal boat of the early to mid-1800s (fig. 9.7). There are three structures on the deck. At the stern is the captain's cabin with a raised deck aft, on which he could stand while directing the boat through a lock. The spacious cabin extends below the waterline; it could accommodate the captain's family and even a stove. In the middle was a stable that carried the

Figure 9.7 *St. Helena III*

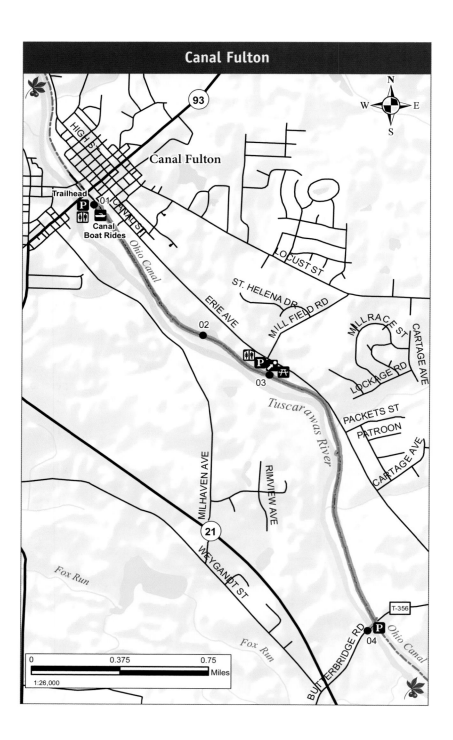

Canal Fulton

horses or mules that pulled the boat. Feed could be loaded through an opening above. The digested grain must have turned the canals into pungent sewage systems. The forward structure was the crew's cabin. At least one of the crew was a young boy who herded the horses along the towpath. He often had to sleep on the deck of the prow.

The first restoration, the *St. Helena II,* was completed in the 1970s using 19th-century tools and materials (mainly wood). She rotted out after 12 years of service on the canal. This latest restoration, when completed, will remain on land to be enjoyed by visitors for many years to come.

Begin the hike at the Canal Fulton Canalway Center (WP 1). This facility was completed in 2003 and serves as a ticket station for the canal cruises as well as offering snacks, information, and rest rooms. If you are hiking from April through October, you will see the *St. Helena III* either tied up at the center or in action along the canal. The St. Helena III's curved hull is built of ferro-cement (concrete over steel mesh) and is, surprisingly, lighter than that of a wooden boat. Visitors may ride in it daily from May through September and on weekends in April and October. The ride may not seem interesting from shore, but hikers, especially children, will enjoy feeling like part of the crew of a working canal boat.

Following the blue blazes to the southeast from the *St. Helena III,* you will pass by its winter dry dock, which has supposedly been in operation since 1860. As you walk further along the canal you will see waterfowl that frequent the canal waterway.

After walking almost a mile you will see a widening of the canal bed (WP 2). This is a turnaround area where canal boats could change direction. Often these areas were used as rest areas for boat repairs. At Lock 4 (WP 3) see a lock tender's house (fig. 9.5). Lock tenders were on duty 24 hours per day. There were no 40-hour weeks. A small park here provides more parking, picnic tables, and portable toilets. Lock 4 is a restored hand-operated lock of the early to mid-1800s. A mill raceway and an old millstone remind us of one of the other functions of the canal—to provide waterpower for agriculture and industry.

As you walk away from Lock 4, note the several culverts that allow streams to cross under the canal. Butterbridge Road (T-356) is the southern end of this hike (WP 4). Further south the BT crosses a reconstructed culvert exhibiting the original sandstone arch. At this point you are within 3 miles of Crystal Springs, which marks the end of the western side of the Little Loop. From here, we will return to Brecksville Reservation and travel north to the west side of the Little Loop, which will continue our trek around the state on the Buckeye Trail.

An option on this hike is to make a return to your car at any point in the walk. Or, you could plan to visit with two cars and can leave one car at the parking area just west of the intersection of the trail and Butterbridge Road.

FEATURED HIKE 3
CHAPIN FOREST

DISTANCE 4 miles.

TIME 2 hours.

DIFFICULTY Moderately easy. The trails in the park are wide and well graveled. The only difficulty is the walk up to Chapin Ledges and Gildersleeve Knob.

To find Chapin Forest Reservation, take I-90 to SR 306 and drive south for 5 miles to the reservation entrance. Drive the park road, Chapin Parkway, to the last parking area—Ledges Picnic Shelter.

Start the hike at the trail leading up the ridge from the kiosk (WP 1). Take a park map to acquaint yourself with all the varied trails in the forest. The trails are maintained with a gravel surface as wide as both arms outstretched.

As you start up the paved trail, Lucky Stone Loop, you will see the blue blazes. Lucky Stone Loop is named for the quartz pebbles that are embedded in the sandstone along this route. Just past the kiosk, you will notice trail junctions that are clearly marked by interpretive posts.

Follow the blue blazes to the right and continue ascending. There are magnificent beeches, maples, and other hardwood trees along the trail. The growth rate of trees for commercial timber production was once studied here. You may notice side trails off to the right as others are making their way to the edge of the ridge to capture a view. In order to protect the fragile vegetation and yourself, signs along the trail warn visitors not to wander off the paved trail to the ledges. One reason you do not have to go off trail to get a good view of the lake plain to the north, is that the blue blazes lead to the best scenic view on the west side of the summit of 1,160-foot Gildersleeve Knob (WP 2).

Standing on the Allegheny Plateau and looking out over the lake plain (see appendix 2), you can see an abandoned stone quarry from where the conglomerate was mined and then separated into sand and quartz pebbles.

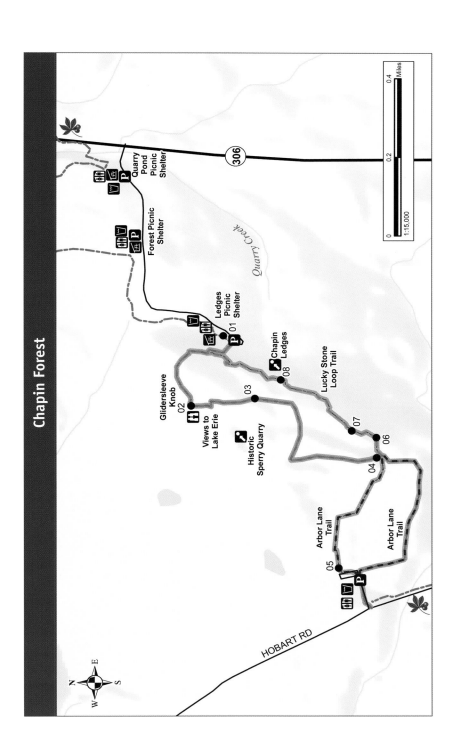

To see the transition in the geologic systems from Gildersleeve Knob (fig. 9.8) to the lake plain, see appendix 2. On most days, you can see the Erie lakeshore, 8 miles to the north, and on a clear day you can see Cleveland skyline, 18 miles to the west. In winter, moisture-laden clouds from Lake Erie rise over this ridge to eventually create the notorious Snow Belt to the east.

When you are able leave this fascinating view, continue with the blue blazes walking south. At WP 3 there is a connector trail leading back to the return leg of Lucky Stone Loop and the parking lot. Stay with the blue blazes. Next you will come upon a trail junction of Arbor Loop and Lucky Stone Loop (WP 4). Follow the blue blazes to the left on Arbor Lane Loop. On Arbor Lane Loop you will see the first of the signs for snowboarding. Of course, you will stay on the graveled trail.

Upon reaching the parking area for the Arbor Lane Loop Trail, the blue blazes will leave the park to Hobart Road. They will be heading south to Brecksville Reservation. You will walk through the parking lot and take Arbor Lane Loop Trail (WP 5) to your right and begin your walk back to the car. For the trip back to the car, unless you choose to retrace the first part of the hike, you will not be following blue blazes.

Figure 9.8 Gildersleeve Knob (Andy "Captain Blue" Niekamp)

After a slight ascent, you reach the junction of Lucky Stone Loop and Arbor Lane Loop (WP 4). Bear to your right on Lucky Stone Loop and then bear immediately left at WP 6. In early spring, you may notice a trail bearing right. This is a snowboard trail and is to be ignored. Notice that the trail to the left is graveled. But, it is quite a different type of trail, with outcroppings of sandstone that must be traversed. The previous trail was so smooth that a stroller could have been used. This stretch of trail takes careful walking. AT WP 7 the trail intersects with another connector trail. Bear to the right on the main trail and stay on Lucky Stone Loop.

This trail is significant because it passes Chapin Ledges (WP 8, fig. 9.9), which are quite impressive outcroppings. These Sharon conglomerate ledges were formed over 300 million years ago, during the Pennsylvanian Period, when Ohio was under a shallow sea interspersed with swamp forest. Deltas from mountains to the north and east that brought the quartz pebbles became a part of the conglomerate, and the weight and movement of glacial ice some 12,000 years ago scored them with prominent grooves.

After coming down a grade from the ledges, the trail intersects the smooth path. Bear right and shortly you are back to the parking/picnic area.

Figure 9.9 Chapin Ledges

The Quarry Pond Loop Trail begins on the far side of the picnic shelter and is well worth your visit. You can walk the 1-mile round trip to the quarry or you can return by car to the first parking area on Chapin Parkway and visit. The quarry provided Berea sandstone used in building foundations like that of the Mormons' Kirtland Temple (1836). Take the earthen side trail around Quarry Pond along the small creek (a tributary of the Chagrin River) that feeds the pond. The footpath is well defined. You will see blue blazes as they come into the park from Lake Erie.

LOCAL CONTACTS

- Brecksville Reservation. www.clevelandmetroparks.com.
- Canal Fulton. www.discovercanalfulton.com.
- Chapin Forest. www.lakemetroparks.com.
- Cuyahoga Valley National Park. www.nps.gov/cuva/.
- Cuyahoga Valley Scenic Railroad. www.cvsr.com.
- Erie Canalway National Heritage Corridor. www.nps.gov/erie/.
- Hale Farm and Village. www.wrhs.org.
- Hiker on the Go map for Brecksville. www.buckeyetrail.org.
- Holden Arboretum. www.holdenarb.org.

WAYPOINT ID'S

WAYPOINT ID	DESCRIPTION	LATITUDE	LONGITUDE
	BRECKSVILLE RESERVATION		
1	Buckeye Trail sign	41.30520600	−81.60894300
2	Deer Lick Cave	41.30529800	−81.61043300
3	Jct BT and Meadow Drive	41.30417100	−81.61132200
4	Meadow Drive	41.30925700	−81.61041900
5	Red leaves Yellow trail	41.31414100	−81.61714900
6	Steps to Nature Center	41.31647700	−81.61530000
7	Jct Yellow with Red and Green	41.31609200	−81.61374500
8	Yellow leaves Red and Green	41.31747300	−81.60673500
9	Yellow joins Red and Green	41.31747300	−81.60673500
10	Creek crossing	41.31624700	−81.60244900
11	Chippewa Creek Picnic Area	41.31624700	−81.60244900
12	Jct BT and Red Trail	41.31066600	−81.60405800
13	BT leaves Red Trail	41.30716700	−81.60762600

WAYPOINT ID	DESCRIPTION	LATITUDE	LONGITUDE
	CANAL FULTON		
1	Canalway Center	40.88843200	-81.59783700
2	Canal boat turn around	40.88004400	-81.58908200
3	Lock Tender's House	40.87745900	-81.58374300
4	Butterbridge Rd	40.86126800	-81.57591000
	CHAPIN FOREST		
1	Kiosk at Ledges Picnic Area	41.59379000	-81.35779100
2	Scenic overlook	41.59516900	-81.36109900
3	Connector trail	41.59273000	-81.36084800
4	Jct of Lucky Stone and Arbor Loop	41.58842400	-81.36378800
5	Arbor Lane Trail from parking lot	41.58981700	-81.36912200
6	Sharp left on Lucky Stone	41.58842600	-81.36280900
7	Jct of Lucky Stone and Connector	41.58929700	-81.36246500
8	Chapin Ledges	41.59177700	-81.35995900

The Upper Cuyahoga River: East Branch of the Little Loop

BTA SECTION MAPS Burton, Mogadore, part of Massillon.

COUNTIES TRAVERSED Lake, Geauga, Portage, Stark.

DISTANCE COVERED 128 miles.

OVERVIEW

Lake Erie (fig. 10.1), one of the five Great Lakes, is a fitting gateway to this chapter. The original Buckeye Trail, then known as the Lake to the River Trail, began here (Point 1, Overview) and ended at Eden Park on the Ohio River (chap. 5).

The large beach at Headlands Beach State Park, the subject of the chapter's first Featured Hike, attracts many visitors during the summer, so

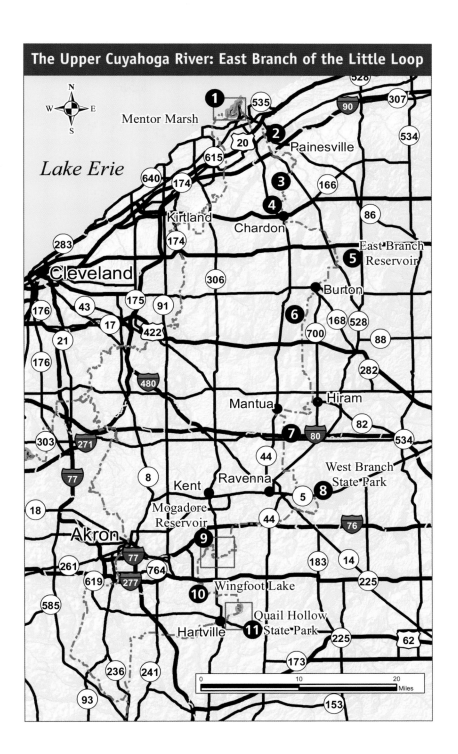

The Upper Cuyahoga River: East Branch of the Little Loop

N W E S

1
Mentor Marsh

535
528
90
307

2
Painesville

Lake Erie

20

615

640 **174**

3

166

534

4

Kirtland

174

Chardon

86

East Branch
Reservoir

283

174

5

Cleveland

306

Burton

176
43
175
91

6

168 **528**

17

21
422

700

88

176

282

480

Mantua

Hiram

303
271

7 **80**

82

534

77

44

Ravenna

West Branch
State Park

8
Kent

5 **8**

Mogadore
Reservoir

44

76

Akron

9

18

77

183 **14**

261

77

764

225

619

277

Wingfoot Lake

10

585

Hartville

11

Quail Hollow
State Park

225

62

236 **241**

173

93

153

0   10   20
Miles

Figure 10.1 Lake Erie (Brent and Amy Anslinger)

hikers may wish to visit the area during the week or in the off-season. The other highlight of the area is Headlands Dunes State Nature Preserve, open during daylight hours only. Here you will find such unique shore plants as sand dropseed, Canada wild rye, wafer ash (a shrub), and wild bean. Over 200 species of birds have been found in this popular flyway. The rather rare old-squaw (or long-tailed duck) is the only diving duck— dark in front and white behind at the waterline. If you see a solid-black duck, it is the common American (or black) scoter.

On a spit of land to the northeast of Headland Dunes is the Grand River Light, which replaced the historic Fairport Harbor Light. Located in Fairport Harbor, just across the Grand River from Mentor Headlands, the lighthouse served as a beacon for one of the northern termini of the Underground Railroad (UGRR), which led slaves to Canada and freedom. The Marine Museum there will interest lighthouse history buffs.

The eastern side of the Western Reserve's Little Loop, from Mentor Headlands to Crystal Springs, is the subject of this chapter (see Overview Map). The BT leads south from the lake to a more urban environment. Nurseries still thrive in the sandy-loam topsoil deposited by the glaciers, giving the county the nickname Nursery Capital of Ohio. The wineries in the area are world class. For lovers of the outdoors, the salient feature is the system of 40 Lake Metroparks established in Lake County (see chap. 9, Chapin Forest).

Other attractions in Lake County include President James A. Garfield's home in Mentor, and the Indian Museum and Rider's 1812 Inn (formerly Rider's Tavern; Point 2), both in Painesville. Rider's Tavern, constructed in 1812, was modeled after George Washington's home, Mount Vernon.

Girdled Road Reservation (Point 3) provides the BT with 2 miles of off-road trail, taking its name from the pioneer road that ran from Cleveland east into Pennsylvania. Before the road was constructed the trees had to be removed. They first were killed by girdling (stripping off a ring of bark around the trunk). The BT, quite steep in parts of this area, crosses scenic Aylworth Creek, a tributary of Big Creek.

The BT next enters Geauga County, part of the glaciated plateau that rises some 500 feet above Lake Erie. As moisture-laden air moves from the lake surface to the plateau, it rises to precipitate as rain or snow. In winter, lake-effect snows can make driving dangerous. The snows come fast and the hiker, somewhat removed from civilization, may be unprepared. It is always a good idea to check the most recent weather reports before planning a hike.

The well-managed Geauga Park District is a crown jewel for the county. Established in 1961, this network of park sites offers programs for an increasing number of outdoor enthusiasts.

Big Creek Park (Point 4) is the first of the Geauga parks to be visited by the BT. The 6.4-miles of trails, including the meandering blue blazes, offer the hiker a restful sojourn. The paved Cascade and Ruth Kennan Trails are designed for people of all abilities.

The blue blazes next cross the watershed divide at the headwaters of Big Creek, whose waters reach Mentor Headlands and Lake Erie via the Grand River. From here, the remainder of the chapter follows the BT along the scenic Upper Cuyahoga River.

After crossing the watershed, the BT leads south to East Branch Reservoir, on the East Branch of the Cuyahoga River. Owned by the City of Akron, the surrounding land is leased by the Geauga Park District to form Headwaters Park (Point 5). The park's off-road, 2-mile hike offers great views of the reservoir. Boats are allowed to use only electric motors, assuring that your hike will be peaceful. Bird-watching opportunities include migratory waterfowl in spring and fall, loons, tundra swans, and even bald eagles.

At Chardon, the off-road BT encounters a new trail, the Maple Highlands Trail, one of the Rails-to-Trails Conservancy's multi-use linear parks, which originally served as railroad corridors. The BTA cooperates with Rails-to-Trails and appreciates their important trail and environmental efforts. The BT leaves the MHT at Headwaters Park.

The BT next visits the village of Burton, which may best be described as a New England village dropped into northeastern Ohio. The blue blazes lead you to Burton's village green, patterned after the Connecticut towns of its founders. One brochure at the log cabin there offers the history and architecture of the village's older buildings and a driving map of the Amish country lying just east of the BT. The Burton Wetlands Nature Preserve, a state preserve with trails and boardwalks, lies southeast of the town. The endangered four-toed salamander, found in the wetlands, can voluntarily disconnect its tail when threatened.

Continue to follow the blue blazes south from Burton on Rapids Road (C-1), along which is the entrance to Eldon Russell Park (Point 6). This Geauga park offers access to the Upper Cuyahoga River, a state-designated scenic river. The flat land along the river was once an Ice Age lakebed. The exit drive and bridge abutments found here formed the infrastructure of an electric interurban railway from 1902 to 1914. This early trolley line was a popular way to travel from the Burton area west to Chagrin Falls, or south to Garrettsville.

The so-called Onion Wars, which took place in this area in 1901, are reminiscent of early western movies. A wealthy farmer named Latham decided that the rich muck on the banks of the Cuyahoga was suitable for growing onions. But first he had to drain the muck, and to do that he needed to dredge the river, in order to increase its flow downstream. All went well until he found that a natural rock dam at Hiram Rapids, to the south, was in the way. His trusty men were sent to dynamite the dam. The valiant townspeople rose up in arms, using shotguns filled with rock salt to chase the "bad guys" off.

Since Latham did not succeed in his nefarious plan, wetland wildlife can still be observed on the 0.6-mile nature trail. The Eldon Russell Park brochure lists beaver, mink, wood duck, and herons. The rare prothonotary warbler, with a head and breast of deep yellow to orange, lives here in the summer and may be found nesting.

Hiram College, next along the BT, is a liberal arts college in Hiram, Ohio. James A. Garfield, the 20th president of the United States, was a student, teacher, and principal (equivalent to today's college president) of

Hiram College. This broadly educated individual taught Greek and Latin as well as mathematics and geology.

The BT is routed past the site of the Mantua Glass Works (1821–29), on Sheldon Road and 0.6 miles south of SR 82. The opening of the Ohio and Erie Canal was the death knell for most early Ohio glass manufacturers, who could not compete with their New England counterparts. Before the canals it was almost impossible to transport products like glass windows. Can you imagine a mule train crossing the Alleghenies with new window glass?

The Mantua Bog and Marsh Wetlands State Nature Preserves are along the BT on Peck Road near Mantua (Point 7). The Department of the Interior designates both as National Natural Landmarks. Mantua Bog may be visited only with a permit due to the fragility of this alkaline fen and cranberry bog. Recently discovered in the bog is a significant population of the brush-tipped emerald, a dragonfly species never before seen in Ohio. Marsh Wetlands, an emergent marsh along the Upper Cuyahoga, is open to visitors. Found here are active beaver lodges, interesting waterfowl, and rare water plants.

As you travel south, the land is flat except for a few striking hills seemingly pasted on its surface. These hills, or kames, and other topographical features are part of the Glaciated Allegheny Plateau, described in chapter 9. The on-road trail passes along the western perimeter of the former Ravenna Arsenal, where during World War II ammunition was produced and tested.

West Branch State Park, surrounds the Michael J. Kirwan Reservoir on the Mahoning River (Point 8). Mahoning, an American Indian word, means salt lick. A salt lick southeast of Warren supplied precious salt to Indians and pioneer settlers. In addition to hiking, the park offers snowmobiling, cross-country skiing, and a horseman's campsite with 20 miles of bridle trails. The staff at West Branch offers many nature programs, including hikes to find and collect the gems of West Branch—gypsum crystals scattered profusely along some parts of the lakeshore.

Continuing south on the Buckeye Trail will bring you to Mogadore Reservoir (Point 9 and second Featured Hike, fig. 10.2), an outstanding example of Akron's efforts to preserve its watersheds. The lands surrounding the reservoir, with their 40-year-old pine plantings, serve as organic filters to protect water quality. The blue blazes are found along the north side of the lake, and the total distance of the BT in this area is 8.5 miles.

Figure 10.2 Mogadore Reservoir (Andy "Captain Blue" Niekamp)

The beauty of the lake is augmented by the variety of flora and fauna found on its shores. The lake is peaceful because electric motors are mandated to prevent water pollution from oil and gas. Hunting is not permitted except for duck hunting, in season.

From Mogadore Reservoir, the BT goes on to Wingfoot Lake, home of the Goodyear Blimps (Point 10). The blue blazes may be followed to Hanger 1 (fig. 10.3), at Suffield on Wingfoot Road. The blimps launched from here help cover sporting events. The first airship to land on a roof—in Cleveland—was launched from Wingfoot Lake in May 1919.

Near the Portage and Stark County line on the BT, soil in some of the lowland valleys is no longer brown but black. This land, locally known as the Hartville mucks, actually evolved from kettle lakes that filled with their own aquatic vegetation over thousands of years. The lake water eventually disappeared, leaving only a rich mixture not unlike that of peat moss mixed with soil. The creeks running through the mucks also turn black.

The rich soil permits local farmers to grow two or three crops of vegetables per year. Carrots, radishes, onions, and several varieties of lettuces are among the produce shipped nationwide. The highly organic soil

Figure 10.3 Hanger 1 (Andy "Captain Blue" Niekamp)

must be first drained by tiling and then constantly irrigated in the summer or it will self-ignite and burn!

Congress Lake is south of Wingfoot Lake, at the intersection of Congress Lake and Pontius Roads. This is one of a relatively few naturally occurring lakes in Ohio formed by glaciers, as were the smaller kettle lakes. Jellyfish live in this lake as well as in other glacial lakes.

Quail Hollow State Park (fig. 10.4) is the site of our third Featured Hike (Point 11). Attractions at the park include a 2-mile bridle trail, a 4-mile mountain bike trail, a primitive camping area, and cross-country skiing trails (with ski rental).

The rich history of Hartville has been documented from the establishment of its first general store, in 1830. It is said that the Hartville Hotel formed part of the UGRR. It is now the Pantry Restaurant, at the junction of SR 619 and SR 43, which is also where the blue blazes lead from Hartville north to Quail Hollow. Just east of this junction is the Hartville Elevator, established in 1909 and, unlike many gristmills in the U.S., still operating as a grain and feed mill.

The Buckeye Trail from Hartville to Crystal Springs will be on roads that may be enjoyed by walking, bicycling, or driving. Following the blue blazes south, you will see small depressions filled with water. These

Figure 10.4 Stewart Manor House, Quail Hollow State Park (Quail Hollow)

"kettles" are the footprints of ancient land-locked icebergs. Some are full of vegetation, a natural succession that eventually produces the muck land described above. At Crystal Springs, the BT joins the Ohio and Erie Canal Towpath Trail and heads south through Massillon.

This chapter ends our tour around the Buckeye Trail's Little Loop that was begun in chapter 9.

FEATURED HIKE 1
MENTOR MARSH

DISTANCE 8 miles for the hike from Headlands Beach State Park to the Zimmerman Trail with a return.

TIME 5 hours.

DIFFICULTY The 2-mile Zimmerman Trail is undulating and can be somewhat difficult. The rest of the hike, on roads or sidewalk, is easy. Hiking poles would be useful on the Zimmerman Trail. Also, depending on time of year, pack mosquito repellent.

The entire south shore of Lake Erie was once under the waters of ancient lakes, creating what is known as the Lake Plain. While hiking, look for the features created by the lake water's changing levels. From the shore you

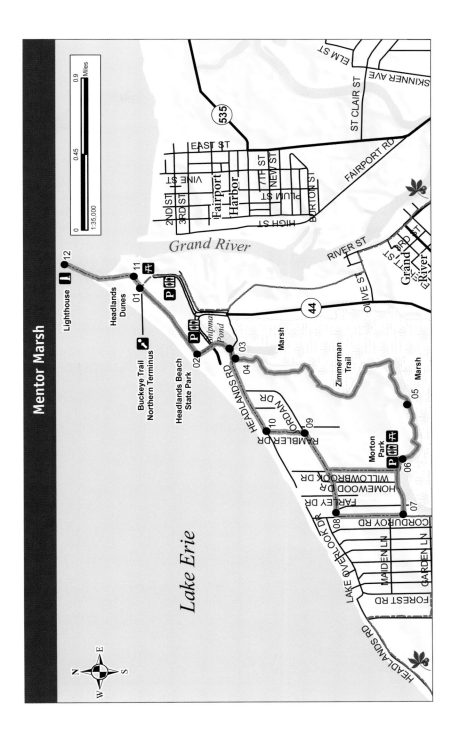

Mentor Marsh

will see Ohio's largest natural sandy beach, Headlands Beach State Park. South of the BT's northern terminus is Mentor Marsh, another artifact of geological history, which hosts a wide variety of flora and fauna. The marsh is one of the country's first National Natural Landmarks. Look for geological artifacts of marsh and lake-level effects, including terraces, dunes, and sandbars. The sandbars, also known as beach ridge formations, are now covered by stands of oak.

Visit the Mentor Marsh Nature Center (also known as the Marsh House) on Corduroy Road before the hike for literature that will help you better understand the geological features mentioned above, the history of the marsh, and the plants and animals living there. The tours offered here are well worth while. Note! Pets are not allowed on the Zimmerman Trail.

The hike begins at Headlands Beach State Park, at the northern end of SR 44, which is accessed from the east of Cleveland off I-90 or SR 2. Park in the northernmost area of the lot and find the interpretive sign announcing the northern terminus of the Buckeye Trail. Be sure to visit the beach and lighthouse (fig. 10.5) either before or after the hike. There are two trails to the north of the sign that lead to the lake (WP 11). The

Figure 10.5 Lighthouse

beach here is the largest natural sand beach in the state. There is a break-water leading to the lighthouse (WP 12), and duck hunting (in season) and fishing are permitted off the embankment. The lighthouse can be accessed from the breakwater.

WP 1 for the hike is at the sign for the northern terminus just south of the entrance to the Headlands Dunes State Nature Preserve (fig. 10.6). The trail follows the paved walkway along the parking lot to the west. Lake Erie, the beach, and dunes are on the right. Swimming is permitted here. There are restrooms along the way. Blue blazes are painted on trees next to the walkway. About 1/3 mile into the hike, there is a turn to the left (WP 2). The trail will go through the parking lot to access a service road for the maintenance area located on the east of the parking lot.

WP 3 is the entrance to the service area from Headlands Road. Ship-man's Pond is to the east. Shipman's Pond is a well-known fishing and birdwatching area. The trail turns right on Headlands Road on a bike path and ascends a small hill to the parking lot for the Zimmerman Trail and the Mentor Marsh State Nature Preserve. The trailhead for the Zimmer-man Trail is at WP 4.

Figure 10.6 Headlands Dunes State Nature Preserve

Because of a large mosquito population in the summer, the best time to visit Mentor Marsh is before late May or after the first frost. At least 26 species of mosquito live and breed in the marshlands. Mosquitoes provide nourishment for many marsh dwellers and do not hesitate to sample an occasional *Homo sapiens.*

The Zimmerman Trail can be steep, with wet, slippery areas, so sturdy hiking boots are recommended. You will find good views of the marsh to the left of the trail. The marsh is the former bed of the Grand River. About 2,000 years ago the forces of erosion changed its course so that now it flows more directly north to Lake Erie.

The marsh was mostly open water until the 1800s; after that it became covered with swamp forest. As recently as the 1960s the landscape changed once again. The beautiful grass you see now is really an invader that thrives on the increased salinity and above-normal water levels the marsh has recently experienced. Common reed (Phragmites communis) has taken over the marsh, causing changes in other life forms.

As you explore, try to find five distinct habitats along the trail—swamp forest, thorn scrub, marshland, open ponds, and sandy ridges. If you have time for birdwatching, there are over 200 different species in the marsh. Look for tundra swans, which nest in the area in June. You may see a pair caring for their cygnets. May through June—spring migration—is one of the best times for birdwatching, for this is when the birds are in their finest feather. There are many opportunities on this hike to catch sight of the white-tailed deer.

The park system has developed ponds along the trail to encourage a return to the natural diversity in the habitat. They have also erected two "exclosures" (WP 5), areas fenced to keep out grazing deer and allow natural flora to flourish. There are so many white-tailed deer in the area that the hillsides are browsed clean. Later in the hike, the trail will pass several residences where homeowners have erected large fences to protect flower and vegetable gardens.

The Zimmerman Trail ends at Morton Community Park (WP 6), where there are facilities and picnic tables. From the park take the Rosemary Lane sidewalk, following the blue blazes, to Corduroy Road. The only road to cross the marsh, it was named for its original construction, in the 1880s, from logs laid perpendicular to the line of travel. The rough and bumpy surface of corduroy roads gave the name to cloth with a similar texture.

At WP 7 turn right on Corduroy Road (the Buckeye Trail goes left) to Jordan Drive. At this intersection, there is a convenience store. The library on this corner will also offer assistance to the Buckeye Trail hiker. If you do not want to take Corduroy, take Willowbrook Drive back to Jordan. The community here is a 1950s development with basically the same house built over and over. Throughout the years, very few changes have been made to these homes.

From Jordan, at WP 9, the trail turns left onto Rambler Road. There will be sidewalk for part of the walk and then the trail is in the street. At Headlands (WP 10), turn right and walk east toward Headlands Beach State Park. This is a quiet street with easy walking and interesting homes and gardens. There are views of Lake Erie to the left. At the intersection of Jordan, Headlands becomes busier and hikers should be on the alert. Shortly, the trail will come upon the bike path. Follow this path down the hill to the maintenance driveway and return to the car. When this hike is planned, consider a side trip to the Wake Robin Trail, a hike into the marsh. From Morton Park, follow the blue blazes on Rosemary Lane to Corduroy. Turn left and, just before reaching the marsh, turn right on Woodridge Road. The Wake Robin Trailhead is at the end of this street. The boardwalk here crosses the marsh and is only one-third mile long. There are good overlooks of the marsh along the trail that may be enjoyed by small children and the physically challenged. Large birds, like hawks and turkey vultures, soar over the marsh here. Signs of beaver are abundant. When you have made the round trip on the Wake Robin Trail, you may choose to visit the Newhouse Overlook, just west on Woodridge Road.

FEATURED HIKE 2
MOGADORE RESERVOIR

> **DISTANCE** Two hikes: the western hike is 4 miles (out and back), the eastern is 2 miles (out and back).
>
> **TIME** 2 hours for the westerly hike and 1 hour for the easterly hike
>
> **DIFFICULTY** Moderately easy. Wooded trail on service road and wooded trail on footpath.

A dam built in 1939 to impound the waters of the Little Cuyahoga River formed Mogadore Reservoir. One of the purposes for the dam was to deliver cooling water to Akron's rubber factories. The dam still provides flood protection for Akron's east side as well as industrial (nonpotable)

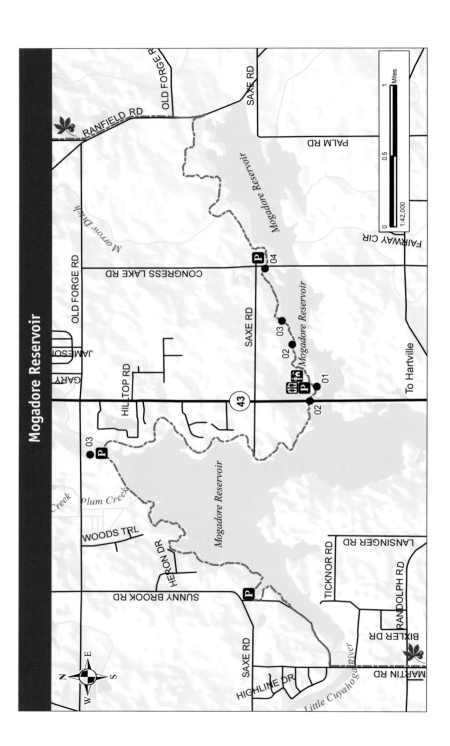

Mogadore Reservoir

water. The Buckeye Trail passes through native and planted forests interspersed with brightly flowered meadows. I talked to a local fisherman, who explained that by using a fish finder from his boat he can see roads, bridges, and even silos that were covered in 1939 by the rising waters of the Little Cuyahoga River.

The trailhead for this hike is on SR 43 at the marina for Mogadore Reservoir. This can be reached from SR 224, east of Akron and going north on SR 43. If you are using two cars, there is occasional parking on Old Forge Road at a fisherman's access road and also on Congress Lake Road at the causeway.

On the east side of SR 43 and the north side of the lake is a maintained parking area with facilities that include toilets, a boat dock with canoe rentals, and a park ranger station. The BT is routed both east and west of this parking area (WP 1). Hiking east from the parking lot you will find a glacial esker (a pronounced ridge of glacial gravel) between Congress Lake and Ranfield Roads and you will also see a number of beautiful granite erratics that the glaciers brought from Canada.

WESTERN HIKE

To begin the westerly hike, cross SR 43 (WP 2) and follow the service road. The Buckeye Trail immediately diverts onto a footpath that follows close to the water, but the path is very narrow and, in the spring, choked with poison ivy. The service road meanders through hardwood forest and then in open lake view fields. It is kept well mowed and brush hogged.

Some of the maintenance is done by a local high school cross-country squad that uses this road for practice. Be prepared to hear and see flickers and song sparrows. The eastern (rufous-sided) towhee will be scratching at the roadsides. The song sparrow will be serenading the walkers through the open fields.

As the trail meanders closer to the lake (fig. 10.7), there will be Canada geese and mallards floating along. Tundra swans also visit occasionally and may be seen from mid-March to early April. Of course in the spring, the lake and surrounding wooded areas offer resting spots for migrating warblers.

At WP 3 there will be a gate across an access road to a service road that exits on Old Forge Road, where there is occasional parking for hikers, joggers, and fisher people. The Buckeye Trail will continue skirting the north side of the lake until it leaves the lake, at Martin Road. There are 3 more miles of hiking on service road and footpath between WP 3 and Sunnybrook Road.

Figure 10.7 Mogadore Reservoir

EASTERN HIKE

The eastern hike also begins at the marina (WP 1) at the northeastern section of parking lot. See a metal fence and blue blazes. You will be following the blue blazes throughout this hike. As soon as you start the hike, note the turn blaze. The double blazes show the direction of the turn, with the top blaze pointing in the correct direction. In this case, the trail stays right and follows the macadam roadway.

At the next intersection, the trail follows a path going straight ahead. Then it turns left and continues to follow the blue blazes. The low areas on this hike have been improved with some board walkways and, farther along, concrete blocks have been laid down.

At WP 2 the trail makes a right turn and follows the blue blazes. After ascending from a low area, the trail bears to the left. It will follow a knife ridge with a low marshy area on the left and the lake on the right. This is easy walking and interesting terrain.

Just after leaving this nice wide walk, the footpath narrows and the maintainers have posted a metal sign that says, Poison ivy everywhere. At WP 3 the trail again intersects with a wider trail and continues straight ahead. After crossing a wooden footbridge, there is a turn blaze, showing that the trail bears right. The trail reaches Congress Lake Road (WP 4) in 1 mile. At Congress Lake Road, parking is available south from the trail toward the lake. The marshy areas along the road play host to many different species of waterfowl. There is another mile of blazed trail from Congress Lake Road to Ranfield Road.

FEATURED HIKE 3
QUAIL HOLLOW STATE PARK

DISTANCE The described hike is 2 miles. Quail Hollow has 13 miles of trail, 2.5 miles of which coincides with the BT.

TIME Less than 2 hours.

DIFFICULTY Easy.

Quail Hollow, dedicated in 1975, is one of our newest state parks. The park entrance is north of Hartville on Congress Lake Road. To reach Hartville, take Exit 118 on I-77 and drive north on SR 241 to SR 619. Turn right (east) to Hartville. Stay on SR 619 to the traffic light at Congress Lake Road and SR 43 South. Turn north on Congress Lake Road to Quail Hollow State Park.

The park road leads through woodlands to the centerpiece of the park, Stewart Manor House (see fig. 10.4). H. B. Stewart and his wife built this vast home, reflecting both Greek Revival and Federal influences, between 1914 and 1929. The 40 rooms include 8 bedrooms with fireplaces, a main bedroom with popular clothing of the period, and a children's bedroom with vintage toys. At a visitor center in the manor, trail maps can be obtained and tours arranged. In the summer there are maps in boxes along the trail. There is a small parking lot at the manor. If that is full, use the lot at the pond and Shady Lane Picnic Area (drive back on the entrance road a quarter mile and turn right). The manor and surrounding gardens are wheelchair accessible and a tour is recommended. If the visitor center and nature center are open, be sure to visit before your hike for brochures and maps.

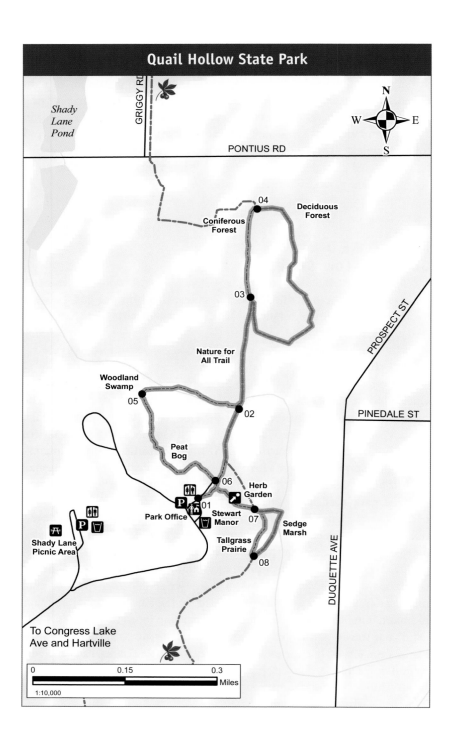

Quail Hollow State Park

Shady Lane Pond

GRIGGY RD

PONTIUS RD

N
W E
S

04
Deciduous Forest
Coniferous Forest

03

PROSPECT ST

Nature for All Trail

PINEDALE ST

Woodland Swamp

05

02

Peat Bog

06
Herb Garden

P
01
Park Office
Stewart Manor
07
Sedge Marsh

DUQUETTE AVE

P

Shady Lane Picnic Area

Tallgrass Prairie

08

To Congress Lake Ave and Hartville

0   0.15   0.3
Miles
1:10,000

Begin the 1-mile hike on the north side of the main house at the Nature for All Trail. This 2,000-foot paved interpretive trail is designed for visitors who are physically challenged or for those unable to hike long distances or over rough surfaces. Begin the hike at the parking area (WP 1) and start walking on the paved Nature for All Trail.

In summer or early fall apply insect repellent for the mosquitoes and deer flies that are abundant. The Buckeye Trail will be accessed on the Nature for All Trail. As you begin the hike, you will pass by a stone archway to a formal garden. We will explore the garden later in the hike.

Follow the blue blazes straight north to the Deciduous Forest Trail, which leads off to the right (WP 3). Do not take any of the side trails; we will visit them later in the hike. In the deciduous forest, you will be seeing older forest trees, mostly hardwoods. As the trail meanders among their stalwart ranks, this appears to be a virgin forest. Actually, it is in late succession, still recovering from land previously farmed in the 1800s and early 1900s. The blue blazes will lead the way through this mature woods.

Early morning and dusk are good times to hear or see the owls prevalent at Quail Hollow. As large as our largest hawks, these voracious predators hunt in the severest winter weather. Dead trees and logs, providing dens for the many animals that otherwise would have no home, are deliberately left in this part of the park. Evidence that the forest is growing older is the return of the pileated woodpecker. This huge bird was extirpated from the area until recently. Listen for its loud kuk-kuk-kuk call.

At WP 4 the BT heads north on a well-defined service road to leave Quail Hollow Park. You will turn left and walk through a coniferous forest. The conifers sigh in the wind, lending tranquility to serpentine walks along the pine needle–strewn trail. This trail returns directly to the Nature for All Trail. Continue on and notice that you have rejoined the BT. You have made a loop. Notice the conifers on your right and the deciduous trees on your left—two very different environments.

 At WP 2 turn right onto the Woodland Swamp Trail. While on this trail try to see, smell, and feel the dark wetlands that once covered much of this area. As in the Great Black Swamp (chap. 7), farmers have converted most of the swampy areas around Quail Hollow to more productive farmland. This vestige may be your best chance to see this part of Ohio as it was in earlier times. In the swamp you will find white pine—with its clusters of five needles—as well as maple, beech, and ash.

Look for the dark muck in the swamp that has made the Hartville area famous. This highly organic soil yields two or three crops per year. However, as mentioned above, this is the land that burns, so the mucks in fields used for agriculture must be constantly irrigated in dry summer weather. Of course, in the swamp the muck is usually under water.

Follow the Woodland Swamp Trail to the Peat Bog Trail and turn left (WP 5). As you walk up a kame, a hill composed of rock and silt deposited by a glacier, it becomes clear that this bog is a remnant of the Ice Age. On the other side of the kame is a kettle, a depression that forms the bog itself. A boardwalk meandering through the bog allows easy access. Peat deposits, which can be 30 feet deep, are composed of the remains of plants and animals, each layer containing the pollen grains of plants that lived long ago. These life forms decompose extremely slowly due to a lack of oxygen in the water. With enough heat, pressure, and centuries of time, coal is the final product. The mucks, mentioned earlier in the Overview, are drained peat bogs.

After leaving the Peat Bog Trail (WP 6), take a right on the Nature for All Trail (paved). Walk though the stone arch (fig. 10.8) and spend time at a recorded message that provides information about the formal garden ahead. It gives the background on the Quail Hollow Herb Society, which maintains and gives a guided tour of the Herb Garden. This garden is planted with many perennials and herbs, which are labeled. From the garden, walk to the southeast, where you will see another interpretive sign and benches (WP 7). Walk into the prairie area and bear to your left and follow the trail to the Sedge Marsh. A marsh is like a bog except that

Figure 10.8 Quail Hollow arch

mostly nonwoody (herbaceous) plants grow in it. Take a moment and look for the sedges. The sedge has sawlike edges you can feel as you carefully stroke the blades; early farmers would cut sedge for hay. The stems of sedges are typically three sided. Stop for a moment, find a sedge stem and touch their rough edges. Stay on the outskirts of the marsh area. There is a very inviting trail leading into the woods, but stay with the blue blazes.

Return to the manicured lawn and gardens of the manor by turning north through the tall-grass prairie at WP 8. Prairies were formed long ago during dry periods in Ohio. Later, during more frequent wet periods, the forests returned, but some prairie lands remained. The Quail Hollow prairie is usually burned off each spring, before the songbirds nest, in order to prevent the otherwise inevitable succession of invading trees. One plant found here is the wild purple coneflower. Native Americans found this native plant useful as an antibiotic, for treating cuts and burns. Cultivated purple coneflower has been planted around the manor.

If you want a longer hike, before you take the Tall-Grass Prairie Trail back to the herb garden, continue to the Meadowlands Trail and then the Beaver Lodge Trail, make a loop, and then return. If you take this longer hike, you will be hiking portions of the Buckeye Trail as it wends its way out of the park.

LOCAL CONTACTS

- Geauga Park District. www.geaugaparkdistrict.org.
- Lake Metroparks. www.lakemetroparks.com.
- Quail Hollow State Park. www.ohiodnr.gov.

WAYPOINT ID'S

WAYPOINT ID	DESCRIPTION	LATITUDE	LONGITUDE
	MENTOR MARSH		
1	Buckeye Trail kiosk	41.75976600	−81.28516300
2	Turn into parking Lot	41.75513800	−81.29276200
3	Service road at Headlands Rd	41.75245900	−81.29221800
4	Entrance to Zimmerman Trail	41.75198800	−81.29333200
5	Exclosure	41.73788500	−81.29883800
6	Morton Park	41.73830900	−81.30499300
7	Corduroy Rd at Rosemary Lane	41.73835000	−81.31129400

WAYPOINT ID	DESCRIPTION	LATITUDE	LONGITUDE
8	Corduroy Rd at Jordan Dr	41.74389100	−81.31098100
9	Jordan Dr at Rambler	41.74640300	−81.30184400
10	Rambler at Headlands Rd	41.74964300	−81.30130400
11	Fisherman's entrance	41.76027000	−81.28375300
12	Lake edge at light house	41.76595000	−81.28226500
MOGADORE			
3	Service road gate	41.08186300	−81.35410500
2	St Rt 43 at Park entrance	41.06007800	−81.34721000
1	Parking lot at Mogadore Marina	41.05933100	−81.34526400
2	Right turn toward lake	41.06172600	−81.33955300
3	Intersection with wide trail	41.06270500	−81.33630900
4	Congress Road	41.06434400	−81.32907400
QUAIL HOLLOW			
1	Parking lot at Stewart Manor	40.98015900	−81.30479200
2	Woodland Swamp Trail	40.98230800	−81.30349000
3	Deciduous Forest Trail to right	40.98504800	−81.30309300
4	Coniferous Forest Trail	40.98722600	−81.30285300
5	Woodland Swamp and Peat Bog	40.98274800	−81.30644000
6	Peat Bog Trail	40.98058200	−81.30424000
7	Kiosk	40.97989000	−81.30306300
8	Tall Grass Prairie	40.97874000	−81.30310600

Lake Country

BTA SECTION MAPS Massillon, Bowerston, Belle Valley.

COUNTIES TRAVERSED Stark, Tuscarawas, Carroll, Harrison, Guernsey, Noble.

DISTANCE COVERED 156 miles.

OVERVIEW

The village of Crystal Springs (Point 1 on the Overview map), at the southern end of the Little Loop (chaps. 9 and 10), is where this chapter begins. From Crystal Springs south, the Buckeye Trail follows the Ohio and Erie Canal Towpath Trail (fig. 11.1), part of the planned 110-mile

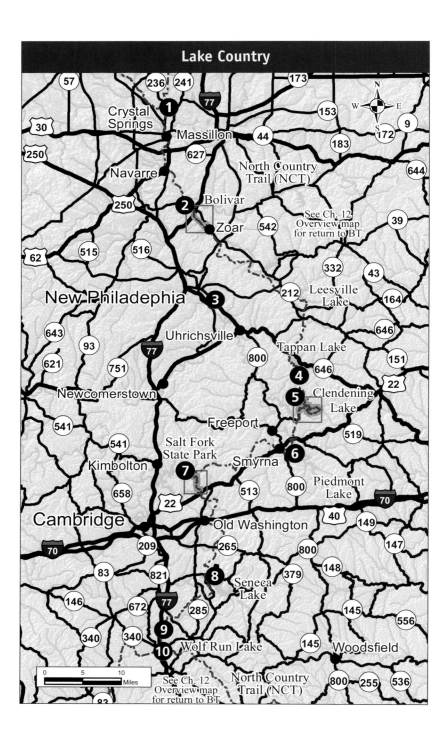

Lake Country

Figure 11.1 Ohio and Erie Canal Towpath Trail
(Andy "Captain Blue" Niekamp)

Ohio and Erie Canal National Heritage Corridor between Cleveland and New Philadelphia, Ohio. Excellent trailheads with portable toilets and horse trailer parking are located along the trail.

In 1825 the Ohio and Erie Canal opened up the lands of the Tuscarawas Valley to more settlers. Goods from the East and even from Europe began to make life easier. Products from local farms could now be shipped relatively cheaply to far-off places, selling for many times more than they were worth locally. For instance, crops grown in previously landlocked central Ohio ended up on tables in England. The canal also brought new ideas that conflicted with the provincialism of the early settlers, but most of these ideas brought the benefits that attend civilization.

The Buckeye Trail follows the OECTT into Massillon. A congregation of the Society of Friends (Quakers) first settled this lovely city in 1812. Principally due to their influence, the city was an important link for the Underground Railroad. Spring Hill Historic Home, built in 1821, is a premier UGRR site that can be seen in the summer.

The mural on First Street shows the city's intense pride in its football teams that came early to this city. The legendary Paul Brown, one of the many great coaches of Massillon Washington High School, is honored here. Paul Brown went on to coach at OSU and the Cleveland Browns and was an owner/coach of the Cincinnati Bengals.

The Republic Steel plant, south of the city, was built adjacent to the old canal. It was convenient to ship coal from southeastern Ohio to be turned into coke. The hot-burning coke was used to charge the furnaces and remove the impurities in the iron ore that was shipped via the canal from the north. Columbus limestone (used to promote the fusing of the metal molecules) was used as a flux in the furnaces and came from central Ohio via the canal.

The Buckeye Trail uses the OECTT to reach Navarre, where canal warehouses still stand. As you hike between Navarre and Bolivar on this trail, you will be traveling over a well-exposed portion of bedrock. This marks the edge of the glaciers that descended from Canada. There are glacial outwash areas as far south as Bolivar. You will discover such geological artifacts as moraines—long, narrow, low ridges with exposed bedrock. In river valleys, or where roads have cut through hillsides, layers of clay, sand, and gravel are revealed.

From the BT (on SR 212) as you enter Bolivar (Point 2), you will see the supports for what was a covered canal aqueduct. Aqueducts were used to lift boats over creeks and rivers, in this case the Tuscarawas. A modern railroad parallels the route of the old canal.

The Turkey Tribe, led by Chief Beaver, who was also called King Beaver, occupied one of the principal towns of the Delaware Nation. The site was east of Bolivar, between the Tuscarawas River and Sandy Creek, where it was known as Tuscarawas or Beaver's Town until 1763, when Chief Beaver moved to a site on the Hocking River. It consisted of some 3,000 acres of cleared ground, protected by 180 warriors, and was strategically located at the Great Crossing Place on the Tuscarawas for the Great Trail as well as other American Indian trails. Europeans lived here as early as 1761, when Moravian missionary Christian Post built a cabin along the river. More than a decade later, Fort Laurens (Point 2), where our first Featured Hike begins, was built there. It was the first and only Revolutionary War fort in Ohio.

Sandy Creek also provided a water source for the Sandy and Beaver Canal, which ran between the Ohio and Erie Canal at Bolivar and the Ohio River at Glasgow. This feeder canal was completed in 1848 to access the large markets in the East.

The North Country Trail (NCT) enters Ohio from Pennsylvania by way of Beaver Creek State Park, which is situated along the Great Trail. The NCT then joins the BT at Bolivar. The first Featured Hike, from Bolivar to Zoar, will follow the two trails where they first join from the east.

The NCT is a National Scenic Trail extending 4,000 miles, from Crown Point in New York to Lake Sakakawea State Park, North Dakota

Figure 11.2 NCT map

(fig. 11.2). At this point it joins the Lewis and Clark National Historic Trail on a water route via the lake. A National Scenic Trail is built specifically for foot travel, and not for use by motorized vehicles. Much of the 700 miles of the NCT in Ohio follows the Buckeye Trail and is maintained by BT volunteers (also see chap. 7).

As the blue blazes go south from Zoar (fig. 11.3), the hills become steeper, offering many scenic vistas. The higher ridges and deeper valleys are due, in part, to the absence of glacier action. Eastern Ohio was left relatively untouched by the huge ice sheets that covered the rest of the state. The convoluted landscape was caused by millions of years of erosion.

Figure 11.3 Zoar (Courtesy of Ohio History Connection)

The rocks and minerals found here, as well as the general profile of the land, are products of the Pennsylvanian Period. The landscape in the rest of Ohio is older because glaciers scraped away the substrata of the Pennsylvanian (see appendix 1).

Most of eastern Ohio's subsurface is composed of thick beds (miles deep) of sandstone, along with deposits of shale and clay. Rivers flowing from the north and east out of the Appalachian Mountains transported this material to Ohio during the Pennsylvanian. Common clay and shale from the many mines in Tuscarawas County are used to manufacture tiles, building brick, and sewer pipe. A special type of clay, fireclay, is used to make firebrick, foundry sand, and vitrified (glassy) sewer pipe. Coal deposits also formed during this period will be discussed in chapter 12.

Erosion of the land in the unglaciated portion of the state was caused mainly by flowing water. The deep river valleys of the region exaggerate the height of the surrounding hills. The tops of the hills do not often exceed 1,400 feet, not far off the average plateau elevation of 1,200 feet. The eroded valleys are around 600 feet above sea level. Of course, when walking this region you seem to be constantly walking uphill or downhill. Eastern Ohio is truly the foothills of the Appalachians.

The other main feature of this land is the abundance of lakes, most of them formed by dams built in the 1930s by the Muskingum Watershed Conservancy District (MWCD). The dams provide valuable flood control for the area's many valleys, and the lakes they create offer a myriad of recreational activities.

The Buckeye Trail in the East-Central Region skirts the shores of seven lakes. From north to south the lakes are Leesville, Tappan, Clendening, Piedmont, Salt Fork, Seneca, and Wolf Run. All are MWCD lakes except Salt Fork and Wolf Run, which are within the Ohio State Parks and are managed by the Ohio Department of Natural Resources. The Muskingum River lies far south of this area, although most of the watershed for the Muskingum is located here.

If you walk, bike, or drive the entire Buckeye Trail through this region of rolling hills, you will see many picturesque villages. You will come upon a variety of farms, most of the larger ones handed down from generation to generation. Sprinkled in with the natives are "hobby farmers" in new homes built on less acreage, most of whom commute fairly long distances to their jobs in more urban counties. The many independent small businesses include auto dealerships, oil- and gas-drilling suppliers, and sand and gravel quarries. Modern malls with their chain outlets seem far away from this land of lakes.

While near New Philadelphia (Point 3), plan to visit Schoenbrunn Village, an Ohio History Connection site (Point 3; fig. 11.4). Schoenbrunn was founded in 1772 as a Moravian mission village for the Delaware Indians. The Moravian missionaries believed in pacifism, striving to remain neutral in a world torn by strife between land-grabbing colonists and the Indian tribes. The Moravians also believed in recording their experiences on the frontier. From their diaries Schoenbrunn Village was reconstructed.

A great way to see Tappan Lake and other features of this part of the Lake Country is to follow the Tappan-Moravian Trail Scenic Byway (Point 4,). See Local Contacts for an auto tour map provided by the Ohio Department of Transportation. The Moravian Trail (now C-2 in Harrison County) was first used by Delaware and Wyandot Indians and early European settlers, when it was known as the Mingo Trail. The trail was later named for Moravian missionaries, who traveled it to establish the Christian Indian villages of Schoenbrunn, Gnadenhutten, and Salem.

The murderers of the Moravian Indians at Gnadenhutten (pronounced by locals as "Ja-NAY-den-hutten") also used the trail. In March 1782 militiamen from Pennsylvania came to the village to seek revenge on

Figure 11.4 Schoenbrunn (Courtesy of Ohio History Connection)

those (or whoever was handy who fit the description of Indian) who had kidnapped or killed some of their own. They rounded up the Christian Indians easily because the Delaware people believed that no harm could come from other Christians. In the end over 90 men, women, and children were horribly massacred.

The Moravian Trail became one of the major stagecoach routes in this area until the railroad bypassed historic Deersville and the ridge route of the trail. Places to see on the drive include the following:

- Tappan Lake—This low-horsepower fishing lake has 24 miles of shoreline, allowing a peaceful walk in the surrounding deep woods. Eaglets have been reported in the area recently.
- Feed Springs—Composed of a church, cemetery, schoolhouse, and the spring (on T-280), the village was once a popular stop for covered wagons traveling the Moravian Trail.
- Brownsville Church—The church was moved in 1941 when the village of Tappan made way for the reservoir. A restored log cabin sits at the intersection of C-2 and Franklin Township Road 280 (T-280), which is also called Eslick Road.
- Deersville—The general store reopened in 2014 and is renowned for ice cream. The BTA Century Barn is located on Tappan and near Deersville (fig. 11.5) This 19th-century barn was remodeled and is used as a hostel for hikers and a meeting space.
- Clendening Lake—The subject of Featured Hike 2 (Point 5).

Not on the BT, but just south of Clendening Lake, in the southwestern toe of Harrison County, is the village of Freeport. Founded by the Society of Friends in 1810, Freeport has a restored Quaker meetinghouse. Begin a tour of Freeport at the northeastern edge of town, on SR 800. You will see the following sites:

- The 1818 Greenmont Union Cemetery offers an impressive vista. Near the crest of the hill, on a huge rock between two pines, is a plaque inscribed with an 1881 poem dedicated to Freeport's Quaker settlers. Fifty-three pioneers rest in this cemetery. The 1817 Quaker Meeting House is found near the cemetery.
- Continuing east on Main Street, on the left-hand side, is a home made from a 1920 Sears Roebuck mail order kit (painted white the last time I saw it). The precut boards, labeled for efficient assembly, were delivered by railroad.

Figure 11.5 BTA Century Barn (BTA)

- Further down the street, still on the left side, is another former Society of Friends (Quaker) meetinghouse, which now contains a collection of vintage cars.
- At the intersection of SR 800 and SR 342 is an 1830s brick home that once served as the village hall. In 1990 it became the community's library.
- Turning South on SR 800, find the 1889 Freeport Lockup. This 148 x 168-foot one-room sandstone jail was used until 1937.

Return to the blue blazes at Piedmont Lake (Point 6). The blue blazes cross the dam, offering one of the most picturesque vistas in Ohio. From the west side of the dam the BT and the NCT enter MWCD property on a road that ends at the site of a historic Sea Scout (BSA) camp. The *SSS Hanna* resting upon the shores of Piedmont Lake was used as a training facility.

From Piedmont Lake the blue blazes pass through the small hillside village of Smyrna on U.S. 22. Less than 2 miles northwest of the village, on Covered Bridge Road (T-611), is the Skull Fork Covered Bridge (fig. 11.6). The bridge can also be reached by turning north off of U.S. 22 onto Skull Fork Road. North of the covered bridge on Skull Fork Road is an unusual hexagonal barn (built in 1921).

Figure 11.6 Skull Fork Covered Bridge (Andy "Captain Blue" Niekamp)

The next off-road section of the BT is in Salt Fork State Park and Wildlife Area (Point 7). This pristine, hilly area offers one of the best off-road hikes in Ohio (see Featured Hike 3). The impoundment for the lake was begun in 1967. The park is one of Ohio's fine resorts and offers a beautiful lodge with dining room, an 18-hole golf course, and 14 miles of hiking trails. The 17,000 acres abound with wildlife.

Old Washington lies on the BT's path, just south of Salt Fork Lake. Its location along U.S. 40, the old National Road (see chap. 6), makes it one of the oldest population centers in Ohio. In the historic district, which is on the National Register of Historic Places, you will see an unusually large number of antebellum buildings. The eastern portion of the National Road in Ohio was built on the former Zane's Trace (chap. 2).

Ten miles east of Old Washington, on U.S. 40, in Middlebourne, is the S-bridge at Bridgewater—one of several built on the National Road. Life must have been slower during the days of the National Road for traffic to negotiate its curves.

Old Washington was a station on the UGRR. Antislavery sentiment was especially strong in this area, and many residents served in the Civil War. Morgan's Raiders ran into a hornets' nest here as they headed north from the Ohio River after being turned back from the vital ford to Virginia (soon to become West Virginia) at Buffington Island, Ohio's only Civil War battlefield. On July 24, 1863, upon reaching Old Washington, the fleeing Rebels skirmished with Union militia. A stone in the local cemetery marks the graves of the three Confederates who lost their lives in the battle.

From I-70 the Buckeye Trail winds south to Seneca Lake (Point 8), the most southerly and largest of the MWCD lakes to be visited and the only one to be stocked with striped bass. The campground has a beach area, hot showers in modern restrooms, and a full-menu restaurant, open year round.

South of Seneca Lake and just north of Wolf Run State Park on the Buckeye Trail is a curious location for a memorial. On the almost impassible Shenandoah Road (T-112) is a granite monument (Point 9) marking the first of several crash sites of the *USS Shenandoah*, the world's first rigid airship kept aloft with nonflammable helium gas. Longer than two football fields, it required a crew of 41. The Shenandoah traveled coast to coast and was heralded as a great advance in air travel. In a 1925 flight many of the crew, including the captain, fell to their deaths near the village of Ava. The tragedy was caused by strong winds from thunderstorms common to the area. Because it broke into several pieces still buoyed by helium, there are several more monuments near where the other pieces finally fell. Across I-77 from the Shenandoah Road site, and just north of the Belle Valley exit, a memorial marked by an American flag can be seen from I-77, looking to the west. Local farmers, clinging to ropes dangling from the airship, captured one other piece near the village of Sharon. The surviving crewmembers jumped out to shoot the helium-filled bags with a shotgun to keep that piece on the ground.

Wolf Run State Park (Point 10) is at the headwaters of the Duck Creek watershed, which feeds into the Ohio River. Follow the blue blazes along the west side of Wolf Run Lake to enjoy a hike of approximately 2.5 miles. Wolf Run is a smaller version of undeveloped Clendening Lake. The family campground here has 138 nonelectric sites, and the public swimming beach provides restrooms and changing booths.

Most unusual is a primitive, fly-in camping area on the north side of the lake. The hillside campsite is within walking distance of the Noble County Airport, overlooking the clear waters of the park's lake. It is open only to fly-in campers, but reservations are not necessary.

Wolf Run Lake is named after an early pioneer family. Oil was discovered in 1814 by some of these early settlers drilling for brine. The well, south of Wolf Run Lake, at the junction of SR 78 and SR 564 near

Caldwell, is one of many touted to be the oldest oil well in North America and can still be viewed by the public. At Belle Valley the Buckeye Trail splits into two segments. The main loop heads westerly, toward Stockport, and the other section forms a 114-mile loop called the Marietta loop. The trails merge just east of Stockport.

FEATURED HIKE 1
FORT LAURENS TO ZOAR VILLAGE

> **DISTANCE** 6 miles for the round-trip. (The off-road trail between Fort Laurens and Zoar Bridge is 3 miles.)

> **TIME** At least 3 hours for the round-trip and an additional hour for touring Zoar Village.

> **DIFFICULTY** Moderately easy. Most of the trail is on flat towpath.

This hike begins and ends at Fort Laurens. From I-77, take SR 212 west into Bolivar at the Bolivar-Zoar exit 93. Fort Laurens is just south of Bolivar (and west of I-77) on County Road 102. Make sure you return to your car before the park closes.

Park your car and begin the hike at Fort Laurens State Memorial. Go to the far end of the park to find the trail.

As mentioned in the Overview, Bolivar and Fort Laurens were near the Great Trail, the American Indian trail connecting Pittsburgh and Detroit. During the American Revolution, an American expedition left Fort Pitt and followed the Great Trail to attack British-held Detroit. They halted for the winter and built the stockade known as Fort Laurens out of local timber.

During the winter of 1778–79, the American troops at Fort Laurens withstood a siege by British soldiers and their Indian allies that left 23 out of 176 dead. Notorious frontiersman Simon Girty (chap. 6) led the Indian allies of the British. The starving Americans boiled ox hides and their own moccasins for soup. The British thought they had won, but the shrewd American commander sent a barrel of flour out to the enemy to make him think there was plenty of food in the fort. The British thus delayed an all-out attack and American reinforcements saved the remaining garrison in March. In August the fort was abandoned, ending General Washington's plan to form a chain of bases to attack Detroit.

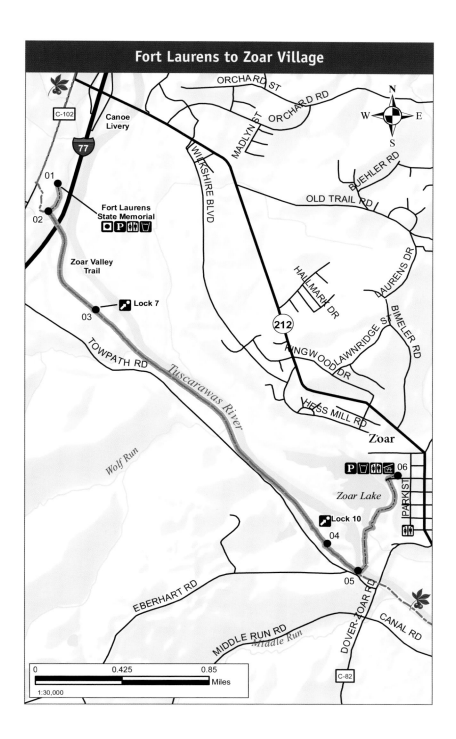

Fort Laurens to Zoar Village

ORCHARD ST
ORCHARD RD
MADLYN ST
C-102
Canoe
Livery
77
01
02
Fort Laurens
State Memorial
WILKSHIRE BLVD
BUEHLER RD
OLD TRAIL RD
Zoar Valley
Trail
LAURENS DR
HALLMARK DR
Lock 7
03
212
BIMELER RD
LAWNRIDGE ST
TOWPATH RD
Tuscarawas River
KINGWOOD DR
HESS MILL RD
Zoar
Wolf Run
P ▽ ♦♦ 🚻 06
PARK ST
Zoar Lake
Lock 10
04
♦♦
EBERHART RD
05
DOVER-ZOAR RD
CANAL RD
MIDDLE RUN RD
Middle Run

| 0 | 0.425 | 0.85 |
Miles
1:30,000
C-82

Now, only a shallow trench marks the shape of the original fort. A museum houses artifacts and the uniforms of soldiers who built the fort. An audio-visual program describes the Revolutionary War and the Fort Laurens campaign. Outside the museum is the Tomb of the Unknown Patriot of the American Revolution, one of the fort's fallen defenders. In the large park is a crypt with the remains of the soldiers who died defending the fort.

You will begin the hike on the Zoar Valley Trail (WP 1). The 17-mile ZVT connects Fort Laurens to Schoenbrunn Village, near New Philadelphia, with an overnight stop at the scout camp, Camp Tuscazoar. Leave Fort Laurens Park on an all-purpose trail and shortly you will intersect with the Buckeye Trail (WP 2) as it comes in from the west from C-102. The trail crosses I-77 on a fantastic pedestrian bridge and continues following the all-purpose trail. You will be on the Buckeye Trail, but because of the nature of the trail, few blue blazes will be seen. Note that the Ohio and Erie Canal prism is on your right and the Tuscarawas River (fig. 11.7) is on the left. As you follow the towpath, note the railroad mile markers. Often towpaths became railroads once the canals were abandoned.

Figure 11.7 Tuscarawas River along the towpath
(Andy "Captain Blue" Niekamp)

You will see the remains of four locks, each about 90 feet long, beginning with Lock 7 (WP 3). Each lock has interpretive signs that give canal history. Further down you will find a towpath footbridge used by the mules and their drivers, known as hoggees. Hoggees, usually children as young as 10, drove the mules, known as long-eared robins (WP 4). Drivers worked long hours in harsh weather and were often undernourished. Many hoggees did not live past 16. President James A. Garfield was one survivor. In 1848, when he was 17, he was said to have jumped a lock 15 feet wide to take on a lock tender who wouldn't let his boat through fast enough. He lost the errant official in a cornfield. (For more on canals and canal boats see chap. 6.)

At Waypoint 5 you reach the newly restored bridge over the Tuscarawas River. This is the end of the 3-mile hike. Retrace your hike to get back to your car. The Buckeye Trail continues south on the towpath. If you want to go into Zoar, climb the steps after crossing the bridge, turn left, and follow paths into Zoar. The trail follows an abandoned roadway and a stone fence. At the first intersection of a mowed path, the trail bears right along a concrete retainer wall. Zoar Lake is on your left and a swampy area is on the right. Next, take a trail to the left and parallel the levy. The levy protects Zoar from Tuscarawas River flooding. The trail you have just taken, brings you up a grade into the Zoar Wetland Arboretum. There is another side trail that would take you closer to the lake if you wish. You will see many interpretive signs explaining trees and shrubs. Walk through the arboretum and take a left as you reach the levy. Follow the mowed grass to a red gate and the picnic area. Leave the area up a grade on a gravel driveway, and when you reach Park Street, turn right and go into Zoar (WP 6).

German immigrants who founded Zoar built the locks in this area. They fled Germany to escape civil and religious persecution. Known as the Separatists for their belief in the separation of church and state, they were perhaps the most successful communal group in Ohio. The Zoarites were active from the early 1800s to the end of that century. But the canal brought its own problems, including a flood of new immigrants. Later cholera, a "wicked" tavern, and more visitors to the village spelled the end of communal life.

Zoar is now a restored village (fig. 11.3). Several original sites, such as Zoar Gardens and Number One House, are administered by Ohio History Connection. During the prosperous days, many of the houses in old Zoar were assigned a number to facilitate distribution of commodities. The village also features Zoar Tavern on Main Street and a modern convenience store just at the edge of town. The historic Zoar Store on Main Street is the place to stop for tours and information on Zoar.

If possible, take two cars on this hike. Spotting a car at Zoar and leaving from another car parked at Fort Laurens will allow you more time to visit Zoar Village at the end of the hike.

FEATURED HIKE 2
CLENDENING LAKE

DISTANCE It is 10 miles completely around the lake: 8 miles off road, 2 miles on SR 799 along a causeway.

TIME At least 7 hours, if you plan to walk around the lake.

DIFFICULTY Difficult, depending on current trail conditions. Open areas, particularly on the north side of the lake, support thorny brush. There are a number of elevation changes (100 to 200 feet) and at times steep climbs. Take hiking poles and prepare for numerous fords over small creeks.

The map also shows parking at the Division of Wildlife boat ramp on Koval Rd. This is an alternative parking site.

A nature lover's paradise, Clendening Lake is the largest undeveloped lake in Ohio, with 1,800 acres of surface area (fig. 11.8). The Muskingum Watershed Conservancy District has designated that the lake remain undeveloped, so you will not find accommodations like those at Salt Fork State Park, but you will enjoy more solitude. The 10-horsepower limit on motorized boats also makes it quieter. There are 80 campsites with electrical hookups at the marina off SR 799.

The surrounding hills offer fabulous views of this pristine lake year round. Great fall colors are assured from hills covered with a variety of hardwoods. Larger animals found in the forest include deer, beaver, and an occasional bear or bobcat. Many types of ducks and other waterfowl are viewed on the lake and along the lakeshore.

To begin the hike, park along the causeway on SR 799, just south of where Long Road (T-305) intersects with SR 799. This point is about 3 miles south of Deersville. The entrance to the wooded area is at the northeast corner of this intersection (WP 1). The Buckeye Trail follows Long Road and Adams Road from Deersville. If you are using two cars,

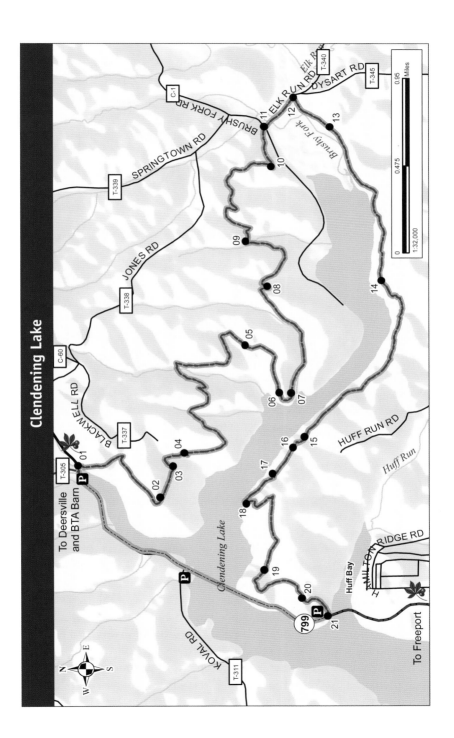

Clendening Lake

Figure 11.8 Clendening Lake

park the second car on SR 799 just north of Huff Bay where the Buckeye Trail exits the woods and turns south on SR 799 (WP 21. There is much casual parking in this area as this is a popular fishing spot.

The trail enters mature woodland and immediately makes a 50-foot ascent. As you begin the ascent, take a good look at the water because this is the last you will see until you have gone 3 miles into this hike. At the top of this ridge, the trail will quickly level out and then drop to the first ford. All the wet areas on the north side of the lake are easily crossed. After this crossing, begin a 140-foot climb gently meandering up the ridge. At the top of the ridge, you will find that a kindly soul has provided a bench (WP 2) dedicated to the Buckeye Trail. This is the time to take a rest and note that you have hiked one-half mile.

Next the trail goes down with switchbacks (WP 3), but more slowly than the ascent. At the bottom (WP 4), you will encounter an old logging or oil service road. Be prepared to make a turn to the left and begin ascending. Note the double blazes that indicate the turn to the left. The ground pine that was discussed in chapter 3 at Davis Memorial is seen here in three distinct swaths about 50 feet apart. After 1 mile you will have climbed three ridges, each climb about 100 feet. The next mile includes two more creek crossings and two more ridges to climb. Just before the 2-mile point, there is a stream crossing. Here, the mature woodland has been replaced by very young growth and shrubs. This area has been logged by a method called clear-cutting. This is the cutting of all vegetation to more easily harvest larger trees. An advantage of clear-cutting that is harder to understand, is that many different species—both flora and fauna—proliferate in cleared areas that in earlier times were naturally cleared by fires. The disadvantage of clear cutting is that the resultant shambles is ugly. And, of course, with the removal of the trees, keeping undergrowth away from the trail is very difficult.

But, just as you might be displeased with this section of the hike, you will shortly encounter a scenic wooded area (WP 5) with very large maple and beech trees. This is a woodlot that should be located on an old estate. It is as though the area has been manicured. You will stand in awe as you feel you can see forever. In the fall, the floor is carpeted in yellow maple leaves and there is a golden radiance. A bit further on, there is more undergrowth, with the habitat becoming far more turkey friendly. You may see the feathered friends or hear them calling.

Related to grouse and pheasants, turkeys are natives of the United States, and their fossils date back to the Oligocene epoch, from 34 to 23 million years ago, when cats and dogs began their evolution. Although such a large bird would appear earthbound, it rises into the sky almost as quickly as a pheasant. The turkey's keen eyesight and quick instincts make it difficult to spot. The best time to see one is in early spring, while they are breeding; but, for safety, go before turkey-hunting season begins, at the end of April. Sitting quietly for an hour or two might produce better results than hiking continuously through the area. Push-button turkey callers are available that will help you coax the birds in. Try to identify the long-bearded gobbler, the year-old male jakes, or the female hens. And remember, hearing the gobble from afar is as thrilling as seeing the gobbler. These birds were extirpated from Ohio by the early 1900s, but in the 1950s the Ohio Division of Wildlife began an aggressive relocation program. Now thousands of wild turkeys may be found in 72 of Ohio's 88 counties.

Finally, at WP 6, 2.5 miles into the hike, you will come close enough to the edge of Clendening Lake to see some distant views. At WP 7 you will pass by foundation stones perhaps from abandoned fishing camps.

Three miles into the hike, you will encounter another logging road. Be alert to an immediate turn left from this road and begin a descent down to a creek. After crossing the creek there is a rather sharp climb and the woods open to allow greenbrier and multiflora rose to proliferate. Unfortunately, the multiflora which was used in the 1940s and 1950s as a "natural" livestock containment system and imported from Japan has escaped the farm confines and has overtaken habitat of native species. This plant is considered a noxious invasive species in Ohio. The Buckeye Trail crew has serious problems trying to keep it from over taking trails.

At WP 8 there is a hard turn to the left from a service road onto a footpath. Whenever the trail is on a service road, it is important to keep a watchful eye on the blue blazes. Missing a turn onto a footpath can make a much longer hike. At WP 9 there is another creek crossing and then a very sharp climb. There are many butternut and hickory trees along the way. Then, the woodland opens up and the greenbrier and wild rose have proliferated. Wild rose was introduced by the U.S. Department of Agriculture in the 1930s to mitigate erosion and as domestic livestock containment. It has also become an invasive species and is quite difficult to eradicate. At WP 10 there is a switchback on the trail with a slight descent. At this point, it is 4.3 miles into the hike.

At WP 11, 4.5 miles into the hike, you will leave the woods at the intersection of Elk Run Road and Brushy Fork Road. Walk the road across the bridge for Brushy Fork Creek, the lake's headwaters. Brushy Fork was dammed in 1933 and it is reported that a village was flooded and remnants of buildings are still found under the water. As you walk the lake's edge on the next part of the hike, you will find ruins of foundations. Are they abandoned lake cottages, or maybe the scars of a flooded village? As you walk this short section of gravel road, you can see and hear a variety of diving ducks in spring and fall, and several species of warbler throughout the summer.

At WP 12 enter the next off-road portion of the hike. The Buckeye Trail follows an abandoned road that volunteers try to keep mowed. The road follows the marshy areas next to Brushy Fork and there is a slight rise to the trail. At WP 13 encounter a wet area that has a bridge and abutments. The bridge is so low that even in dry times, there could be damp boots. Walking sticks will help here as you maneuver the wetness. The broad leaves of the skunk cabbage are seen in low areas that stay wet most of the year.

Shortly after 5 miles into the hike, the trail will go up into the woods. This higher trail is dryer and it is pleasant walking with the lake views off to the right. It is quite apparent that four-wheelers are using this trail. Whenever the trail narrows because of downed trees, the four-wheelers have made a new path around the obstruction. There will be a couple of stream crossings on this side of the lake but they are not deep.

At 6 miles you will encounter a pine forest (WP 14). These are refor-estation projects from more than 60 years ago. After the pine forest, keep your eye out for a sharp turn to the left. After this, you will encounter a couple of short ups and downs to creekbeds. These are minor crossings and will not present problems with wet boots. You will encounter more abandoned roads. When you are walking trail on abandoned road, it is easy to become lulled into complacency and not notice turns from the road onto more narrow paths. Always make sure you are following the blue blazes.

At WP 15 there is an opening between two wooded areas and a rest-ing place for a metal boat (fig. 11.9). This old treasure has been the talk of hikers for the many years that the Buckeye Trail has traveled here. After the boat, the trail is wooded again and follows the easy tread of aban-doned road. Just before WP 16, at 6.5 miles, the trail will take a sharp turn to the left, but the road will continue down to the lake. You will pass aban-doned building sites with sandstone foundations strewn about. The

Figure 11.9 Rowboat at Clendening Lake
(Andy "Captain Blue" Niekamp)

sandstone outcroppings are abundant. The builders did not have to go far to get their building materials.

The next turn is rather tricky. From the footpath, at WP 17, the trail encounters an abandoned road and a large area of downed trees. Follow the road to the right and in 50 yards, make a right onto another footpath. There is blazing on a tree and a survey post that has a blue blaze. This portion of the hike is again, very close to the lake. Be ever vigilant for the elusive *Homo sapiens* fishing out on the lake.

At WP 18 the trail begins a sharp ascent to the top of the ridge. There are four switchbacks that will help during the 200-foot climb. After the switchbacks, the trail encounters another old roadbed. Follow the blue blazes to the right. The fascination of hiking near a lake is being able to see the water. High on this ridge, during summer, you will catch only silver glimmers through the leaves. You must be here in late fall, early spring, or winter to get the best views. The road the trail is following gradually becomes a footpath that will then meet another roadbed. Be prepared to make an immediate left from this road onto a footpath (WP 19). At WP 20, 7.5 miles into the hike, the trail enters a pine forest and immediately descends to Huff Bay. Now, the water will be on your left. When you encounter SR 799, either find you car or begin the 2-mile hike back to your car parked near Long Road (T-305).

FEATURED HIKE 3
SALT FORK STATE PARK

DISTANCE 3 miles out and back.

TIME 2 or 3 hours.

DIFFICULTY Moderately difficult due to 200-foot elevation changes.

Park your car at the Salt Fork primitive camping area. The campground is located on Parker Road (T-587), off U.S. 22 and just east of the main entrance to Salt Fork. This is a group campground and the gate may be closed if groups have not registered to use the campground. Individual hikers on the BT may contact the Park Office to obtain permission to camp. Day hikers may park off to the side of the entrance driveway to the campground if the gate is locked.

If you are using two cars, park the second car on Park Road 55. To get there, take Parker Road until it intersects with Gunn Road. Turn left on

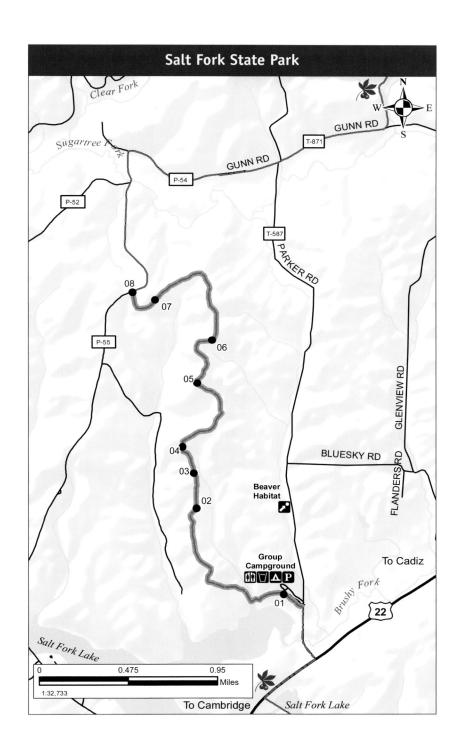

Gunn (P-54), following the blue blazes, and then left on Park Road 55, cross the bridge over Sugartree Fork, and go up the hill. Watch for the blue blazes on P-55 and note where they enter the woods on the left side of the road. You may park off the road here.

Please note that you will be hiking in a wildlife hunting area. It is dangerous to hike during hunting season, especially during shotgun season for deer. Contact information for Ohio's Division of Wildlife is at the end of chapter 1.

In case you are a hiker prone to complain about hunters, be aware that they provide us with green space. The habitat you will hike through is maintained by the Ohio Division of Wildlife, which is funded by revenues from hunting and fishing licenses. Since 1990 the division has acquired almost 60,000 acres of reclaimed strip-mine land. This land will be used by hikers many more months of the year than by hunters. Active BTA members learn quickly that it "takes a village" to protect our environment.

Beginning at the campsite (WP 1), follow the blue blazes to the west through a wetland area, past an open meadow, and then into a wooded area on a well-defined state fire trail. In spring and early summer, the wetland's frog and toad denizens will greet you if you quietly walk past. The fire trail is a gradually undulating roadway with mostly wooded areas and a couple of open meadows. The meadows offer the most variety in bird life. Look and listen for the field sparrows and the eastern goldfinches (commonly called yellow canaries). The red-winged blackbirds will be plentiful, particularly as you leave the wetland. During summer months, take time to look at the edges of the meadow for blackberries and raspberries. You don't need a hunting license to search for these treasures.

The trail is continually climbing into the wooded lands above lake level. Pileated woodpeckers will often make themselves heard and, in the fall, the chipmunks will be chattering and scurrying about. Blue jays will scream at you for disturbing their quiet. The woods are mature deciduous trees, mostly maple, oak, tulip (yellow poplar), and beech. All of the forest is second growth, as the land surrounding Salt Fork was heavily lumbered and then farmed, before the conservation efforts begun in the 1940s. At WP 2 you have walked 1 mile on a wide shaded service path and are about ready to begin a significant climb. At WP 3 bear right on the clearly marked Buckeye Trail and begin climbing a steep roadbed to reach Devils Knob. On your way up, listen for the gobble of the American turkey. This bird has made a remarkable recovery from extirpation and is hunted in these woods in the spring.

When you reach the summit of Devils Knob (WP 4), you are ready for a deserved rest. Take time and look out over the woodland. You will be able to see great distances from this vantage point. Except for the last couple hundred feet, you may not have noticed how far you have climbed on the hike. At WP 5 the altitude is 1,112 feet above sea level and the trail has climbed 470 feet. The trail continues northerly along a ridge with remnants of homesteads (WP 6). Shortly after WP 6 walk through a reforestation of pine. The eastern (rufous-sided) towhee is often rustling the leaves at the road's edge. The woods will then abruptly turn from pine to deciduous. At WP 7 the trail will leave the woods and skirt the right edge of an open grassy area. The scrubby growth, on the edges of the meadow, does not offer much in the way of trees to paint blazes on. Shortly, you will bear right at a Game Break. A Game Break is an area maintained by the Division of Wildlife to gain access to their properties. The Buckeye Trail leaves via the Game Break to P-55. If you are using two cars for this hike, you may park a car near this entrance.

If you drive on Parker Road, note the ponds on the west side of the road. This area is noted for beaver activity and they have created ponds along the many creeks.

The search for beaver was a major economic reason for exploring and settling this wild continent. It was all about hats—but not hats that merely keep us warm. The fine inner fur of the beaver pelt was easily turned into felt for the finest top hats. Early New England settlers and French traders in the interior exchanged manufactured items such as blankets, beads, iron pots, and axes for pelts harvested by American Indians. The pelts were then sold to European mercantile firms. Steel axes, traps, and bullets were too much for the beaver population. Indian tribes often fought over the rights to hunt beaver. The Beaver Wars resulted in many deaths, making it easier for the Europeans later to extirpate the American Indian from the Ohio Country.

As you are leaving the Salt Fork area, look for osprey nests along U.S. 22, east of the entrance to Salt Fork State Park. Like the beaver, the osprey has recovered recently due to the ban on DDT as well as other conservation programs. These large raptors, with a wingspan of 5 to 6 feet, live on every continent except Antarctica. Ospreys catch fish by either diving in the water or simply snatching them from the surface. Osprey nests, usually built in snags or trees over water, can be identified by the large platforms they construct of sticks, sod, and wetland material. Often called fish eagles or fish hawks (they actually are hawks), ospreys migrate south in winter, some as far as South America. Thus some of the ospreys you see in spring and fall may be just passing through.

LOCAL CONTACTS

- Fort Laurens State Memorial. www.ohiohistory.org.
- Ohio and Erie Canalway Coalition . www.eriecanalway.org
- North Country Trail Association. www.northcountrytrail.org.
- Ohio Department of Transportation. www.dot.state.oh.us/ OhioByways.
- Salt Fork State Park. http://parks.ohiodnr.gov/saltfork.
- Schoenbrunn Village Historic Site. www.ohiohistory.org
- Wolf Run State Park. http://parks.ohiodnr.gov/wolfrun.
- Zoar Village Historic Site. www.ohiohistory.org.

WAYPOINT ID'S

WAYPOINT ID	DESCRIPTION	LATITUDE	LONGITUDE
FORT LAURENS TO ZOAR			
1	Fort Laurens	40.63717100	−81.45610800
2	Junction ZVT and Buckeye Trail	40.63522000	−81.45678200
3	Lock 7	40.62780400	−81.45270100
4	Lock 10	40.61060400	−81.43141900
5	Bridge over Tuscarawas River	40.60859700	−81.42860600
6	Picnic shelter at Zoar Arboretum	40.61556400	−81.42482300
CLENDENING LAKE			
1	North trail at SR 799	40.26559600	−81.18685500
2	Bench on top of ridge	40.25946700	−81.19018600
3	Switchbacks	40.25844200	−81.18708600
4	Logging/service road	40.25758000	−81.18574400
5	Scenic woodland	40.25285700	−81.17495300
6	2.5 miles lake views	40.25033000	−81.17980900
7	Foundations	40.24945300	−81.17984500
8	Left off logging road	40.25109000	−81.16893600
9	Creek crossing - sharp climb	40.25269100	−81.16429700
10	4.3 miles into hike	40.25065500	−81.15662000

WAYPOINT ID	DESCRIPTION	LATITUDE	LONGITUDE
11	Brushy Fork Rd	40.25116400	−81.15247400
12	Elk Run Rd	40.24891200	−81.14957700
13	Concrete bridge	40.24620600	−81.15262300
14	6 miles	40.24249700	−81.16852500
15	Metal boat	40.24851900	−81.18433400
16	6.5 miles	40.24936700	−81.18538200
17	Tricky turn to right	40.25093400	−81.18799600
18	Steep climb	40.25295800	−81.19097800
19	Footpath to road bed	40.25171900	−81.19769700
20	Descent to Huff Bay	40.24890900	−81.20061100
21	SR 799 southern entrance	40.24698300	−81.20247900
SALT FORK			
1	Campground	40.09726300	−81.44710900
2	Fire Trail 1 mile point	40.10402400	−81.45564200
3	Steep climb	40.10675800	−81.45588400
4	Devils Knob	40.10874500	−81.45699100
5	Top of the ridge	40.11390800	−81.45540100
6	Foundation stones	40.11735400	−81.45413200
7	Open grassy area	40.12042200	−81.45975800
8	Game Break	40.12139400	−81.46169700

Hill Country

TOLEDO

CLEVELAND

OHIO TURNPIKE

I-90

I-80/90

I-80

I-80

I-76

AKRON

CANTON

I-75

I-71

I-77

PIQUA

COLUMBUS

CAMBRIDGE

DAYTON

I-70

ZANESVILLE

I-70

I-71

US 23

US 33

I-77

MARIETTA

CINCINNATI

PORTSMOUTH

BTA SECTION MAPS Stockport, New Straitsville, Road Fork, Whipple.

COUNTIES TRAVERSED Noble, Washington, Morgan, Athens, Perry.

DISTANCE COVERED 224 miles.

OVERVIEW

The BT takes you south from the northern perimeter of the American Electric Power's ReCreation Land (Point 1 on the Overview Map and site of the first Featured Hike, fig. 12.1) on a combination of off-road trails and township roads. The foothills of the Appalachian Mountains offer the hiker or cyclist great exercise and superb vistas. The Hill Country was one of the first sections of Ohio to have been settled, but it is

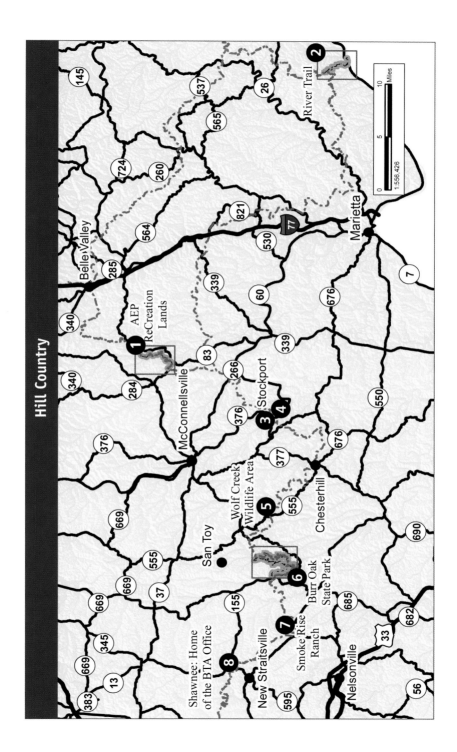

Hill Country

Figure 12.1 Buckeye Trail in AEP's ReCreation Land
(Andy "Captain Blue" Niekamp)

relatively unpopulated today. Large cities or major industries are nonexistent, and the natural areas that are no longer mined are returning to their pristine state.

Southeastern Ohio is part of the unglaciated Allegheny Plateau. The bedrock is of the Pennsylvanian Period (see chap. 11 and appendix 1). During the Pennsylvanian, Ohio was near the equator, with a climate similar to that of present-day Central America! As a result of that orientation, a flat and swampy forest covered all of Ohio, where rainforest vegetation abounded and giant insects roved the skies in search of prey. Periodically the swamp water rose and fell, burying plants and animals under a silt of sand and clay, which sealed their remains from decay. Over the span of 35 million years the rising and falling water created huge coal deposits.

The coal deposits have been a mixed blessing: environmental problems plague the region today. During the 1800s plentiful resources of timber, coal, clay, and oil were harvested from the land. In the early 1900s one of the world's largest coal-mining operations was located in southeastern Ohio. By the 1970s most of the mines were closed. Before serious government cleanup regulations were initiated in 1972, gob piles (waste from mining operations) covered the soil and leached into watersheds. The result was polluted rivers and streams, depleted forests (with subsequent erosion), and ghost towns like San Toy (see below).

Today, in spite of environmental problems and sparse population, the natives of this region are optimistic. They see opportunity in attracting tourists to the magnificent forests and waterways of southeastern Ohio. Cleanup efforts are already in place. A strong tourist industry, with local people acting as tour guides and support staff, will provide an economic boost so that the people here will no longer need to randomly log the forests for a living.

If you are looking for coal mines in this region today, you will not see mine shafts burrowed deep in the ground. You will instead see strip mines, large trenches in the land from which coal is stripped. There are strip mines near the BT, and the trail must be relocated when a mining operation moves across it. Although strip mining causes an enormous impact to the environment, the American Electric Power Company reclaims its mines by planting trees and building lakes, ponds, and campsites. As you travel this region you will see active, inactive, and reclaimed strip mines. (Longwall mining is becoming more common in eastern and southeastern Ohio since the 1990s. This form of underground mining, in which coal is taken from a face up to 1,100 feet across and 3 miles deep, does not require the removal of overburden, or land on the surface).

Ten years ago, the Buckeye Trail created a second loop trail, similar to the Little Loop in northern Ohio. This second loop begins at Belle Valley, winds south to Wayne National Forest, where it follows the North Country Trail, and then turns north to intersect the Big Loop of the Buckeye Trail at the southern edge of the AEP recreation lands. It is called the Marietta Loop and is mapped with two maps, Whipple and Road Fork. This loop adds 114 miles of trail to the BT, with 33 miles off-road in the Wayne National Forest. In the forest, the trail goes through campgrounds such as that at Ring Mill. At this site, the sandstone building, dating from the mid-1800s, was the mill owner's home and is listed on the National Register of Historic Places (fig. 12.2). The remaining 80 miles follow little-used township and county roads. The largest town encountered is Whipple, with fewer than 1,000 residents.

The Wayne National Forest is the only national forest in Ohio, and it showcases some of the finest hardwood trees in North America, but it was not always so. Most of the forest in this area was removed in the 1800s. The Wayne was created in the 1930s so that the government could acquire barren and eroded land abandoned by the hill farmers. The renewed

Figure 12.2 Ring Mill (Andy "Captain Blue" Niekamp)

forest covers about 210,000 acres. Special Areas are identified and protected in the Wayne. They include remnant tallgrass prairies, wetlands,
and older-growth forests. The second Featured Hike is the Scenic River
Trail (Point 2), from deep in the forest down to the edge of the Ohio river.

National forests usually contain a good deal of private property (80
percent of the Wayne is private). Please be careful not to trespass on private lands. The U.S. Forest Service is chiefly concerned with timber management (especially reforestation), watersheds (often polluted by acid
mine drainage), maintenance of present forests, and fire control. All
national forest lands are available for primitive camping (dispersed camping is permitted), hiking, hunting, and fishing.

The Buckeye Trail has been traversing the huge Muskingum watershed since Barberton, more than 300 miles to the north (almost 400 trail
miles), but it does not cross the Muskingum River until it reaches Stockport. The Muskingum is one of Ohio's longest and widest rivers. The
name was taken from the Delaware *moos-kin-gung* (elk eye river). There
once were elk (*moos*) in the Ohio Country.

Draining 20 percent of the state, the Muskingum was important to
the first settlers. Marietta, the first permanent settlement in Ohio, was

established in 1788 across the river from Fort Harmar, at the junction of the Muskingum and Ohio Rivers.

The BT crosses the Muskingum at Lock 6 (Point 3) and passes the Stockport Mill (fig. 12.3). The 10 locks along the river are the only functioning hand-operated locks in the nation. They have been in use since 1841 and served an active steamboat trade as recently as 1913. The gates are made of Douglas fir from Washington state and weigh 33,000 pounds each. Nevertheless, two people, each pushing a lever to turn cogs (for mechanical advantage), can move them. From SR 266 you will see Lock 6 and the falls it creates. The falls are spectacular during high-water periods in the spring.

The BT continues through the picturesque village of Stockport, so named because it was a major port for shipping cattle down the Muskingum. For a short hike through part of the village, follow the BT across the lock. Turn left almost immediately onto County Road 2. Following the blue blazes along C-2 and Salt Works Hill Road (T-23) will lead you uphill to a dissected plateau—a plateau cut into ridges, in this case, by erosion rather than glaciation. The view of the village below is well worth the hike or drive. Return to the village and walk down the old

Figure 12.3 Stockport Mill (Richard Lutz)

tree-lined, brick Main Street. You will see a dozen buildings built before 1850. The current four-story feed mill, at the Muskingum River, was built in 1907, replacing a mill built as early as 1849. In the mill is a popular bed-and-breakfast with a restaurant.

Drive 1 mile southeast of Stockport, along SR 266, to Big Bottom State Memorial Park (Point 4). This park on the Muskingum offers a picnic area with restroom facilities. Here in 1791 settlers fought the Delaware and Wyandot Indians. Since the Indians won, it was called a massacre, resulting in four years of war against the Indians of the Ohio Territory. In the end the Treaty of Greenville (chap. 6) ceded most of the lands in Ohio to the White Man.

Near a sharp bend on Township Road 21, northeast of the quaint village of Chesterhill (see Overview Map), is a covered bridge built in 1872 using multiple king post trusses (a superstructure with upright posts and diagonal braces). This bridge is unique because of an arch of timbers built in as a brace. Once known as the Barkhurst Mill Covered Bridge, it is now known locally as the Williams Bridge.

Members of the Society of Friends (Quakers) founded the village of Chesterhill, and it became a busy stop on the Underground Railroad. Just west of Chesterhill the BT passes several Amish farms that seem to be in keeping with their oldest traditions. If you hike through the area on a Monday, freshly washed clothes will be hanging from clotheslines. In the summer sheep grazing in the front yards preclude the need to mow. Some Amish and Mennonite communities have shifted their economies from farming to cottage industries, but you will see no evidence of that here.

The blue blazes pass through a small portion of the Wolf Creek Wildlife Area (Point 5). This 3,600-acre wilderness has been set aside for public hunting and fishing. Here the BT is entirely on-road, because the Ohio Department of Natural Resources, Division of Wildlife, does not permit off-road trail through this land used by hunters.

Known as the Little Cities of Black Diamonds, the ghost towns left by closing coal mines were former boomtowns that sprang up to prepare the coal for transport to other regions. Historians note that life in the coal towns of the 1800s and early 1900s was as rough as that in the frontier towns of the West. San Toy (see Overview Map), in the Burr Oak Region, was one of the roughest. A gunfight was once held over a $20 debt. The streets were cleared as the two "coalboys" got ready to shoot it out. One ended up dead and the other critically wounded.

Most of the mine workers walked the 4 miles from Corning to San Toy, returning to their lodging at the end of each grueling workday. The town's demise came in 1924 when fire destroyed its coal tipple, the apparatus used for loading coal wagons. Several other buildings were also engulfed in the flames. The foundations of many buildings, including the old jail, can still be seen on T-452, just north of T-16. You can also find the San Toy covered bridge on T-16, west of SR 555 and north of Ringgold.

The blue blazes next enter the Burr Oak Region as well as the Athens Ranger District of the Wayne National Forest on Sunday Creek Road (C-58), which connects with SR 78 south of Ringgold. This country lane offers a lovely introduction to the Wayne for the summer hiker. In July, C-58 is lined with teasel, whose thistlelike lavender flowers attract many tiger swallowtail butterflies. Chicory, a brilliant-blue flower, is also abundant along the roadside. Other wildflowers found in the area are tall bellflower, wild bergamot, downy wood mint, crown vetch, daisies, and black-eyed Susan. In the spring find violets, Dutchman's breeches, trillium, rare orchids, bloodroot, and hepatica. Look for pawpaw trees on the slopes along Sunday Creek and around the lake. The fruit of these large shrubs or small trees in the custard apple family is edible when ripe. You might also see box turtles, beaver, and ruffed grouse, which will startle you with a booming release when flushed from cover.

Burr Oak State Park (Point 6), site of our third Featured Hike, is one of Ohio's eight Park Lodges and Conference Centers, offering a 60-room lodge and 30 family cabins, a full-service dining room, indoor pool, and facilities for tennis and basketball. More important to BT hikers are the two camping areas, with water and pit toilets available from June to Labor Day. The camping areas are located at boat docks along the trail. Tom Jenkins Dam offers picnic facilities, toilets, water, and plenty of parking.

From Burr Oak State Park the BT again enters the Wayne National Forest, where there is off-road trail passing through the Trimble State Wildlife Area. Smoke Rise Ranch Resort, the next stop on the BT (Point 7), has allowed the Buckeye Trail to bring its off-road trail over its lands. This working cattle ranch lets guests live and work like a Western cowboy. Nestled in the Appalachian foothills, and close to the BT, the 200-acre resort offers cattle drives, team penning, cow cutting, and guided trail rides.

The BT is easily accessed again at Tecumseh Lake (known locally as Tecumsey; Point 8). Nearby is the village of Shawnee, which has changed little since the 1870s and bears an amazing resemblance to many Old West towns (fig. 12.4). Main Street, with its frontier-style wooden buildings, is on the National Register of Historic Places. Shawnee is the hometown of the Buckeye Trail office.

New Straitsville, host of the Moonshine Festival in the summer, is south of Shawnee. Two miles further south, on SR 595, is Payne Cemetery. Buried

Figure 12.4 Shawnee (Richard Lutz)

here are five (perhaps six) Civil War veterans who served in the Ohio regiments of the U.S. Colored Troops. Two of the veterans belonged to the 5th USCT, and it is believed that the only USCT burial sites other than the Payne Cemetery are in Arlington Cemetery in the nation's capital.

Just north of the BT's Stone Church Trailhead are found the skeletal ruins of St. Peter's Catholic Church and an old cemetery of almost 100 tombstones. The church was built in 1845 to support the village, which was vacated shortly after the Civil War. The Wayne National Forest office has several pamphlets about the historical sites in the forest.

The BT continues generally west from the national forest lands to the village of Enterprise, northwest of Logan and on the Hocking River, where we began our tour of the blue blazes in chapter 2. When planning a trip to any location on the Buckeye Trail in Ohio consult the appropriate chapter Overview. Also, intend to walk at least one of the Featured Hikes in this chapter to see what the Hill Country has to offer.

FEATURED HIKE 1
AMERICAN ELECTRIC POWER RECREATION LAND

DISTANCE 6.5 miles of off-road trail one way.

TIME 4–5 hours.

DIFFICULTY Moderately difficult. Take hiking poles for creek crossings.

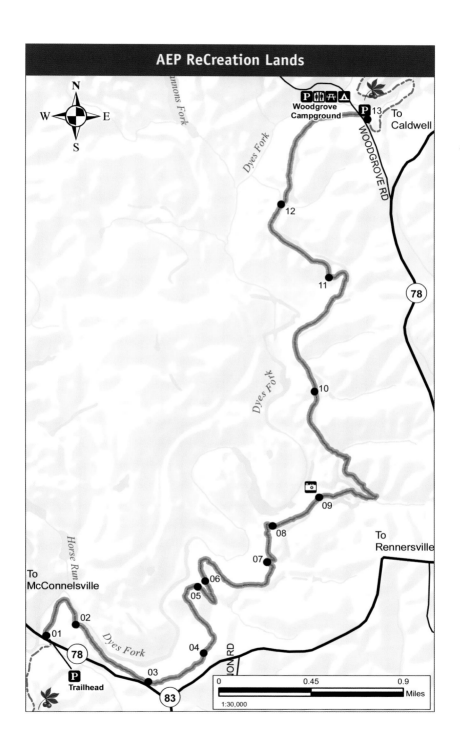

AEP ReCreation Lands

Woodgrove
Campground

To
Caldwell

WOODGROVE RD

78

12

11

Dyes Fork

10

09

08

07

To
Rennersville

06

05

To
McConnelsville

Horse Run

02

04

JON RD

01

78

Dyes Fork

03

Trailhead

83

0	0.45	0.9

Miles

1:30,000

N
W E
S

Park your car at the parking area next to the bridge crossing Dyes Fork on SR 78/83 just west of the southern junction of SR 78 and SR 83. There is a sign at the footpath entrance to the wood (fig. 12.5). If you use two cars, park the second on Wood Grove Road at the entrance to the trailhead for the Buckeye Trail.

The American Electric Power Company (AEP) has built and maintains the recreation lands here. Free permits to use the area and maps can be obtained by contacting AEP (see Local Contacts). You do not need a permit for day hiking.

Begin your hike at the sign (WP 1) and walk a footpath on abandoned railroad bed following the blue blazes northeast along Dyes Fork. In early May you will see many wildflowers, including Virginia cowslip (Virginia bluebells), wild ginger, trout lily, spring beauty, hepatica (both white and violet varieties), and bloodroot. Two related invasive trees are proliferating in this area. The Russian olive was imported in the 1800s to be used for windbreaks and to control erosion. The autumn olive is an

Figure 12.5 AEP trailhead

ornamental that has escaped to the wild. These trees crowd out native trees and easily adapt to poor habitat. The fruit is popular with birds, hence the widespread dispersion.

The Osage orange trees found on this portion of the trail were used by early farmers as livestock containment and planted as windbreaks. The fruit (hedge apples) litters the trail during the fall. Folklore has it that the fruit, laid around home foundations, will deter insects. Shortly, the trail leaves the roadbed and goes up into deciduous second-growth forest of maple, oak, and beech. All this land was deforested and farmed by the 1920s. At WP 2 there is a large gnarled tree surrounded by a grove of pawpaw. The pawpaw is a small fruit tree that has purple bell-shaped flowers in the spring and edible fruit in the fall. The fruit is nicknamed the Indiana banana. As you stand here in the midst of the pawpaw, look down at Dyes Fork meandering along the valley floor. Ghostlike sycamores follow the waterway. Their trunks are a patchwork of grays, browns, and whites. In the winter, you can look down over this valley and see the small beech trees that hang tightly onto their leaves, well into the spring.

At WP 3 you will cross a bridge over a gully. The trail has climbed 200 feet, but you will not notice the climb because the BT trail crew has worked many hours benching this trail and easing the ascent. At the bridge you are about 1 mile into the hike. As you are walking high up on the ridge, you will have sweeping views of the valley below. The trail used to follow closer to the river, but it offered too many "ups and downs." This is a much nicer trail.

The trail next intersects an old oil service road (WP 4). Go to the right. Then, immediately leave the road to the right on the footpath. Strangely, the footpath crosses that same road and continues straight ahead on a slight descent. From this trail, you can look out to the northwest and see the rolling acres of land that have been strip-mined and reclaimed.

The trail now crosses through a mowed area where there are very few trees to mark with blazes. Mother Nature hates a void and takes great pleasure in undoing the efforts of the Buckeye Trail mowers. Watch for a split in the trail and stay to your left. At WP 5 the trail will be hugging sandstone outcroppings. One rock in particular has been entirely straddled by a large tree. At 2 miles into the hike, the trail weaves through sandstone outcroppings. At one point (WP 6) it seems as though the rocks have parted like waves for your passage. The woodland trees here are more mature than those walked previously. Perhaps this land was not as hospitable to the farmer. The forest floor is littered with pine straw.

After a sharp ascent from a creek crossing (WP 7), you will now begin to encounter the lake part of the hike. The trail meanders close to many man-made lakes that were created as part of the mining process and now offer recreational opportunities. Many species of waterfowl, including mallards, geese, and coots use these lakes. The lowlands present a wet-boot possibility to the hiker depending on the time of year. The trail crew has spent many hours installing culverts in an attempt to dry out the trail (WP 8). A fall hike would be the driest, but the spring and early summer will provide the most excitement. Then, the toads, frogs, and red-winged blackbirds will serenade your journey. The butterflies, cardinals, and gold-finches will take your mind off a muddy boot.

At WP 9 there is a significant creek crossing and could present an opportunity for trash-bag boots in the spring. The trail will then ascend steeply. Almost to the top of the ridge, there will be an evergreen area. Next to the trail is a larch tree. This evergreen has tufts of needles on the branches and, in the fall, sheds its needles. If you are hiking in the winter, it will look like a dead pine. After this area, the trail follows the edge of a very steep ridge. Do not venture close to the rim, and if you are hiking with "man's best friend," put them on leash. The woodland is mature maple, oak, beech, and dogwood.

Be alert to make a sharp turn to the left (3.5 miles into the hike) and begin a steep descent. Hiking poles are a necessity. If you do not have poles, consider using your posterior if the ground is wet. This is truly a slippery slope! After crossing through the wetland, ascend on a wide ser-vice road (WP10). The trail will follow road, then mowed footpath, and back to service roads. The trek will be undulating, with easy up-and-down terrain. AT WP 11 pass discarded oil well storage tanks (5 miles into the hike). This sight is very common in southeastern Ohio. Tanks, gas lines, plastic tubing, and pumps are left to decompose into the earth. There seems to be no incentive for the driller to take the trash off the land. At WP 12 there is another service road intersection. The trail goes to the right. The hike ends at Wood Grove Road (WP 13). The Buckeye Trail continues on the other side of the road for 2.7 miles, to SR 78. There is occasional parking at this juncture. As the Buckeye Trail continues to the north, it will pass a number of small lakes created by strip mining.

As an alternative to the two-car process, you can camp in the AEP's Woodgrove Campground. Then you can hike both ways on the BT over several days. In order to camp here, be sure to send for the free permit (see Local Contacts). Bring your fishing gear, as the ponds along the BT offer good fishing.

FEATURED HIKE 2
SCENIC RIVER TRAIL IN WAYNE NATIONAL FOREST

DISTANCE The hike is 4 miles from the trailhead on top of the ridge to the picnic area in Leith Run Campground. This is an out-and-back hike, but two cars are recommended if you do not wish to walk back up the ridge.

TIME 2 hours one way.

DIFFICULTY Moderately difficult walking down to the river. The walk up is difficult. The hike from the river to the top of the ridge is a strenuous 500-foot climb for the first half mile. Hiking poles are recommended.

To get to the trailhead, use SR 7 east from Marietta. Just past Wade, take Archers Fork Road (C-14) north to C-9. Go right on C-9. In less than a mile see signs for parking on the North Country Trail and the Scenic River Trail. If you are using two cars, park the second car at an abandoned roadside park, just east of Archers Fork Road. There are trail shortcuts from this parking area to the River Walk Trail. Or, during the season, you can park at the Leith Run Campground picnic area, about a mile further on.

The Buckeye Trail leaves from this parking spot to go southwest into the woods. Begin this hike at the signs for the two trails, the Scenic River Trail and the Greenwood (fig. 12.6). Follow the yellow diamonds from the parking area (WP 1). The woods are second-growth deciduous, maple, oak, and tulip trees. There are many smaller pawpaw, which have a pretty purple flower in the spring and edible fruit in the fall. The deer are very fond of pawpaws, so your chances of finding fruit on these trees are not very great. At WP 2 there is a switchback to the right and then immediately to the left. From the start of the hike until this point, the trail has been undulating with gentle rises and falls of 50 feet. The trail is used by mountain bikers, who help keep the downfalls and debris cleared. The undergrowth is shared by ferns and many springtime woodland flowers. The woods are shaded enough and the deer sufficiently plentiful so that there is little shrubby undergrowth. This gives the hiker a panoramic view of the hillside, to the right, as it descends to the bottom. As with many of the trails in southeastern Ohio, there are many exposed sandstone outcroppings and scattered stones along the way. Even with the slight descents, there are switchbacks to ease the hike.

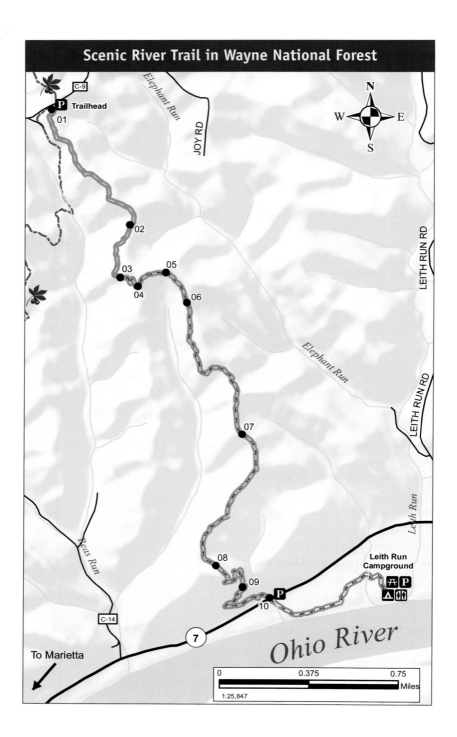

Figure 12.6 Scenic River trailhead

At WP 3, 1 mile into the hike, the Greenwood and the Scenic River Trails split. The Greenwood Trail goes to the right and the Scenic River Trail goes left. You will be following the solid-yellow diamond blazing to the left. Just after this turn, the trail will go through three switchbacks to climb 50 feet to get back to the top of the ridge. The trail levels out and at WP 4 crosses an oil service road. Follow the blazes into the woods on the other side of the road. At WP 5 a mighty tulip tree has come down on the path. Hikers and bikers have carved a new path around. Tulip trees are notoriously tall with a shallow root system that makes them vulnerable to high winds. Their soft, fine-grained wood made them popular with the Native Americans for making dugout canoes. It was quite handy to have these trees here on the Ohio River.

You will probably never see a bobcat in Ohio (or anywhere else), but it is encouraging to note the comeback of these shy cats, for they were extirpated from Ohio in the mid-1800s. (They are probably migrating in from Kentucky.) If you were to see one in Ohio, the Wayne National Forest would be a likely place.

As you walk up on the ridge, you will cross a couple of oil service roads and cables and tubing for oil and gas use (WP 6). It is a fact of life that after the oil production has ceased, there is no incentive to remove the used equipment and it is left to decay into the forest. Don't be surprised to come across relatively new production and the unmistakable aroma of natural gas.

But, these man-made leftovers do not trump the beauty that nature offers. In the spring, trillium, violet, and toothwort are found along the trail. Can you find the wild ginger under the leaf mold? In the fall, lady's thumb graces the trail (note the dark "thumbprint" on the leaf). There are many species of fern just off the beaten track. And overhead there are warblers that will spend the summer. The ovenbird will be singing all spring and early summer. The pileated woodpecker, Ohio's largest woodpecker, screams out his Amazon forest call as you walk along.

AT WP 7 the trail will be wandering among mature maple, oak, and beech trees. The pawpaw is ever present. Anyone who is walking "down to the river" is doing so with the expectation they will see the river from afar. But the woodland does not easily give way to the view of the river. This hike wanders for 3 miles (WP 8) before you can see the water off to the left (fig. 12.7). Just after this glimpse, the trail starts down. There are

Figure 12.7 View of the Ohio River

numerous switchbacks that make the rapid descent safe but awe inspiring. The trail hugs the side of the cliff as it goes down. The hiker will be walking around exposed sandstone outcroppings. It is quite exciting to feel secure in your footing while looking to the right at a precipitous drop.

At WP 9 the Greenwood Trail intersects the Scenic River Trail. The hiker can choose to go right and follow the Greenwood back to the top of the ridge and parking area, or continue down to the left and intersect with SR 7.

Across the road from the parking area at SR 7, there is a white-blazed trail that leads to the Leith Run Campground. This hike adds another mile to the trek.

FEATURED HIKE 3
BURR OAK BACKPACK HIKE

DISTANCE It is almost 24 miles around the lake.

TIME Plan for at least 3 days to journey around the lake with camping at approved campsites. Take hiking poles for creek fordings.

DIFFICULTY Moderately difficult as there are numerous ascents and descents around the lake.

There is a Hiker on the Go map for this section of the Buckeye Trail.

This backpack adventure begins at Burr Oak State Park. Make sure you contact the front desk at the lodge before beginning. It is a good idea to also contact the park and the Wayne National Forest ahead of time to obtain current information about the possibility of flooded trails, availability of water, and other trail conditions. From the intersection of SR 13 and SR 78, near Glouster, follow the Burr Oak Lodge signs past the roads leading to Dock 1 and Dock 2 until reaching Burr Oak Lodge Road on the left. Follow this entrance road to the old Ranger Station (WP 1), where the road splits, left to the lodge and right to cabins. Parking is available at the old Ranger Station for 6 to 10 vehicles.

The Burr Oak Backpack Trail is an excellent resource for the beginning backpacker. Even though the rugged terrain presents a physical challenge, the location of trailheads, designated camping sites, and water

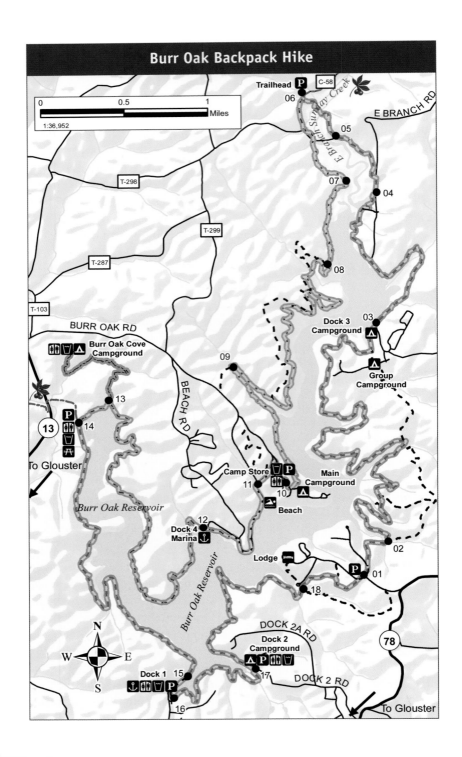

provides several options for planning this trip. Much of the preparation for day hiking discussed in chapter 1 can be applied to backpacking with a few important additions that are summarized in the Checklist below.

Around Burr Oak, water not only comes from above, but below as well. A strong storm can raise stream levels relatively quickly and make your trail impassable. The East Branch of Sunday Creek feeds Burr Oak Reservoir and must be crossed by fording. The trail is located at the best possible crossing but if water is high on the banks, it could be 6 feet deep in the middle. The surrounding floodplain of Sunday Creek could also have standing water a foot or two deep. While East Branch Road and Sunday Creek Road may provide a route around the stream crossing, they may delay your planned route enough that it is better to call it a weekend and head back to the lodge. Be smart; don't attempt to cross flooded streams. They could be deeper and more swiftly moving than they appear.

MINIMAL BACKPACKING CHECKLIST
(also read chapter 1, Day Hiking Checklist)

BACKPACK There are many quality packs to choose from. A pack supported by a hip belt is definitely recommended. When shopping for backpacks, do your research thoroughly. Ultralight (UL) backpacking is becoming increasingly popular, but it requires experience the average hiker might not have.

It is up to you how much weight you want to carry on your back all day long up and down the rugged hills. The walking will obviously be more enjoyable with less weight, but there are the evenings to think about also. Remember that you are heading out to get away from it all. If you don't need it to survive the elements or enjoy the adventure, consider leaving the extra weight in your car.

TENT

SLEEPING BAG

COMPASS/GPS/MAP/CELL PHONE Necessary tools to prevent becoming lost.

RAIN GEAR A backpacking poncho is best because it covers the pack and is long enough to provide protection to your legs.

WATER Carry plenty. In addition, do not count on potable water being available at campsites. Be sure to bring a source of water purification, for which there are many options: tablets, droppers, pumps, and even ultraviolet-light devices.

HEADLAMP

FOOD At a local outfitter, and even at larger grocery stores, there is a greater variety of nutritious and delicious food geared toward backpacking than ever before. You'll need the calories after a lot of physical exertion, so don't limit yourself. But, like gear, you are going to have to carry the weight of that food on your back. That is the benefit of meals that require water for preparation— you add the weight later. Cook stoves require fuel but enhance the comforts on the trail. Backpackers generally do not need campfires; enjoy the sunset and the night sounds instead of wandering around in the darkness looking for fuel.

EXTRA BATTERIES FOR ELECTRONIC DEVICES

OVERVIEW

The Burr Oak Backpack Trail highlights many reasons why this area is so special. Burr Oak is a relatively underused park, as are its trails. Located in the central Appalachian hardwood forests and surrounded by Wayne National Forest lands, the wider landscape boasts some of the highest plant and animal diversity in the world. Related to biodiversity is the concentration of migratory warblers that spend their summers with us and their winters in Central and South America. The trails that provide access to forests in different stages of succession, the ridges, waters, and wetlands here are a birder's paradise. For enthusiasts of other wildlife, the hills are host to the occasional black bear, bobcat, coyote, wild turkey, grouse and white-tailed deer. Mature forests and old fields in succession are rich with a great diversity of wildflowers and native medicinal plants such as goldenseal, black cohosh, and wild ginger. Burr Oak is also known for its peace and quiet, so all this beauty can be experienced on a personal level.

Even though the scene may seem pristine, it was not always this way. The industrial revolution extracted from this landscape the timber, clay, and coal that it needed. The hillsides were barren of trees, and erosion and the siltation of streams made hill farming a poor investment. The East

Branch of Sunday Creek was dammed by the Army Corps of Engineers to control flooding, provide drinking water for the region, and provide recreation. Local sources say that even before there was a state park here, this valley was a destination for recreation; picnicking and fishing were the choices in the late 1800s. Today, if you take SR 78 from Nelsonville east past the entrance to the Burr Oak Lodge on the Morgan County Scenic Byway, you will see the vista to the west known as the Rim of the World. The view of the Sunday Creek watershed looks like a sea of trees.

DAY 1

DISTANCE 4.4 miles.

When you arrive at Burr Oak Lodge, take a moment to stop at the front desk and inform the attendant of your planned trip and that you are leaving your vehicle in their parking lot. It is wise to leave your name, cell phone number, and license plate number for emergency purposes. An overnight stay at Burr Oak Lodge or cabins before or after your hike would be an added treat to your plan. The lodge has a bar and restaurant that also help to make a good start or end to your hike—one less meal to prepare or eat on the highway.

This first day is short, providing a good opportunity to test your legs, readjust your pack, and ease into the weekend. Once you are ready you will take a short hike up Burr Oak Lodge Road to the old Ranger Station (WP 1). At the Ranger Station look to the north to follow the blue blazes on the shared Buckeye Trail, Burr Oak Backpack Trail (yellow blazed), and Buckeye Loop Trail (white blazed). The segment of trail ahead is also designated in honor of Bob and Mary Lou Paton, who championed the development of the Buckeye Trail (see chapter 13). The combined trails soon head downhill, where the white-blazed Buckeye Loop Trail diverts to the right. Remain on the blue-and-yellow-blazed trails to the left to take in glimpses of Burr Oak Lake stretching north and south through the foliage. In addition to the vistas from the rock outcroppings on the lip of the ridge are several sandstone recess caves (outcroppings) including Buckeye Cave (fig. 12.8) and Cave of the Leaves. Buckeye Cave is the largest recess cave in Burr Oak State Park and is worth the short hike on a spur trail that leads downhill on the left.

You will also pass the red-blazed Tanager Trail, which connects the Burr Oak Backpack Trail with the Buckeye Loop Trail. At WP 2 the three trails combine again for a short distance. Then, the white trail heads right

Figure 12.8 Buckeye Cave, Burr Oak (BTA)

and the yellow and blue go left toward the lake. WP 2 is about the halfway point in the first hike, and Boat Dock 3 lies 2 miles ahead. While the distance for this hike is relatively short, there are a few significant changes in elevation during this first day.

When you arrive at Dock 3 (WP 3), you can self-register to camp if you have not reserved a site already. There is an expansive view of the forested hills rising out of the lake. Just above you on the ridge is the Group Camp, which may be available for camping with special permission. After watching the sunset below the ridgeline reflecting across the water, grab your headlamp and walk back up the hill in the evening for a little night hike. The Group Camp has an area devoted to astronomy and is known for having one of the darkest skies in the region. In the early summer the open fields in the Group Camp offer a spectacular show of fireflies that rivals the stars themselves. Keep your ears open for screech owls and the thrill of coyotes singing from the ridges.

DAY 2

DISTANCE 10 miles.

The hike for Day 2 will take you around the northern tip of Burr Oak State Park at the Wildcat Hollow Trailhead then down the west side to your campsite, near the camp store at the Main Campground. The northern end of Burr Oak is lush with wildlife and scenery lending much to the wilderness character of the region. The East Branch of Sunday Creek is the main source of water for Burr Oak Lake. This watershed escaped the major impacts of the coal-mining era experienced in the Little Cities of Black Diamonds region. This stretch of your hike is one of your best chances spot bald eagles fishing across the lake as you hike silently above. The East Branch empties into the lake, creating a long thin waterway that is a local catfishing destination.

From Dock 3 head north into the woods. The yellow and blue blazes will lead you on a nice hike along the lake. After navigating through an open field of grasses that is a recently retired settling pond for lake dredging, follow the footpath until it ends on East Branch Road for a short stretch (WP 4). Turn left onto abandoned East Branch Road and keep your eyes open for a footpath going back into the woods on your left. You will cross an abandoned service road in the middle of the woods that used to be the route of the trail. The trail continues by footpath across the service road and gently rises up the side of the ridge. The trail provides a treetop view and Wildcat Hollow is on the other side of the valley (fig. 12.9). From the upland hardwoods you will descend by switchback to the floodplain. Near this point is an oxbow lake, the former streambed of the East Branch, now a linear pond that is great habitat for the colorful wood duck. This particular floodplain can often be impassable during strong rains. Flooding here may last several days. *Do not attempt to cross flooded streams!* WP 5 is an intersection of an abandoned road with the backpack trail. Recently, the Buckeye Trail was rerouted from this roadway. The trail continues straight ahead.

The crossing of the East Branch of Sunday Creek at a small riffle is a good place to take a short break under large sycamore and buckeye trees. Listen for the large pileated woodpeckers, kingfishers following the stream, and great blue herons traveling from an upstream rookery to fish the shores of the lake during the day.

The Burr Oak Backpack Trail and the Buckeye Trail part ways at the Wildcat Hollow Trailhead (WP 6), on Sunday Creek Road. This is

Figure 12.9 Burr Oak Reservoir (BTA)

2.5 miles from Boat Dock 3. Dispersed camping and 17 more miles of trail lie on the other side of the parking area. The first half mile of Wildcat Hollow is a seasonal destination for its showy display of native wildfowers. Virginia bluebells, blue-eyed Mary, trillium, and Dutchman's breeches are abundant and worth a brief visit for the wildflower enthusiast. The patches of white pine that you experience around the lake are not native; they were planted decades ago by the Civilian Conservation Corps to combat soil erosion on abandoned hill farms. The replanting and restoration efforts to improve watershed health all make the surrounding Wayne National Forest one of the nation's first environmental restoration efforts.

From its northern apex, the Backpack Trail is marked with yellow blazes all the way to Tom Jenkins Dam, where the Buckeye Trail coincides again. The trail parallels Sunday Creek Road a short distance before turning south. Just uphill from this entrance is the entrance for the red-blazed horse trail that also heads to the Main Campground on higher ground.

As you follow Sunday Creek, Burr Oak Lake will come back into view (WP 7). You will be able to see how the creek forms a delta effect, with many peninsulas and backwaters. Beaver are very active in this area; maybe you will hear the slap of their tails on the water when they sense your approach. In the foreground and middle ground are stands of bald cypress, fairly rare this far north. You can tell this tree by the "knees" that protrude from the waterlogged roots near its base. The flat areas between the trail and the water have helped create vernal pools, which are ecologically important features for salamanders and frogs. These will be great places to hear the chorus of spring peepers in March and April.

For the rest of the day's hike, keep to the lake, following the yellow blazes in a generally southern direction. There will be intersections with the red-blazed horse trail. The first of these crossings will occur at WP 8. The red trail will get you to the campground, but continue follow the yellow trail markers for an easier hike. Within a mile of the campground the trail turns into a hollow (WP 9) typical of the area, crosses the stream, and follows along the other side. Take a moment to observe the difference between the southwest-facing slope and the north-facing slope. South-facing slopes receive more sunlight, are drier, and naturally erode more than north-facing slopes. As you walk into the hollow you'll see more exposed rock outcroppings on the drier hillside dominated by oak and hickory. If you are looking for more moist-soil-loving forest wildflowers with dominant beech and maple, you will find them on the north-facing slope on the way out of the hollow.

Near your night's destination some hikers get a little confused. The trail will take you uphill and then through the outdoor amphitheater, from there you will be able to see the Camp Store (WP 10). The Camp Store is where you register for your campsite, purchase treats well earned after a long hike, and find restrooms and showers.

DAY 3

DISTANCE 9 miles.

Day 3 will take you around the southern end of the lake and back to Burr Oak Lodge. But first you'll have to head north on the paved road running through the Main Campground. The trail to the left, marked in yellow, is an abandoned road that heads straight down the hill to Burr Oak Beach (WP 11). At the beach there are running water, flushable toilets, swimming, outdoor showers, cell phone service, and a great view of the lake. The route continues on the lakeside road to the Dock 4

Marina and back onto the hiking trail at the south end of the marina parking lot (WP 12).

From here until Tom Jenkins Dam the trail is known as the Lakeview Trail as well. The Lakeview Trail goes from Boat Dock 4 to Tom Jenkins Dam, with a side trail up to Burr Oak Cove Campground, managed by the Wayne National Forest. The Lakeview Trail is aptly named, but it also provides a great view of the hills. You've probably noticed that the height of all the hills is relatively consistent. It is not that the hills are so high, but that the valleys are so low. The entire region is part of the great Allegheny Plateau, dissected over time by rivers and streams to form the cuts in the hills you see all around you.

When the trail reaches WP 13, the Lakeview Trail goes north and also continues with the backpack trail straight ahead to the west. Stay with the yellow blazes unless you need facilities at the campground, including water and restrooms.

At Tom Jenkins Dam (WP 14) the Burr Oak Backpack Trail meets the Buckeye Trail again. Take a moment to take in the view from the dam, obtain water near the shelter house, and use the restroom. A peaceful moment at the dam might provide a glimpse of the bald eagles or ospreys that call Burr Oak home. You can see why the East Branch was chosen as the site for the dam: steep hillsides a short distance apart. When the dam was created, in 1950, the rising lake waters claimed several covered bridges down below. Around the rim of the lake, foundation stones can still be found and daffodils and wisteria mysteriously appear where rural residences once stood.

In case of any emergency needs the U.S. Army Corps of Engineers has an office with regular hours just down the entrance road on the right. To continue the hike, walk across the dam following the yellow and blue blazes; the trail will be very wide and visible. As you walk look for paw-paw trees, with their long, tropical-looking leaves. They bear North America's largest native tree fruit, which ripens in September. If you like banana custard, you'll love pawpaws. Follow the trail along the lake passing through the large emergency spillway and past unmarked trails that lead to the right, keep left.

The Burr Oak Marina Dock 1 (WP 15, fig. 12.10) can provide you with water, convenience items, and restrooms, and is staffed during regular summer hours in case of emergencies. Continue to follow the yellow and blue blazes out the back of the marina parking area toward Dock 2 (WP 16). Dock 2 (WP 17) provides the last water and restrooms before returning to the lodge. For future reference, there is also camping here.

Figure 12.10 Burr Oak Marina Dock 1 (BTA)

When you arrive at the Burr Oak Lodge Boat Launch (WP 18), the combined Buckeye Trail, Backpack Trail, and Chipmunk Trail head toward the Ranger Station.

LOCAL CONTACTS

- American Discovery Trail. www.discoverytrail.org.
- American Electric Power. www.aep.com/environment/conservation.
- Burr Oak State Park. http://parks.ohiodnr.gov/burroak.
- Burr Oak Lodge and Conference Center. www.stayburroak.com.
- Hiker on the Go map for Burr Oak. www.buckeyetrail.org.
- Leith Run Recreation Area Campground. http://www.fs.usda.gov/wayne.
- North Country Trail. www.northcountrytrail.org.
- Wayne National Forest. http://www.fs.usda.gov/wayne.

WAYPOINT ID'S

WAYPOINT ID	DESCRIPTION	LATITUDE	LONGITUDE
AEP			
1	Parking at Dyes Fork	39.68167800	−81.69793900
2	Pawpaw patch	39.68245500	−81.69526100
3	Bridge over gully	39.67824200	−81.68865200
4	Footpath at oil service road	39.68030100	−81.68358000
5	Sandstone outcroppings	39.68514700	−81.68405600
6	Parting of the stones	39.68555500	−81.68337100
7	Creek crossing	39.68692000	−81.67769500
8	Marsh land	39.68955000	−81.67714600
9	Creek crossing	39.69158400	−81.67287900
10	Service road	39.69929200	−81.67319800
11	Oil storage tanks	39.70767800	−81.67177000
12	Service road	39.71309200	−81.67609700
13	Kiosk	39.71932500	−81.66813800
RIVER WALK			
1	Parking on C-9	39.47500500	−81.17719200
2	Switchbacks	39.46758500	−81.17117900
3	Jct Scenic River and Greenwood	39.46425500	−81.17198400
4	Service road	39.46367000	−81.17062200
5	Blowdown HUGE	39.46454000	−81.16839700
6	Oil service road	39.46257900	−81.16678600
7	Mature woodland	39.45420400	−81.16255000
8	3 miles river view	39.44599700	−81.16469900
9	Jct Scenic River and Greenwood	39.44464500	−81.16262700
10	SR 7	39.44394300	−81.16051500
BURR OAK			
1	Parking	39.52920500	−82.02634000
2	Jct Tananger Trail and BT	39.53217300	−82.02350200
3	Dock 3	39.55191000	−82.02469500
4	CR 15	39.56376400	−82.02452200
5	Old Trail	39.57045900	−82.02562000
6	Wildcat Hollow	39.57281000	−82.03279700
7	View of Lake?	39.56482000	−82.02791500

WAYPOINT ID	DESCRIPTION	LATITUDE	LONGITUDE
8	First Horse Trail	39.55725300	−82.03008600
9	Spur to the top of the hill	39.54795500	−82.04079200
10	Camp Store	39.53751800	−82.03494000
11	Beach	39.53740700	−82.03815400
12	Dock 4	39.53355800	−82.04434600
13	Spur to Burr Oak Cove	39.54500300	−82.05496900
14	Dam	39.54310100	−82.05819900
15	Dock 1	39.52026700	−82.04623100
16	Tr leaving Dock 1	39.51829500	−82.04781300
17	Dock 2	39.52085300	−82.03859700
18	Lodge Boat Dock	39.52797400	−82.03316300

Making It All Possible— The Blue Blazes, of Course!

On June 17, 1959, the Buckeye Trail Association (BTA) officially came into being. The BTA is an organization of volunteers. The Buckeye Trail, as you find it today, exists only because committed people are willing to give their time freely for the benefit of many. The vision of its pioneers was a trail from Lake Erie to the Ohio River. Now forming a complete circle within the state's boundaries, the 1,400-mile BT was designated Ohio's Millennium Legacy Trail by the U.S. Department of Transportation in 1999. There is only one such trail award per state.

THE PIONEERS

Wildlife biologist and poet Merrill Gilfillan created the spark that ignited this magnificent volunteer achievement. On October 2, 1958, Gilfillan (1910–1996), author of *Moods of the Ohio Moons*, published an article in the Columbus Dispatch under the pen name Perry Cole, outlining his ideas for a Buckeye Trail. The proposed trail would be modeled after the venerated Appalachian Trail, granddaddy of all trails in the United States.

Merrill's article piqued the interest of many, a few of whom were eager to take action. A 14-member executive committee first met in May 1959. Some of the attendees became major influences on the fledgling BTA. These vital pioneers included Bill Miller, Roy Fairfield, Emma Gatewood, and Robert Paton, along with prime mover Merrill Gilfillan. Several representatives of the Ohio Department of Natural Resources (ODNR) attended this important beginning as well, and Bill Price of the Division of Parks and Recreation contributed much to the ragging of the new trail. (Ragging is the process of laying out new trail with colored cloth or ribbons before clearing and blazing take place.)

Merrill Gilfillan and Bill Miller are the two people credited as the creators of what is now the record-setting Buckeye Trail. Bill was a marine during the Second World War and as a combat correspondent landed during the fierce fighting on Iwo Jima in the Pacific theater. Bill later served as president of the BTA (1964–67).

Dr. Roy Fairfield, then professor of political science at Ohio University, was the first president of the Buckeye Trail Association. Other charter members elected him for his experience with building and leading the Appalachian Trail effort in Maine. Born in 1918 in Saco, Maine, he later returned to his hometown and contributed to building a new system of trails in that area. During Roy's tenure as president of the BTA (1959–64), about 150 hard-earned miles of BT were completed, mostly in Hocking County. The progress of trail development after four years was revealed in the minutes of the board of directors in October 1963: "It was also noted that there are about 100 miles of continuous trail, with many added miles in Noble County, which it is hoped will be linked with Morgan County in 1964. The total distance from lake to river was estimated at 500 miles." Pretty good for people starting from scratch.

In these early years many other decisions had to be made. First of all, how was the trail to be blazed—with white blazes, as is the Appalachian Trail, or with blue blazes, used to mark side trails on the AT? Blue was chosen because it contrasted well with the green and brown forest colors and could be more easily seen than white when hard-driven snow coated the tree trunks.

One of the willing workers and advisers throughout all these early efforts was Emma Gatewood (1887–1973). Grandma Gatewood, as she was affectionately called, brought experienced hiking knowledge to the many startup decisions the board of directors made in the early years. (She also blazed a lot of trail and contributed $20 to purchase the first blue paint for blazes.)

Long before the BT was even thought of, Grandma Gatewood gave birth to and raised 11 children in the southern Ohio counties of Gallia and Jackson. As if this were not enough to do, she also worked as a licensed practical nurse. Later in life, after reading a National Geographic article in 1954, she decided it was time for another challenge. The article stated that no woman had hiked the Appalachian Trail in one season.

Emma became famous for being the first woman to hike the 2,000-mile Appalachian Trail. This mostly mountainous trail has brought many young, strong men and women to their knees. Grandma was 67 years old when she completed the trail for the first time, in 1955. It took her 146 days, and her average hiking rate was an impressive 15 miles per day. She completed the arduous trail twice more, then took on the 2,000-mile Oregon Trail in 1959, at age 72, in honor of that trail's centennial. She hiked with the barest of necessities, spurning modern hiking equipment. Her pack was an old rucksack and her hiking shoes were sneakers.

Trails are still being dedicated to this legendary hiker. In 1977 a hiking trail on the Bob Evans Farm, near Rio Grande, Ohio, was named the Gatewood Trail. Emma, who grew up in the Gallia County area and hiked there often, deeply desired that the BT traverse her area. She built trail and put in blue blazes there, but this area was destined to be bypassed by the present-day trail. The many trails on the Bob Evans Farm make it a worthwhile place for hikers to visit.

A portion of the Buckeye Trail is dedicated to Grandma. It was one of her favorites, because it was an annual BTA hike early on that has evolved into an annual Winter Hike hosted by the ODNR. This portion of the trail, from Old Man's Cave to Ash Cave in the hills of Hocking County (chapter 2), has been certified by Congress as a National Recreational Trail. At the 10th annual meeting of the Buckeye Trail Association, in April 1969, Emma (Grandma) Gatewood was named Director Emeritus of the BTA and presented with a lifetime membership by President Victor Whitacre and Director John Bay for her pioneering work on the trail (fig. 13.1).

Figure 13.1 Grandma Gatewood receives lifetime membership in the BTA (Courtesy of Ohio History Connection)

Also present from the beginning was Robert Paton (1901–1995). Because of his long-term commitment to the trail, he is aptly known as Mr. Buckeye Trail. When I joined the association, in the early 1980s, and had the pleasure of getting to know Bob, he had just completed more than 10 years as executive director. During our visits along the trail or at his lovely home in Wooster, he patiently shared many personal remembrances. One of those memories involved Governor James A. Rhodes signing Senate Resolution 22, designating the BT as an official state hiking and riding trail, in 1967 (fig. 13.2).

Bob Paton's proudest accomplishment was to see the first 500 miles from the lake to the river completed—the original goal of the BTA—which would not have been accomplished without his efforts. He was quoted during the dedication of that original trail, at Mogadore Reservoir in 1969: "This last blue blaze marks the completion of the trail from the lake to the river, but not the completion of the Buckeye Trail. We are

Figure 13.2 Ohio Senate Resolution signing. (*Left to right*): Kenneth Crawford, Merrill Gilfillan, Senator Harry Armstrong, Governor Rhodes, William Miller, Senator Ralph Regula, and Robert Paton. (Courtesy of Ohio History Connection)

making plans for another branch to stretch from the Ohio River to Toledo. The BT will also tie in with the North Country Trail thus making it a national trail."

Bob witnessed the BT's completion from Lake Erie to Eden Park in Cincinnati in just over 10 years, an amazing accomplishment. The dedication of the completed trail at Mogadore Reservoir took place October 10, 1970, and included both branches of what is known now as the Little Loop. He was also active in the BTA when the connection at Brecksville was made, on March 20, 1981. The Robert and Mary Lou Paton Trail was dedicated at Burr Oak State Park in 1991 and is part of chapter 12's Featured Hike at Burr Oak. How much the state of Ohio owes to the foresight and energy of the people who worked early on to realize what began simply as one person's yearning! The Buckeye Trail Association was destined to be an organization to set records. The Buckeye Trail became the longest contiguous hiking trail within any one state, the longest loop trail in the world, and the only trail to encircle the majority of land within a state. Most impressive of all, these achievements required a minuscule amount of taxpayer money and little in the way of government support.

THE MAINTAINERS

One set of leadership qualities is required to bring an organization into existence. Another distinct set is required to maintain an established organization. After 1980, new leadership was required in the administration of the organization, and new strategies had to be developed for the continued advancement of the Buckeye Trail. Two outstanding people, Emily Gregor and Jim Sprague, provided the necessary bridge between the new and the continuing Buckeye Trail Association.

As president in the 1980s, Emily Gregor (fig. 13.3) brought unique leadership skills to a critical juncture in the BTA's evolution from an obscure regional trail to a world-class organization. Emily combined a love of the outdoors—a prerequisite for all trail leaders—with a superb knowledge of group dynamics gained from her experiences in teaching, her volunteer efforts in many organizations in the Cleveland area, and especially her leadership with the Cleveland Hiking Club. Her son, revealed some of these formative experiences in the June 1999 issue of the organization's newsletter, the *Trailblazer*, designed to pay her special tribute: "It's fair to say I was raised in the Cleveland Hiking Club. As I got

Figure 13.3 Emily Gregor at kiosk
(Courtesy of Ohio History Connection)

older there were the near-regular Sunday 5-mile hikes and the social events (potluck suppers, bowling, canoeing, and Christmas parties) that I remember pleasantly to this day. Several of my best lifelong friends were children of other CHCers—friendships that were begun when we were one or two years old."

Emily continued to change the BTA throughout her years as president by constantly bringing new people to leadership positions. The board of trustees changed over her administration to include people from a more diversified background—members of the financial community and government representatives as well as skilled trail maintainers.

In 1999, on the BTA's 40th anniversary, U.S. congressman and former vice president of the BTA Ralph Regula commended Emily Gregor for her "devotion to the preservation of the trail." Congressman Regula's speech was entered into the *Congressional Record,* granting this "Lady of the Buckeye Trail" a permanent place in U.S. history.

Although the BTA promotes and encourages hiking, of even greater importance is its mandate to continually build new trail and maintain what is there. Jim Sprague, BTA president from 1987 to 1992, recognized the importance of Article II of the BTA's constitution, written by the prescient pioneers in 1960:

> *The purpose of the Association is to promote the construction and maintenance, in the State of Ohio, of a system of trails extending from Cincinnati to Lake Erie, to be supplemented by side trails and a system of public campsites so as to render accessible for hiking and horseback riding some of the historical and beauty spots of the Buckeye State.*

You might be wondering what it would be like to adopt a section of the trail. Every year, about 150 maintenance volunteers walk or drive around their adopted areas of the Buckeye Trail freshening up existing blazes or adding new ones. They carry kits assembled by other volunteers, including brushes and cans of the correct color of paint. One of the decisions a trail adopter must make is how often and where to paint a blaze. If blazing on-road, is every half mile good enough, or should a blaze be painted every tenth of a mile? Is it OK to paint a turn blaze on the back of a stop sign? If off-road, should blazes be painted as the trail is walked in both directions to make sure hikers traveling in either direction will have a better chance of staying on it? Experienced maintenance volunteers know that, no matter how carefully they plan, someone will always manage to become lost. The only way you can truly appreciate the value of blazing trails or performing other maintenance is to become a volunteer and adopt a portion of trail. Of course, the BTA always enthusiastically welcomes new members, whether or not they decide to become maintenance volunteers.

Jim Sprague's greatest source of pride is the formation and continuing work of the Buckeye Trail Crew. In his own words: "I began the Buckeye Trail Crew and Work Party Weekends as an excuse for a camping weekend at which BTA members would build new trail and enjoy lots of camaraderie. It has evolved into a top-notch team that builds exceptional foot trail." In figure 13.4, Jim is shown training a new work crew member.

The Work Party Weekends bring together 10 to 30 experienced BTA maintainers to complete planned projects along the trail. The volunteers rise early and have breakfast from the chuckwagon (fig. 13.5). In the evening, the chuckwagon produces the evening meal and a campfire offers camaraderie. In between times, the volunteers work diligently with such primitive implements as the McLeod (pronounced like McCloud), Pulaski, and fire rake. When I worked with them I somehow felt connected to the ancient Moundbuilders, whose earthworks have revealed their existence

Figure 13.4 Jim Sprague and Adelade Bashaw (Andrew Bashaw)

Figure 13.5 Chuckwagon, Herb Hulls and Jay Holwick (BTA)

to our civilization. The association's newsletter announces the yearly work party schedules. New volunteers are always welcome.

The editor of the first *Trailblazer*, in January 1968, was Mr. Buckeye Trail, Bob Paton. In the quarterly newsletter, members find scheduled hikes and other activities from around the state, trail coordinator reports, ADT and NCT National Trail updates, and tips on hiking safety.

One of the most exciting and safest ways to hike and enjoy the entire Buckeye Trail is to join a Circuit Hike, led by one of our knowledgeable and experienced members. A circuit hike is the name given to a series of weekend hikes, the culmination of which leads to hiking the entire trail. The *Trailblazer* communicates where the circuit hikers will meet on specified weekends in the month and how far they will hike.

The Buckeye Trail Fest is an annual weekend gathering of Buckeye Trail hikers, maintainers, and friends. The goal of the association is to move the event around the state to explore various parts of Ohio. The event features hiking, birdwatching, and short seminars on backpacking and trail building. Most important is a weekend of chatting with folks who share your interests. Membership in the BTA is not required.

If you are not a member and want to know more about the BTA, all you need is a computer to access www.buckeyetrail.org. Explore it to find an overview map of the BT, supported by section map outlines and section supervisor contacts. (It is recommended that for actual hiking, other than this book's short hikes, you purchase the weatherproof section maps that can be obtained from the site's online store.) The website also has Web Alerts explaining recent trail closures or other problems, plus links to related sites offering further information. Updates on Circuit Hikes and Work Party Weekends are also included, and the photos on the site show lovely scenes along the trail (fig 13.6).

The objective of this chapter is to celebrate the founders of the Buckeye Trail Association. Their personal contributions to the association make it easier for each of us to appreciate the great diversity in the natural world and Ohio history. Their wishes for us were that we explore, enjoy, care for, and better understand our natural surroundings, while participating in the sense of community offered by the BTA. Join with us. Come along on a Work Party Weekend or adopt a piece of trail to maintain. Your life will be richer and your vision will be expanded beyond imagining. Happy Trails.

Figure 13.6 Buckeyes on the trail (Brent and Amy Anslinger)

Appendix 1
Bedrock Geologic Map
of Ohio

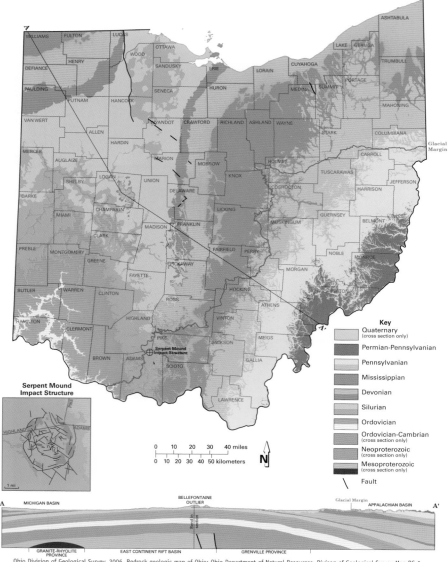

Serpent Mound Impact Structure

Key

- Quaternary (cross section only)
- Permian-Pennsylvanian
- Pennsylvanian
- Mississippian
- Devonian
- Silurian
- Ordovician
- Ordovician-Cambrian (cross section only)
- Neoproterozoic (cross section only)
- Mesoproterozoic (cross section only)
- \ Fault

0 10 20 30 40 miles
0 10 20 30 40 50 kilometers

N

A — MICHIGAN BASIN — BELLEFONTAINE OUTLIER — Glacial Margin — APPALACHIAN BASIN — A'

GRANITE-RHYOLITE PROVINCE   EAST CONTINENT RIFT BASIN   GRENVILLE PROVINCE

Ohio Division of Geological Survey, 2006, Bedrock geologic map of Ohio: Ohio Department of Natural Resources, Divison of Geological Survey Map BG-1

Appendix 2
Physiographic Provinces
Sections of Ohio

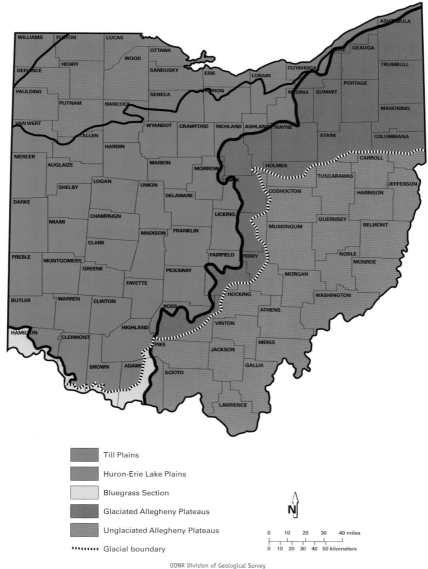

Till Plains

Huron-Erie Lake Plains

Bluegrass Section

Glaciated Allegheny Plateaus

Unglaciated Allegheny Plateaus

••••••• Glacial boundary

N

| 0 | 10 | 20 | 30 | 40 miles |
| 0 | 10 20 30 40 | 50 kilometers |

ODNR Division of Geological Survey

Index

Aberdeen, 71
Adena, 38, 46, 121
adopting a trail segment, 12, 304
Akron, 193–208
Allegheny escarpment, 56, 67, 174
American Discovery Trail (ADT), 2–3 (map), 75, 89
American Electric Power (AEP) ReCreation Lands, 269–80
Amish, 222, 274
Anthony Wayne Trail, 151
Anti-Horsethief Society Monument, 69, 70 (fig.)
Antioch College, 96, 98 (fig.)
Appalachian Highway, 41
Appalachian Mountains, 43, 246; foothills of, 268
Appalachian Trail, 2, 12, 298–300
aqueduct. See canal: aqueducts
Archbold, 146
Ash Cave, 19 (fig.), 20, 23, 300
Auglaize River, 148, 154

backpack hike, 285–95
backpacking checklist (minimal), 287 (table)
Ballville Dam, 169
Battle of Fallen Timbers, 150, 164–65
barn, 134, 249; BT, 248–49 (fig.)
bear, 10, 33, 76
Beard, Dan, 100
Beaver's Town, 244
Bedford Reservation, 202
Bellevue-Castalia area, 171
Bend View Metropark, 164, 166
Bentonville, 66, 69
Bicycle Museum of America, 126–27 (fig.)
bicycle transportation, 118–20. See also bike trails; mountain bike trails
Big Bottom State Memorial Park, 274

Big Creek Park, 221
bike trails, 11–12, 15, 174. See also mountain bike trails
Bill Miller Trail, 17, 19
bison, 67, 172
Black River, 172, 174, 184
blazes, 12, 299; triple, 72 (fig.), 86, 206; turn, 12 (fig.); white, 95, 108, 124, 289, 299
Bloody Bridge, 142
Blue Hole, 115 (fig.), 171
bobcat, 33, 76, 256, 283, 288
Bob Evans Farm, 300
Bolivar, 125, 244, 252
Boone, Daniel, 37, 96, 100, 113
Boy Scouts of America, 100
Brecksville Nature Center, 204
Brecksville Reservation, 167, 183, 194–98
bridge: bow, 188; cable-stayed, 71; concrete arch, 100; covered, 124, 140, 170, 178, 199, 250 (fig.), 274, 275; Daniel Carter Beard Bridge, 100; Jeremiah Morrow Bridge, 108 (fig.); John A. Roebling Suspension Bridge, 91; S-bridge, 237
Buckeye Trail Crew, xiv, 260, 304
Burr Oak Backpack Hike, 285–96
Burr Oak Reservoir, 289, 291–93 (fig.)
Burr Oak State Park, 15, 275, 285, 289, 291
Burton, 195, 218, 222
Burton Wetlands Nature Preserve, 222
Butterworth House, 93
Buzzardroost Rock, 67–68

Caesar Creek, 94; section map, 89, 94; Lake, 95; State Park, 90, 94
Caldwell, 252; Lake, 35–37
Camp Dennison, 93
Camp Deposit, 164
Camp Onwego, 175

Camp Tuscazoar, 241
canal: aqueducts, 137–38 (fig.), 142–43,
    199, 244; boats, 120, 124, 125 (fig.),
    132–34, 136, 140–41 (fig.), 142–43, 151,
    157, 164, 199–201, 209 (fig.), 211;
    feeder canal, 136, 138, 244; Hocking, 17;
    locks, 39, 91, 120, 124, 126, 128, 132–37
    (fig.), 140–42 (fig.), 151, 156, 164, 199–
    200, 209–11, 255, 273; Miami and Erie,
    91, 120, 124, 123–28, 134, 136, 138,
    141–42, 147–48, 156; Ohio and Erie, 17,
    36, 39, 195, 198–99, 209–12 (fig.), 209,
    223, 243–44 (fig.), 254; Sandy and
    Beaver, 244; Wabash and Erie, 128
Canal Fulton, 202, 198–202 (fig.), 209–11
canoeing, 130, 172
Carsonite signs, 12, 33
cave: fracture cavern/Seneca Caverns, 171.
    See also Ash Cave; Old Man's Cave
Cedar Falls, 19, 24 (fig.), 28–29 (fig.)
cemetery: Evergreen Hill Cemetery, 203;
    Feed Springs, 248; Fort Laurens crypt,
    254; Greenmont Union Cemetery, 248;
    Hill Cemetery, 170 (fig.), 177–78 (fig.);
    Old Washington, 251; Payne Cemetery,
    275–76; Red Oak Cemetery, 71
Chagrin Falls, 203
Chapin Forest, 203, 212–16
Chapman, John, 156
Chesterhill, 274
Chief Logan, 35, 138
Chillicothe, 17, 20–21 (fig.), 30, 35, 37, 43,
    94–96, 106
Cincinnati, xv, 82, 89, 91–92, 95, 102, 115,
    120, 124, 141, 164, 302; Central
    Riverfront, 91; Cincinnati Arch, 94
Cincinnati-Pittsburgh Stagecoach
    Trail, 115
circuit hikers, 5–6 (fig.), 306
Clendening Lake, xiv, 248, 251,
    256–61 (fig.)
Cleveland, 95, 170, 175–76, 180, 190–96,
    199, 201, 214, 221, 224, 228, 243, 302–3
Cleveland Hiking Club, 175, 302–3
Clifton Gorge, 96–97 (fig.), 112–17 (fig.)
Clifton Mill, 97, 113–14 (fig.)
Cole, Perry, 298
compass, 5, 8, 30, 287

Congress Lake, 225
Connecticut's Western Reserve.
    See Western Reserve
Continental Divide Trail, 2
Counterfeit House, 68 (fig.)
coyotes, 10, 199, 290
Creekside Trail, 95
Crystal Springs, 196–97, 202–3, 211, 220,
    225–26, 241
Cuyahoga River, 155, 180, 195, 198–99, 221
Cuyahoga Valley National Park (CVNP),
    198 (fig.), 202, 206 (fig.)
Cuyahoga Valley Scenic Railroad, 199,
    206 (fig.)

Davis Memorial State Nature Preserve,
    46–47 (fig.), 57–63 (fig.)
day hiking checklist, 6 (table)
Dayton, xv, 11, 95, 97, 109, 120–23,
    130–31
Dayton Aviation Heritage National
    Historic Park, 120
Deeds Point MetroPark, 122, 131
Deep Cut, 128, 142
Deep Lock Quarry Metropark, 199
Deer Lick Cave, 195 (fig.), 206–7
Deersville, 248, 256
Defiance, 148–49 (fig.), 153–56
Delphos, 126, 128
Democracy Steps, 23, 28
Demoiselle, 120
Dunbar, Paul Laurence, 122
Dunbar House, 122

Eager Inn, 43–44 (fig.)
East Branch Reservoir, 221
East Fork State Park, 72, 83–85, 87
Eastwood MetroPark, 122, 128–30 (fig.)
Eden Park, xv, 72, 89, 92, 98–102 (fig.),
    218, 302
Edge of Appalachia, 67–68, 70
Eldon Russell Park, 222
Emerald Necklace, 175, 190, 193
Enterprise, 17, 276
Erie, Lake, 69, 147–48, 150–51, 155, 158,
    169, 171, 184, 195–97, 214, 220–21
    (fig.), 226–31, 298, 302, 304
Everett (a restored village), 199

Fairborn, 97
Fairfield, Roy, 298, 299
Fallen Timbers, 150, 155, 164–65
Farnsworth Metropark, 151–52 (fig.), 163–64
Feed Springs, 248
Findley State Park, 172–74, 181–85 (fig.)
Firelands, 172
fly-in camping, 251
Fort Ancient, 93–94, 103–5, 108 (fig.); culture, 46, 105, 107
Fort Defiance, 148–49 (fig.), 153–56
Fort Hill State Memorial, 44–45 (fig.), 51–57 (fig.)
Fort Laurens, 125, 155, 244, 252–55
Fort Loramie, 124–25, 155
Fort Meigs, 151, 165
Forty Acre Pond, 142–43
fossil collecting, 85, 94–95, 171
Frazee-Hynton House, 202
Freeport, 248–49
Fremont, 147, 153, 167–69, 177
French Indian Apple Tree, 153; monument, 154 (fig.)
Fugitive Slave Law, 77, 174

Garfield, James A., 222; as hoggee, 255; home, 221
Gatewood, Emma (Grandma Gatewood), 12, 23, 25 (fig.), 298–300 (fig.)
Geauga Park District, 221
General Harrison Canal Boat, 125 (fig.), 132, 134–35
Georgetown, 72
Gildersleeve Knob, 212, 214 (fig.)
Gilfillan, Merrill, 298, 301 (fig.)
Gilliland, Reverend James, 70–71
Girdled Road Reservation, 221
Girty, Simon, 97, 127–28, 252
Girty's Town, 127
glacier: effect on landforms, 17, 25, 30, 51, 55, 69–70, 113, 120, 147, 149–50, 183–84, 195, 197, 220, 225, 233, 238, 245–46; glacial boundary, 37, 244, 308–9; Illinoian, 70, 72, 85; Wisconsinan, 72, 118
Glen Helen Nature Preserve, 96, 109–11

Gnadenhutten, 247
Goll Woods State Nature Preserve, 147
Grandma Gatewood. See Gatewood, Emma
Grand Rapids, 150–51, 158, 163
Grand River, 220–21, 230
Grant, Ulysses S., 72
grave: of Johnny Logan, 156; of Civil War veterans, 276; of Unknown Soldier, 50 (fig.); of War of 1812 veterans, 170
Great Black Swamp, 146–47, 150–53, 158, 167, 237
Great Miami River, 113, 122, 124, 131, 135
Great Seal State Park, 21
Greenfield: Gardens, 174; dolomite, 59–60
Green Springs, 161
Greenville Treaty, 43, 125, 138, 155, 274
Gregor, Emily, 302–3

Hale Farm and Village, 197, 199
Happy Days Visitor Center, 199
Harriet L. Keeler Memorial, 204
Harrison, William Henry, 151, 165, 171
Hartville, 225, 235, 237
Hartville mucks, 224
Hayes Presidential Center, 169
Headlands Beach State Park, 218, 226–28, 231
Headlands Dunes State Nature Preserve, 220, 229 (fig.)
Headwaters Park, 221–22
Hinckley Reservation, 175–76, 186–90 (fig.)
Hocking Canal, 17
Hocking River, 17, 244, 276
Holden Arboretum, 203
Hopewell, 20–21, 43, 46, 51, 53, 57, 94, 105–7, 111
Hopewell Culture National Historic Park, 20
Huffman Dam, 121–23
Huffman Prairie Flying Field, 120–22
Hunt Farm, 199

Independence Dam State Park, 148, 150 (fig.), 153, 156
Indian Lake, 136

John Bryan State Park, 96–97, 113, 115
Johnny Appleseed. *See* Chapman, John
Johnston, John, 124, 132
Johnston Farm and Indian Agency
    Historic Site, 124, 132–35 (fig.)
Junction, 128

karst formations, 67, 171
Kern Effigy, 108
Kirtland Temple, 203, 216
Kossuth, 142
Krohn Conservatory, 101–2

Lake Logan, 17–19
Lake Logan State Park, 17
Lake Loramie State Park, 125
Lake to the River Trail, 195, 218
Land of the Cross-Tipped Churches, 126
Leesville Lake, 246
Lester Rail-Trail, 174 (fig.)
lighthouse, 228; Grand River Light, 220;
    Fairport Harbor, 220
Lincoln Highway, 128
Little Cities of Black Diamonds,
    274, 291
Little Cuyahoga River, 231, 233
Little Loop, 176; west branch, 193–217;
    east branch, 218–26, 271, 302
Little Miami River, 11, 72, 83, 85, 92, 97,
    103–5, 108, 112–13
Little Miami Scenic Park & Trail (LMST),
    72, 92–93, 103–4, 108–9
Lockington, 124
Lockington Locks, 135–37 (fig.)
locks. *See* canal: locks
Logan (city), 17, 276
Logan, Chief, 35, 138
Logan Elm, 35
Logan Trail, 33–35
Loramie: Creek, 135, 137; Mill, 135;
    Summit, 124–26
Ludwig Mill, 152 (fig.), 163–64
Lytle, 94

Mad River, 11, 128–31
Mahoning River, 223
Manchester (and the three islands
    area), 69

Mantua, 223
Mantua Bog and Marsh Wetlands State
    Nature Preserves, 223
manufacturing: aluminum, 173; auto tires,
    200; bicycle tires, 200; drainage tile,
    147; glassmaking, 200, 223; steel, 244;
    St. Marys Woolens, 140
Maple Highlands Trail, 222
maps (as resources or adjuncts): Preface,
    How to Use This Guide, BT maps,
    13–15 (fig.); Gazetteer, 5
Marietta, 311
Mary Jane Thurston State Park, 151
Massillon, 226, 243
Maumee and Western Reserve
    Turnpike, 153
Maumee River, 138, 148, 153–57
Mentor Marsh, 228, 230
Mentor Marsh Nature Center, 228
Mentor Marsh State Nature
    Preserve, 229
Miami and Erie Canal Towpath Trail, 126,
    138–42
Michael J. Kirwan Reservoir, 223
Milford, 72, 92–93
mill, 137; Clifton, 97, 113–14 (fig.);
    Hartville Elevator, 225; Lock 4, 137;
    Loramie, 124, 135; Ludwig, 152 (fig.),
    163–64; Patterson, 113; St. Marys
    Woolen, 140; Ring Mill, 271–72 (fig.);
    Stockport, 273–74 (fig.)
Miller, Bill, 298, 291
mining: coal, 270–71, 280, 291; limestone,
    46, 100, 153, 244; sand and quartz, 212;
    strip mining, 271, 280; in Tuscarawas
    County, 246
Minster, 126 (fig.)
Mirror Lake, 102
Mogadore Reservoir, 195, 223–24 (fig.),
    231–34 (fig.), 301–2
Moravian: early settlers, 244, 247; Trail,
    247–48
Morgan's Raiders, 51, 250
Mormon, 103
mound builders, 20, 42, 69, 107
mountain bike trails, 30, 85, 172, 184,
    225, 281
Mount Logan, 21

museums: Allen Memorial Art Museum,
173; Bicycle Museum of America, 120,
126–27 (fig.); Boston Store, 199; Canal
Fulton Heritage Society Old Canal
Days Museum, 209; Cincinnati Art
Museum, 102, 115; Firelands Museum,
172; at Fort Ancient, 107; at Fort Hill,
51; at Fort Laurens, 254; at Glen Helen,
111; Hale Farm and Village, 199; Indian
Museum, 221; John J. Parker House,
79–81 (fig.); Johnston Farm and Indian
Agency Historical Site, 124, 132–35;
Marine Museum, 220; National
Afro-American Museum and Cultural
Center, 95; National Museum of the
USAF, 122, 130–31; Ripley Museum, xii,
80–81; Wilderness Trail Museum, 125
Muskingum River, 246, 272, 274
Muskingum Watershed Conservancy
District (MWCD), 233
Mustill Store, 200

Napoleon, 149
National Road, 250
Native Americans, extirpation of, 138
Native American towns: Gnadenhutten,
247; Schoenbrunn Village, 247 (fig.),
254; Snaketown, 148
Native American trails: Belpre, 17; Great,
170, 244, 252; Maumee, 150; Mingo,
247; Scioto, 37; Watershed, 170
natural arch, 55
natural bridge, 51, 55
Natural Landmark (designation):
National, 51, 68, 113, 233, 228;
Ohio, 171
Navarre, 244
Navigation Monument, 100
Nesmith Lake, 201
New Bremen, 120, 124, 126
Newman, Steven, 83–87 (fig.)
Newman Worldwalker Perimeter Trail,
83–87 (fig.)
New Philadelphia, 199, 243, 247, 254
Newport, Ky., 100
New Straitsville: city, 275; map, 13–14
Nipgen, 21
North Chagrin Reservation, 203

North Country Trail (NCT), 2–3, 33, 75,
85, 103, 126, 147, 149, 244–45 (map),
271, 281; from Ohio to Michigan, 161;
from Pennsylvania to Ohio, 244
Northern Terminus of BT, 203, 228–29
Norwalk, 170, 172
Nursery Capital of Ohio, 221

Oak Openings Preserve Metropark, 149,
158–61 (fig.)
Oberlin, 173–74
Ohio and Erie Canal National Heritage
Corridor, 199, 243
Ohio and Erie Canal Towpath Trail
(OECTT), 198–202 (fig.), 243–44 (fig.)
Ohio Brush Creek, 67 (fig.)
Ohio Department of Natural Resources
(ODNR), 10, 12, 19, 95, 246, 274, 298, 300
Ohio Division of Wildlife, 259, 264
Ohio History Connection: Fort Ancient,
93–94, 103–8 (fig.); Fort Hill State
Memorial, 51–57 (fig.); Fort Laurens
State Memorial, 252; Hayes Presidential
Center, 169; Johnston Farm and Indian
Agency Historic Site, 124, 132–35 (fig.);
Schoenbrunn Village, 247, 254; Serpent
Mound, 45–46, 55; Zoar Village, 252,
252–53
Ohio River, xv, 17, 20, 65–66 (fig.), 69–72
(fig.), 77, 80, 82, 89, 91–93 (fig.),
98–100, 169, 197, 244, 251, 283–84
(fig.) 298; origin of, 69
Ohio River to Erie Trail, 95
Ohio's Millennium Legacy Trail, 2, 298
Ohio Trails Partnership, 12
Old Chillicothe, 94, 96
Old Man's Cave, 16–19, 23–27 (fig.), 300
Old Military Road, 171
Old Mist'ry River, 171
Old Town, 94–95
Old Washington, 250–51

Paint Creek, 55, 59
Parker, John, 77–81
passenger pigeon, 43
Paton, Robert, 289, 298, 301–2 (fig.), 306
Payne Cemetery, 275–76
Peebles: city, 41, 44–46, dolomite, 59–60

Pemberville, 151, 153
Peninsula, 199
Perry, Oliver Hazard, 151, 171
Peter's Cartridge Company, 93
Pickawillany, 132, 135
Piedmont Lake, 249
Pike Lake State Park, 22, 43, 47–48
Plowing Match and Conservation
    Exposition, 46
Pompey's Pillar, 111
Pontiac Park, 148, 153, 156
portage, 113, 120, 124, 197, 200; path, 200;
    river, 153
prairie, 67–68, 72, 122, 130, 158, 204, 206,
    238–39, 272
Presidents' Grove, 102
Price, Bill, 298
Price, John, 173
Providence Dam, 151, 163
Providence Metropark, 150–52 (fig.),
    161–63

Quail Hollow State Park, 225–26 (fig.),
    235–237
Quaker. *See* Society of Friends

Rankin, John, 77–79, 82
Rankin House, 71 (fig.), 81–82 (fig.)
rappelling, 19, 97, 190
rattlesnake: Kern Effigy, 108; Massasauga,
    95; timber, 32, 76
Ravenna Arsenal, 223
Red Garter Saloon and Inn, 136
Red Oak, 70–72, 77,
Regula, Ralph, 195, 301(fig.), 303
Rhodes, Gov. James, 301 (fig.)
Rider's 1812 Inn, 221
Ringgold, 275
Rio Grande, 300
Ripley, 70–71, 77–82 (map); and Liberty
    Monument, 77
Roche de Bout, 151, 165 (fig.)
Rogers Rangers, 155, 170
Rowe, Richard, 27

Salt Fork Lake, 250
Salt Fork State Park and Wildlife Area,
    250, 256, 263–65

Saltpetre Cave State Nature Preserve, 19
sand dunes, 149, 158, 160
Sandusky River, 147, 167, 169, 170,
    177–79
San Toy, 274
Scheick Hollow State Nature Preserve, 19
Schoenbrunn Village, 247 (fig.), 254
Scioto River, 17, 20–21, 37, 39, 73
Scioto Trail: State Forest, 21; State Park,
    35–39 (fig.)
Sea Scout (BSA) Camp, 249
Seip Mound, 43
Seneca: Caverns, 171; Lake, 251
serpent effigies, 46, 109
Serpent Mound, 45–46 (fig.), 55
Shawnee, village of, 275–76 (fig.)
Shawnee State: Forest, 73–75 (fig.); Park,
    67, 76
Shenandoah airship, 251
sinkholes, 44, 61, 67, 171
Sinking Spring, 45, 51
Smith, Joseph, 203
Smoke Rise Ranch Resort, 275
Smyrna, 249
snake bite, 9
snakeroot: and milk sickness, 54
Society of Friends, 93, 243, 248–49, 274
Sojourner Truth, 101
Solstice, 106–7 (fig.)
South Chagrin Reservation, 203
Southern Terminus of BT, 89, 91–92
    (fig.), 100
Spencer Lake Wildlife Area, 174
Sprague, Jim, 302–5 (fig.)
Spring Valley Wildlife Area, 95
Squaw Rock, 203
Stan Hywet Hall, 200, 206
Stanwix Treaty of 1768, 69
steamboat, 22, 71, 100, 273
Steamboat Rock, 115
Stewart Manor, 226 (fig.), 235
St. Marys, 126, 127–28, 138–43; Belle of
    St. Marys, 140 (fig.)
St. Marys River, 127, 138, 140–42
Stockport, 252, 272–74 (fig.)
Stowe, Harriet Beecher, 80, 92
Stuart, Noble, 190
Suffield, 224

Summit Lake, 199, 201
Sunday Creek, 275, 287, 289, 291–93

Tadmor, 123–24 (map)
Tappan Lake, 247–48
Tappan-Moravian Trail Scenic Byway, 247
Tar Hollow, 20, 30–35
Taylorsville Reserve, 122–23
Teays River, 69
Tecumseh, 37, 95, 107, 138, 150, 165
Tecumseh Lake, 275
Tiffin River, 147, 156
Tight, William, 69; Lake Tight
   (ancient), 69
Tinkers Creek Gorge, 203
trail alerts, 14–15
Trailblazer, 13, 302, 306
Trail crew (builders) and maintainers, 13,
   47, 105, 235, 260, 279–80, 302–4
Treaty of Greenville, 43, 125, 138, 155, 274
turkey vulture, 175–76 (fig.), 186, 231
Tuscarawas River, 197, 200–201, 244, 254
   (fig.), 255; Great Crossing Place, 244
Twin Lakes, 98

Uncle Tom's Cabin, 80
Underground Railroad (UGRR):
   Butterworth House, 93; Fairport
   Harbor Light, 220; Grand Rapids, 151;
   Hartville Hotel, 225; Oberlin, 173–74;
   Old Washington, 250; Rider's Tavern,
   221; Ripley, 77–82; Spring Hill Historic
   Home, 243
Upper Cuyahoga River, 221–22

Vietnam War Memorial, 103
Virginia Military District, 43

Wabash and Erie Canal, 128
Wabash Cannonball Trail, 149, 161
Wake Robin Trail, 231

War of 1812 monument, 172
waterfall, 20, 61, 101, 112, 114 (fig.), 175,
   198, 207
Waterville, 149, 151, 163–65
Waterville Electric Bridge, 164
Wayne, Gen. "Mad Anthony," 155, 164–65
Wayne National Forest, 2, 271, 275–76,
   281–83 (fig.), 285, 288, 292; Athens
   Ranger District, 275; Marietta Unit, xiv
Wellington, 172–74
West Branch State Park, 223
Western Reserve, 153, 172, 175–76, 197,
   199, 203, 220
West Union, 75
wheelchair accessible trails, 20, 235
Whipp's Ledges, 175, 189–90 (fig.)
Wilberforce University, 95
Wildcat Hollow Trail, 291–92
wild turkey, 15, 33, 259, 264, 288
William H. Harsha Lake, 72
Williamsburg, 72, 85
Wingfoot Lake, 224–25
Wolf Creek Park, 170, 177–79 (fig.)
Wolf Creek Wildlife Area, 274
Wolf Run: Lake, 246, 251; State Park, 251
Woodgrove Campground, 280
Woodville, 153
Worden's Ledges, 190
Wright Cycle Company, 122
Wright Memorial, 121 (fig.)
Wright-Patterson Air Force Base, 97, 121

Xenia, 94–95

Yellow Spring, 111–12 (fig.)
Yellow Springs, 96, 109, 113, 116

Zane's Trace, 21–22, 44, 69, 71, 250
Zimmerman Trail, 226, 228–30
Zoar Valley Trail (ZVT), 254
Zoar Village, 199, 244–45 (fig.), 252–56